PENGUIN BOOKS

WHO'S WHO IN THE AGE OF JESUS

Geza Vermes was born in Hungary in 1924. He studied in Budapest and Louvain, where he read Oriental history and languages and in 1953 obtained a doctorate in theology with a dissertation on the Dead Sea Scrolls. From 1957 to 1991 he taught at the universities of Newcastle and Oxford. His pioneering work on the Dead Sea Scrolls and the historical figure of Jesus led to his appointment as the first Professor of Jewish Studies at Oxford, where he is now Professor Emeritus. Since 1991 he has been director of the Forum for Qumran Research at the Oxford Centre for Hebrew and Jewish Studies. Professor Vermes is a Fellow of the Jewish Academy and of the European Academy of Arts, Sciences and Humanities, the holder of an Oxford D.Litt. and of honorary doctorates from several British universities. His books include *The Complete Dead Sea Scrolls in English* (most recent edition 2004), *The Changing Faces of Jesus* (2000), *The Authentic Gospel of Jesus* (2003) and *The Passion* (2005), all published by Penguin.

D1114723

GEZA VERMES

Who's Who
in the Age of Jesus

PENGUIN BOOKS

PENGUIN BOOKS

Published by the Penguin Group

Penguin Books Ltd, 80 Strand, London WC2R ORL, England
Penguin Group (USA) Inc., 375 Hudson Street, New York, New York 10014, USA
Penguin Group (Canada), 90 Eglinton Avenue East, Suite 700, Toronto, Ontario, Canada M4P 2Y3
(a division of Pearson Penguin Canada Inc.)
Penguin Ireland, 25 St Stephen's Green, Dublin 2, Ireland
(a division of Penguin Books Ltd)
Penguin Group (Australia), 250 Camberwell Road,
Camberwell, Victoria 3124, Australia (a division of Pearson Australia Group Pty Ltd)
Penguin Books India Pvt Ltd, 11 Community Centre,
Panchsheel Park, New Delhi – 110 017, India
Penguin Group (NZ), cnr Airborne and Rosedale Roads, Albany,
Auckland 1310, New Zealand (a division of Pearson New Zealand Ltd)
Penguin Books (South Africa) (Pty) Ltd, 24 Sturdee Avenue,
Rosebank, Johannesburg 2196, South Africa

Penguin Books Ltd, Registered Offices: 80 Strand, London WC2R ORL, England

www.penguin.com

First published 2005
Published in paperback 2006
1

Copyright © Geza Vermes, 2005
All rights reserved

Typeset by Rowland Phototypesetting Ltd, Bury St Edmunds, Suffolk
Printed in England by Clays Ltd, St Ives plc

ISBN-13: 978-0-141-01703-7
ISBN-10: 0-141-01703-1

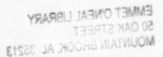

Contents

CONTENTS

List of Illustrations

Foreword

The principal primary source of Jewish history in the Graeco-Roman era is the work of the first-century CE historian Flavius Josephus, supplemented by the Apocrypha, Pseudepigrapha and the Dead Sea Scrolls as well as by Tacitus, Suetonius and Cassius Dio. The relevant Christian evidence is borrowed from the New Testament and from the *Ecclesiastical History* of Eusebius of Caesarea.

While compiling the work, I regularly consulted the 'New English Schürer', the three volumes of *The History of the Jewish People in the Age of Jesus Christ* (175 BC–AD 135) by Emil Schürer, revised and edited by Fergus Millar, Martin Goodman and myself (T. and T. Clark, Edinburgh, 1973–87).

Dr Susan Walker, Keeper of Antiquities in the Ashmolean Museum, Oxford, kindly advised me in the domain of the Roman illustrative material, for which I am very grateful.

G.V.
Oxford, November 2004

Introduction

Roman Emperors and Statesmen

POMPEY, Cnaeus Pompeius Magnus (106–48 BCE); general and
 statesman
CAESAR, Caius Iulius Caesar (100–44 BCE), general and statesman
MARK ANTONY, Marcus Antonius (c.83–30 BCE), general and
 statesman
AUGUSTUS, Caius Iulius Caesar Octavianus (63 BCE–14 CE),
 emperor (31 BCE–14 CE)
TIBERIUS, Tiberius Claudius Nero (42 BCE–37 CE), emperor
 (14–37 CE)
CALIGULA, Gaius Iulius Caesar Germanicus (12–41 CE), emperor
 (37–41 CE)
CLAUDIUS, Claudius Tiberius Drusus (10 BCE–54 CE), emperor
 (41–54 CE)
NERO, Claudius Caesar Germanicus Nero (15–68 CE), emperor
 (54–68 CE)
VESPASIAN, Titus Flavius Vespasianus (9–79 CE), emperor (69–79
 CE)
TITUS, Titus Flavius Sabinus Vespasianus (39/41–81 CE), emperor
 (79–81 CE)
DOMITIAN, Titus Flavius Domitianus (51–96 CE), emperor (81–96
 CE)
NERVA, Marcus Cocceius Nerva (30–98 CE), emperor (96–98 CE)
TRAJAN, Marcus Ulpius Traianus (53–117 CE), emperor (98–117
 CE)

HADRIAN, Publius Aelius Hadrianus (76–138 CE), emperor
(117–138 CE)

Jewish/Herodian Rulers

HASMONAEANS
Judas Aristobulus II (67–63 BCE)
John Hyrcanus II (63–40 BCE)
Matthias Antigonus (40–37 BCE)

HERODIANS
Herod the Great (40/37–4 BCE)
Archelaus (4 BCE–6 CE)
Antipas (4 BCE–39 CE)
Philip (4 BCE–33/4 CE)
Agrippa I (37, 40, 41–44 CE)
Herod of Chalcis (41–48 CE)
Agrippa II (50–c. 92/3 CE)

ADIABENE
Izates (c. 35–60 CE)

Roman Governors of Judaea

Coponius (6–9 CE)
Marcus Ambivulus (9–12 CE)
Annius Rufus (12–15 CE)
Valerius Gratus (15–26 CE)
Pontius Pilate (26–36 CE)
Marcellus (36/7 CE)
Marullus (37–41 CE)
Cuspius Fadus (44–46 CE)
Tiberius Julius Alexander (46–48 CE)
Ventidius Cumanus (48–52 CE)
Antonius Felix (52–60 CE)

Porcius Festus (60–62 CE)
Lucceius Albinus (62–64 CE)
Gessius Florus (64–66 CE)
Sextus Vettulenus Cerialis (70–72 CE)
Lucilius Bassus (72–3 CE)
Lucius Flavius Silva (73/4–81 CE)
Atticus (c. 99/100–102/3 CE)
Quintus Roscius Coelius Pompeius Falco (c. 105–107 CE)
Lusius Quietus (c. 117 CE)
Quintus Tineius Rufus (132 CE)

Roman Governors of Syria

Marcus Aemilius Scaurus (65–62 BCE)
Aulus Gabinius (57–55 BCE)
Caius Sosius (38–37 BCE)
Publius Quinctilius Varus 7/6–4 BCE)
Publius Sulpicius Quirinius (6 CE)
Publius Petronius (39–41/2 CE)
Lucius Vitellius (35–39 CE)
Cestius Gallus (63–66/7 CE)

Proconsul of Achaia

Lucius Iunius Annaeus Gallio (51–53 CE)

Jewish High Priests

HASMONAEAN HIGH PRIESTS (63–37 BCE)
Hyrcanus II (76–67 BCE, 63–40 BCE)
Aristobulus II (67–63 BCE)
Antigonus (40–37 BCE)

HIGH PRIESTS APPOINTED BY HEROD (37–4 BCE)
Ananel (37–36, 34–? BCE)
Aristobulus III (35 BCE)
Jesus son of Phiabi (?)
Simon son of Boethus (24–5 BCE)
Matthias son of Theophilus (5–4 BCE)
Joseph son of Ellem (4 BCE)
Joazar son of Boethus (4 BCE)

HIGH PRIESTS APPOINTED BY ARCHELAUS (4 BCE–6 CE)
Eleazar son of Boethus (4 BCE–?)
Jesus son of See (?)
Joazar (?–6 CE)

HIGH PRIEST APPOINTED BY QUIRINIUS (6 CE)
Ananus or Annas son of Sethi (6–15 CE)

HIGH PRIESTS APPOINTED BY VALERIUS GRATUS (15–26 CE)
Ismael son of Phiabi (15–16 CE)
Eleazar son of Ananus (16–17 CE)
Simon son of Kamithus (17–18 CE)
Joseph Caiaphas (18–36 CE)

HIGH PRIESTS APPOINTED BY VITELLIUS (35–39 CE)
Jonathan son of Ananus (36–37 CE)
Theophilus son of Ananus (37–? CE)

HIGH PRIESTS APPOINTED BY AGRIPPA I (41–44 CE)
Simon Cantheras son of Boethus (41–? CE)
Matthias son of Ananus (?)
Elionaeus son of Cantheras (?)

HIGH PRIESTS APPOINTED BY HEROD OF CHALCIS (44–48 CE)
Joseph son of Camei/Camydus (?)
Ananias son of Nedebaeus (47–59)

HIGH PRIESTS APPOINTED BY AGRIPPA II (52?–92/3 CE)
Ismael son of Phiabi (59–61 CE)
Joseph Kabi son of the high priest Simon (61–62 CE)
Ananus son of Ananus (62 CE)
Jesus son of Damnaeus (62–63 CE)
Jesus son of Gamaliel (63–64 CE)
Matthias son of Theophilus (65–?)

HIGH PRIEST APPOINTED BY THE PEOPLE DURING THE JEWISH
    WAR (67/8 CE)
Phannias/Phanni/Phanasos son of Samuel (? CE)

Leading Women

Cleopatra
Salome, sister of Herod
Alexandra
Mariamme
Herodias
Salome, daughter of Herodias
Bernice
Drusilla

Rabbis

Simeon ben Shetah
Samaias and Pollion
Hillel
Shammai
Gamaliel I
Simeon son of Gamaliel
Yohanan ben Zakkai
Gamaliel II, Rabban

Jewish Charismatics and Ascetics

Honi
Menahem the Essene
Abba Hilkiah
Hanan
Simon the Essene
Bannus
Hanina ben Dosa
Jesus son of Ananias
Eleazar
Jacob of Kefar Sekhaniah

Jewish Revolutionaries

Ezechias
Judas son of Sapphoreus
Matthias son of Margaloth
Simon the Peraean
Athronges
Judas the Galilean
Theudas
The 'Egyptian'
Menahem
Eleazar son of Simon
John of Gischala
Simon bar Giora
John the Essene
Eleazar son of Jairus
Simeon ben Kosiba

Writers

Nicolaus of Damascus
Philo
Josephus
Justus of Tiberias

New Testament Personalities

Joseph
Mary
John the Baptist
Jesus
Peter
Andrew
James son of Zebedee
John
Philip the Apostle
Matthew
Bartholomew
Thomas
James son of Alphaeus
Thaddaeus
Simon the Zealot
Judas Iscariot
Matthias
Mary Magdalene
James brother of the Lord
Jude
Barnabas
Paul
Exorcist, Anonymous
Cornelius
Agabus
Elymas

Simon Magus
Mark
Luke
Philip the Deacon
Stephen
Silas/Silvanus
Timothy
Titus
Philemon
Symeon son of Clopas
John the Elder

THE HASMONAEAN FAMILY

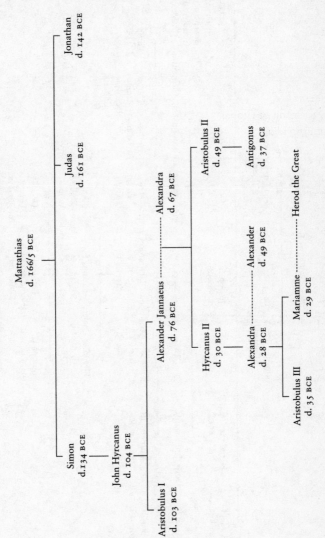

Mattathias
d. 166/5 BCE

Simon
d. 134 BCE

Judas
d. 161 BCE

Jonathan
d. 142 BCE

John Hyrcanus
d. 104 BCE

Aristobulus I
d. 103 BCE

Alexander Jannaeus
d. 76 BCE

Alexandra
d. 67 BCE

Hyrcanus II
d. 30 BCE

Aristobulus II
d. 49 BCE

Alexander
d. 49 BCE

Antigonus
d. 37 BCE

Alexandra
d. 28 BCE

Mariamme
d. 29 BCE

Herod the Great

Aristobulus III
d. 35 BCE

THE HERODIAN FAMILY*

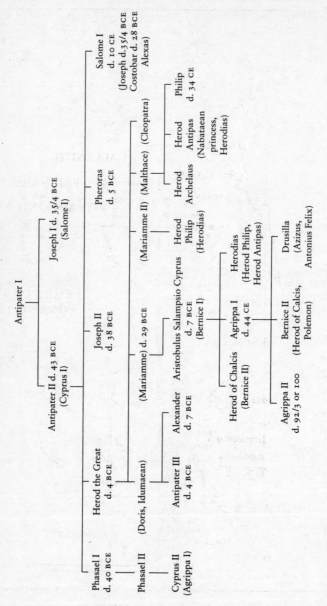

*In ( ) spouses, in succession.

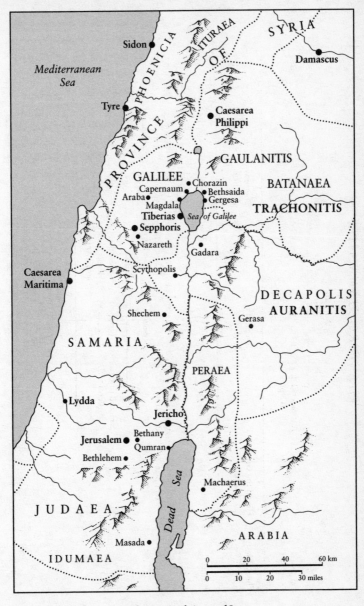

Palestine in the age of Jesus

The Age of Jesus in its Wider Context

In 1906 Albert Schweitzer solemnly declared the quest for the historical Jesus to be an unattainable task, yet despite his eloquent funeral oration the Jesus of history has refused to lie down or disappear. In fact, with the exception of a handful of inveterate doubters, most present-day scholars go to the other extreme and take the existence of Jesus so much for granted that they do not bother to inquire into the meaning of historicity. Yet the truth is that Jesus and the movement which arose in his wake did not exist *in vacuo*: they were integral parts of first-century Jewish society, a society formed by the forces and influences of previous generations and by the impact of Hellenism and the political power of Rome. These Jewish and Graeco-Roman influences interacted and created the matrix out of which Christianity emerged.

The purpose of this book is to make the reader aware of the amalgam of ideas, inspirations and impulses that penetrated the age of Jesus. To achieve this purpose in a vivid fashion, I have chosen to present a series of biographical vignettes. The wider world will be made tangible through the depiction of individuals who in their various ways were influential in the making of history. *Who's Who in the Age of Jesus* portrays personalities from the New Testament, from the works of first-century Jewish writers, from rabbinic literature and from the sources of Graeco-Roman history. These personalities occasionally appear in various records. Rulers of Judaea, Jewish leaders and Roman dignitaries such as *Herod the Great, *Antipas, *Ananus or Annas and *Caiaphas, *Gamaliel the Elder, *Augustus,

---

* Prefixed asterisks indicate personalities with a separate entry in *Who's Who*.

*Tiberius, *Pontius Pilate, etc. are mentioned in the New Testament, and some New Testament characters (*Jesus, *John the Baptist, *James the brother of the Lord) make a fleeting appearance in *Josephus and in the accounts of Roman historians like Tacitus. Other Jewish characters such as *Hillel the Elder, *Honi and *Hanina ben Dosa and *Jesus son of Ananias, who are recorded in Josephus and in rabbinic literature, shed important light on the Gospel story. In consequence, a multi-pronged approach to the age of Jesus promises to open up unexpected fresh vistas.

The broader scope thus conceived demands also an elastic definition of the time scale of the inquiry. The net will be cast wider than the presumed life span of Jesus (c. 6/5 BCE–30 CE). One reasonable starting point would be the Maccabaean revolution against the Seleucid (Syrian) Greek empire in the 160s BCE, when Jews first experienced religious persecution. The forceful and ultimately successful Jewish resistance to Hellenistic tyranny led to the creation of an independent Jewish state, which was governed for the best part of a century (152–63 BCE) by the priestly family of the Maccabees-Hasmonaeans. However, to call 150 years of the pre-Christian era the age of Jesus seems something of an exaggeration. Hence it is preferable to choose instead the next significant watershed in Jewish international history, the switch from Seleucid-Greek to Roman rule in Palestine, inaugurated in 63 BCE by *Pompey's conquest of Jerusalem. This happened less than two generations before the birth of Jesus. The ideal finishing line would lie roughly two generations after the crucifixion. However, the absence of any remarkable event in the closing years of the first century CE prompts one to opt for the end of the second Jewish uprising against Rome in 135 CE. These two boundary posts encompass one of the very crucial periods of the intellectual and religious history of the Western world.

The 200 years in question can be neatly divided into five stages.

1. From Pompey to the end of the Hasmonaean priestly rule (63–37 BCE).
2. The reign of Herod the Great (40/37–4 BCE) – The birth of Jesus (c. 6/5 BCE).
3. Herod Archelaus (4 BCE–6 CE) – Roman prefects (6–41 CE);

Herod Antipas (4 BCE–39 CE) – The public ministry and death of Jesus (29–30 CE).

4. *Agrippa I (41–44 CE) – Roman procurators (44–66 CE) – First rebellion (66–70 [73/4] CE) – The beginnings of Judaeo-Christianity and the career of St *Paul.

5. From the fall of Jerusalem to the end of the second rebellion under *Hadrian – The departure of Christianity from its Jewish social setting (70–135 CE).

Two features distinguish this work from any run-of-the-mill *Who's Who in the Bible*: the first is its dominant strictly historical, as opposed to denominational, religious perspective and the second is the illustrative material selected for it, which consists exclusively of sober ancient artefacts (statues, coins, buildings and inscriptions) rather than beautiful medieval mosaics or early modern paintings. The first-century CE fishing boat retrieved from the bottom of the Lake of Galilee is valued more highly than the artistic imagination of Renaissance painters for bringing the reader close to St *Peter.

The rise and glory of the Hasmonaeans (164–67 BCE)

After two and a half centuries of Babylonian and Persian domination, followed by Greek overlordship introduced by Alexander the Great's conquest of the Near and Middle East, in 164 BCE the Jews recovered their independence and complete self-government as a result of their successful armed resistance to the cultural and religious Hellenization imposed on them by the Greek monarch Antiochus IV Epiphanes (175–164 BCE). The Hasmonaean Jewish priestly family of Mattathias and his sons, surnamed the Maccabees, triumphed over the Seleucids of Syria and restored the Jewish worship, which had temporarily been transformed by Antiochus into the cult of Olympian Zeus, whose statue he had installed in the holy place in Jerusalem. The upheaval caused by the Hellenists, aided and abetted by Jewish upper-class allies, inaugurated a feverish anticipation of the final age, of the eschatological and apocalyptic era, which was expected to culminate in the arrival of the final Redeemer, the King-Messiah, foretold by the biblical prophets and anxiously awaited by pious Jews dreaming of freedom under God. The victorious Judas Maccabaeus (164–161 BCE) and his brother Jonathan (161–143/2 BCE) defeated the enemy and restored a Jewish state. Jonathan, though not a scion of the sacerdotal dynasty which had held the pontificate since the time of King David, proclaimed himself high priest in 153/2 BCE, and Simon, another of the Maccabee brothers, established himself as hereditary religious and political head of the Jewish nation in 143/2 BCE.

Simon's son John Hyrcanus I (135/4–104 BCE) and John's successors, Judas Aristobulus I (104–103 BCE) and Jonathan or Alexander Jannaeus (103–76 BCE), extended the frontiers of the new Jewish state and compelled the neighbouring peoples, the Idumaeans in the south and the various foreign clans in and around Galilee, to recognize them as their rulers and embrace Judaism as their religion. This entailed submission to circumcision as far as the male population was concerned. Their Judaizing missionary activity did not stop these Hasmonaean priest-kings from practising harsh secular tyranny at home. Alexander Jannaeus in particular is notorious for his cruelty in wreaking vengeance on his political opponents, the Pharisees. He ordered 800 of them to be crucified, while he and his mistresses, eating, drinking and merrymaking, were mesmerized by the unholy spectacle.

On Alexander's death his widow, the pious Alexandra Salome or Shelamzion, a great friend of the Pharisees, occupied the royal throne, with her elder son John Hyrcanus II inheriting the high priesthood (76–67 BCE). His more vigorous and envious younger brother Judas *Aristobulus II was determined to dispossess him of his office, however. When Queen Alexandra died, civil war broke out between the two priestly rivals, and with the ensuing conflict there opens a new era leading to the age of Jesus.

1. From Pompey to the end of the Hasmonaean priestly rule (63–37 BCE)

The attempt by Aristobulus II to unseat Hyrcanus II, the legitimate holder of the high priesthood, and the forceful riposte by Hyrcanus, backed by the clever Idumaean strong man Antipater, the father of Herod the Great, and the Nabataean king Aretas III, formed the preamble to the Roman invasion of Judaea by Pompey in 63 BCE. The trio of Hyrcanus, Antipater and Aretas laid siege to Jerusalem, where Aristobulus was forced to withdraw. The innocent victim of the battle was the renowned miracle-working man of God, *Honi, whom the partisans of Hyrcanus stoned to death for refusing to put a curse on Aristobulus and his party. Here we are faced with a politically motivated murder with religious undercurrents. The trend repeated itself in the case of John the Baptist, Jesus, James the brother of the Lord, and others.

The stalemate between the two forces induced both Aristobulus and Hyrcanus to ask for Pompey's intervention. Each hoped to find favour with him. Instead, Pompey, accompanied by the army of his general Marcus Aemilius *Scaurus, conquered Jerusalem and without further ado turned the Hasmonaean state into the Roman province of Judaea. Hyrcanus was reinstalled in the high priesthood, but the title of king was removed from him, while the deposed Aristobulus was sent to Rome as a prisoner. A little later he escaped and began to organize resistance to Rome at home, but he was soon arrested and returned to captivity in the capital. At the start of the Roman civil war between Julius *Caesar and Pompey, Caesar released Aristobulus, seeing him as a potential ally, but the Jewish leader was poisoned by Pompey's partisans before he could set sail to support Caesar in Syria.

After the battle of Pharsalus in 48 BCE, where Pompey was defeated, Hyrcanus and Antipater switched their allegiance to the victor. Caesar, who generally showed himself sympathetic to the Jews in both Palestine and the Diaspora, rewarded them by reappointing Hyrcanus II as nominal head of state or ethnarch of the Jews and placing the administration of the province in the hands of the Idumaean Antipater, who shared his duties with his two sons, *Phasael and Herod.

While governor of Galilee, the young Herod overstepped the boundaries of legality and ordered the execution without trial of the rebel leader *Ezechias and his men. He was summoned before the Jewish Sanhedrin, but with Roman help and the connivance of Hyrcanus, the president of the court, Herod escaped conviction and was confirmed in

his position by Caesar's colleague *Mark Antony, the Roman plenipo-
tentiary in the eastern Mediterranean provinces. In 40 BCE the mighty
Iranian tribe of the Parthians invaded Judaea and gave their patronage
to *Antigonus, the son of Aristobulus II and a rival of Hyrcanus II.
On his coins, Antigonus called himself high priest and king. To ensure
his position as high priest, he maimed his uncle Hyrcanus, apparently
by biting off one or both of his ears, with a view to making him unfit
to act as a pontiff. However, the ephemeral rule of Antigonus came
to an end in 37 BCE, when the Romans captured and beheaded him
by order of Antony, who in 40 BCE had already nominated Herod as
king of Judaea. In 37 BCE, after his conquest of Jerusalem with the
helping hand of *Sosius, the Roman governor of Syria, and of his
legions, Herod, the Idumaean upstart, actually became the ruler of
the Jewish nation and terminated the century-long dominion of the
Maccabaean-Hasmonaean dynasty.

2. The reign of Herod the Great (37–4 BCE) – The birth of Jesus (c. 6/5 BCE)

The reign of Herod covers the decades of Jewish history which directly
open the 'age of Jesus', who was born shortly before Herod died. The
friendly Roman oversight of the government of Judaea and the iron
fist of the new monarch substantially affected the Jewish society in
which Jesus lived. Herod was a cross between a genius and a monster;
he was a master tight-rope-walker whose steps seem to have been
constantly protected by Fortune. His climb to power was hard. As the
protégé of the Roman Mark Antony Herod was first looked on with
suspicion by the Jews, but he managed to gain their approval thanks
to the help of the Pharisees, whose leaders, *Samaias and Pollion,
spoke up for him out of gratitude for sparing their lives when Herod
took revenge on the judges of the Sanhedrin who had tried him in
Galilee. The clever king also succeeded in softening the opposition of
the pro-Hasmonaean Sadducee upper classes, for whom he was no
more than a 'half-Jew', by marrying the Jewish princess *Mariamme,
the granddaughter of the ethnarch and high priest Hyrcanus II. In
addition to the Pharisees and Sadducees, Herod was also on good

terms with the Essenes, by then a long-established community, first mentioned in Josephus in the mid-second century BCE. They owed this favourable treatment to the prophecy of the Essene *Menahem, who foretold Herod's elevation to the kingship of Judaea. With the deaths of Antigonus and Hyrcanus II, the Hasmonaean hereditary pontificate came to an end and Herod, being the secular head of state, arrogated to himself the right to appoint and dismiss Jewish high priests. This right was granted in New Testament times to his grandsons, Agrippa I and Agrippa II, by the emperors, and exercised in the meantime by the Roman governors of Judaea between 6 and 41 CE.

To secure his position, Herod had to ensure friendly relations with Rome and overcome the continuing hostility of some members of the Hasmonaean family. Remaining on good terms with Mark Antony became rather tricky because of the influence of *Cleopatra, the Egyptian queen, on Herod's patron. This *femme fatale*, first the lover and later the wife of Antony, had cast an envious eye on the Judaean kingdom. Herod succeeded in minimizing his territorial losses – only some coastal towns and the area of Jericho were annexed to Egypt – while briefly contemplating, but wisely abandoning, the idea of a love affair with Cleopatra which he thought might provide him with an opportunity to get rid of her. The deteriorating relationship between Antony and Octavian, the future Augustus, created a new dilemma for Herod, but with his customary good luck he contrived to gain first the trust and later the close friendship of Augustus.

Herod's feud with the Hasmonaean royalty was harder to settle as it was kept alive by the continuous intrigues of the female members of the court, led by the king's Idumaean mother, Cyprus, and his sister *Salome on the one hand and, on the other, by his Hasmonaean wife *Mariamme, with whom he was passionately in love, and her mother *Alexandra. The outcome was bloody for the Hasmonaeans. The long list of family members executed by Herod includes his beloved wife Mariamme and her two sons, Alexander and Aristobulus; her brother, the young high priest *Aristobulus III, drowned in an arranged swimming-pool accident; Mariamme's mother and her old grandfather, the harmless former high priest Hyrcanus II. The king's sister Salome also used her brother's good services to get rid of two of her husbands, one of them Herod's own uncle. Nevertheless, shortly after the execution in 4 BCE of Antipater, Herod's eldest son by the first of his ten wives, Salome and her third husband frustrated the dying king's final mad murder project by setting free a large group of Jewish notables whom they had been instructed by Herod to assassinate on his death so as to guarantee widespread mourning at the moment of the royal funeral in 4 BCE.

Herod the Murderer, a suitable model for the man who stands behind the Gospel legend of the Massacre of the Innocents, was none the less also Herod the Great. His foreign policy was outstandingly successful despite the fluctuations of fortune in the Roman world, and he was quite often solicitous and generous towards his Jewish subjects too. He went so far as to introduce substantial tax cuts to help the national economy after the severe famine of 25 BCE. He was a great promoter of Greek culture and, above all, excelled in grandiose building projects at home and abroad. Among his achievements with New Testament relevance should be mentioned the construction of the port and city of Caesarea, named after Caesar Augustus, the seat of the Roman governors of Judaea in the first century CE where St Paul spent two years in prison. Herod restored the city of Samaria and renamed it *Sebaste* (Greek for *Augusta*), again in honour of the emperor. He erected a pagan temple in Caesarea Philippi, the city where the apostle Peter was to acknowledge the Messiahship of Jesus. But, above all, his greatest architectural memorial was the rebuilding of the Jerusalem sanctuary known as Herod's Temple, some of whose remains, especially the Western or Wailing Wall, still stand today.

The life of Jesus began in the closing years of the reign of Herod the Great; this is one of the few points on which the Infancy Gospels of *Matthew and *Luke agree. But the main events which occurred during the final year of Jesus' career (29/30 CE) belong to the next period of Jewish history.

3. Herod Archelaus (4 BCE–6 CE – Herod Antipas – Roman prefects (4 BCE–41 CE) – The public ministry and death of Jesus (29–30 CE)

Jesus did not bring peace into this world. His early years coincided with quarrels about who would be the heir of Herod and with political turmoil caused by a series of uprisings. The succession, confused by contradictory wills of the dying king, was decided by Augustus: the realm was divided into three parts among the surviving sons of Herod, with *Archelaus being put in charge of Judaea, Idumaea and Samaria (4 BCE–6 CE), Antipas of Galilee (4 BCE–39 CE), and *Philip of the territories north and east of Galilee (4 BCE–33/4 CE). None of them inherited the royal title. Archelaus was made an ethnarch and the other two were given the lower rank of tetrarch. But while the settlement was still in the making, the death of the strong ruler encouraged revolutionary forces to come into the open. The Peraean *Simon, the giant shepherd, *Athronges, and especially Judas son of Ezechias revolted, but they were soon overcome by the army of Archelaus and especially by the legions of *Varus, the Roman governor of Syria, who after crushing the rebellion crucified 2,000 Jewish revolutionaries outside Jerusalem, thus foreshadowing the harsher times to come in the first century CE.

No doubt this same Judas from Gamala, nicknamed *Judas the Galilean, raised the flag of rebellion again in 6 CE, when as a preliminary to the annexation of Judaea as a Roman province after Archelaus' dismissal, *Quirinius, the governor of Syria, organized a property registration with a view to reassessing taxes. This is the census of 6 CE, the date of which is clearly stated by the Jewish historian *Josephus. Quirinius' census is the event that the Gospel of Luke wrongly attributes to the reign of Herod the Great in association with the legendary journey of the parents of Jesus, *Joseph and *Mary, from Nazareth to Bethlehem. The uprising of Judas the Galilean petered out, but the revolutionary movement, which he launched in association with a Pharisee called Zadok, persisted throughout the next sixty years; it was responsible for most of the subsequent political unrest among Jews and culminated in the catastrophic war which between 66 and 70 CE devastated the country and destroyed Jerusalem together with all the Jewish state institutions. The eschatological discourse attributed to Jesus in the Synoptic Gospels (Mk 13; Mt 24; Lk 21) is the echo of those dreadful events.

In 6 CE the political landscape of Palestine underwent a marked change. Galilee, where Jesus was growing up, continued its apparent political independence. As long as its ruler Herod Antipas maintained peace and paid his tribute to the emperor, he was allowed to rule unmolested. In Judaea, by contrast, after the deposition and banishment of Archelaus the government of the country was transferred to a Roman prefect, appointed by Augustus.

Rome in general preferred to delegate administrative power (the keeping of the peace and the collection of taxes) to the Jewish ruling classes, the chief priests and the Sanhedrin. Rome also abstained from direct interference with Jewish religious life. Indirectly the extensive powers of Roman governors included the appointment and dismissal of Jewish high priests. Most of them remained in office only for a short period, one year or a couple of years, with the exception of two, both of whom played an important part in the trial of Jesus: the former high priest Annas (6–15 CE) and his son-in-law Joseph Caiaphas, who sat on the pontifical throne from 18 to 36/7 CE. Annas interrogated Jesus and Caiaphas delivered him to Pilate. The Roman governors also kept the vestments of the high priest under their custody and thereby controlled the high priest's functions, which required the wearing of certain ceremonial robes. The Pharisee teachers, mostly active in Jerusalem and the Judaean cities, enjoyed full freedom. Three famous masters, Hillel, some of whose ideas are reflected in the teaching of Jesus, *Shammai, Hillel's opposite number, and *Gamaliel the Elder, who is mentioned with approval in the Acts of the Apostles, flourished during the lifetime of Jesus in the early decades of the first century CE. There is no doubt that the ascetic Essenes, described by the writers *Philo of Alexandria and Josephus, and represented by the sectarian Dead Sea Scrolls, were pursuing their reclusive religious existence at Qumran and elsewhere. They influenced Jewish life more by their fame and moral authority than by direct impact: the instruction of non-members was forbidden by their rules. Nevertheless their community may have served as a model for the organization of the first

Christian Church in Jerusalem, which, like the Essene sect described by Josephus, Philo, Pliny the Elder and the Community Rule of Qumran, lived out of a common kitty administered by the apostles. Some of the charismatic rainmakers and healer-exorcists like the grandsons of Honi, *Abba Hilkiah and *Hanan, and the Galilean man of God Hanina ben Dosa, also belonged to the same country, and lived in the period preceding the first Jewish war.

The public activity of Jesus fits neatly into the reign of the emperor Tiberius (14–37 CE). It occurred during the governorship of Pontius Pilate (26–36 CE) and the high priesthood of Caiaphas (18–36/7 CE). According to Luke, John the Baptist appeared on the scene in the fifteenth year of Tiberius (29 CE), and was soon followed by Jesus, who was crucified under Pontius Pilate, most probably in 30 CE. Of the two great Jewish authors of the first century CE, Philo (20 BCE–40 CE) was Jesus' contemporary and Flavius Josephus (37–c. 100 CE) belonged to the next generation, which witnessed the beginnings of the Jewish-Christian community. As all the significant figures of the New Testament have their own entries in this Who's Who, it seems superfluous to list them here. The information about John the Baptist and Jesus contained in the Jewish Antiquities of Flavius Josephus, which sometimes does and sometimes does not tally with the story contained in the Gospels, is judged authentic by the best scholarly opinion of today, and will be treated as such in the relevant articles.

By the end of this period (41 CE), Augustus and Tiberius were gone, but the insane Gaius *Caligula was still there to make a nuisance of himself in Jewish affairs by insisting that his statue be installed in the Temple of Jerusalem and that he should be venerated as a god. Herod Antipas and Pontius Pilate were simultaneously sacked by the Romans and sent to exile in southern France. Caiaphas was also removed from the high priesthood. The leadership of the Christian movement in Judaea was in the hands of Peter and *James the brother of the Lord, soon to be dominated outside the Land of Israel by the towering figure of Saul of Tarsus, St Paul. The Jesus movement was still rooted in Palestinian Jewish society, but was almost ready for a unilateral declaration of independence and to devote itself to the evangelization of the Gentile world in the Roman empire.

4. Agrippa I (41–44 CE) – Roman procurators (44–66 CE) – First rebellion (41–73/4 CE) – The beginnings of Judaeo-Christianity and the career of St Paul

The period from Agrippa I, the grandson of Herod the Great who was appointed King of the Jews by Caligula in 41 CE, to the fall of Jerusalem and Masada at the end of the first war against the Romans (66–73/4 CE) attests a steadily worsening political situation. The Roman procurators in charge of the Jewish state from the death of Agrippa I in 44 CE until the outbreak of the rebellion in 66 CE were rarely able to exercise full control. Nor was the expert and willing help offered by Agrippa II, the son of Agrippa I, the reformed playboy of Roman high society to whom the emperor Claudius assigned the kingdom of Gaulanitis, Batanaea and Trachonitis, sufficient to resolve the troubles. The murderous faction of Jewish revolutionaries known as *Sicarii* (daggermen) made life impossible. They remained unaffected by the example made of two of the sons of Judas the Galilean whom Tiberius Julius *Alexander, the Roman governor of Judaea, caught and sentenced to crucifixion. The incompetent and corrupt last procurators further aggravated matters.

Nascent Christianity, too, had its ups and downs during those years. In Judaea two leading figures of the Palestinian Church met with violent death. For reasons untold by the author of the Acts of the Apostles, the otherwise notoriously mild Agrippa I is said to have condemned *James son of Zebedee to decapitation, a secular form of death penalty no doubt for a secular crime, and the high priest *Ananus son of Ananus ordered – unjustly according to Josephus – the execution by stoning of the saintly *James the brother of the Lord for having 'transgressed the law'. Church tradition places the martyrdom of the apostles Peter and Paul to the final years of *Nero, whose reign ended in 68 CE. On the positive side the preaching of the gospel to Palestinian Jews continued, though without spectacular progress, but the decision of the council of the apostles in Jerusalem in 49 CE gave the green light to Paul and *Barnabas for their remarkably efficacious mission among the Gentiles of the Diaspora once the pre-condition of the acceptance of Judaism was cancelled and non-Jewish men could be baptized without being obliged first to undergo circumcision. Paul and his helpers were proclaiming the gospel among the inhabitants of Asia Minor and mainland Greece between 49 and 58 CE and the Pauline letters were all written in the fifties and possibly the early sixties of the first century CE. Events of Paul's career fit neatly into Roman history. His appearance before the tribunal of *Gallio, brother of the philosopher Seneca, took place in Corinth between 51 and 53 CE, while Gallio was proconsul of Achaia, and Paul was arrested in Jerusalem in the closing years of the procuratorship of *Felix (52–60 CE). As he was still a prisoner in Caesarea two years later when *Festus replaced Felix in 60 CE, his captivity must have begun in 58 CE. He was transferred to Rome for trial before Nero after surviving a shipwreck close to Malta at the end of 60 CE.

The storm clouds were gathering and despite the initial efforts of the Jewish upper classes the catastrophic war against the Roman empire became inevitable. We know all the details from Josephus, who at the beginning was himself a half-hearted leader of the revolt. Soon the command passed to men of violence, like *John of Gischala, *Simon son of Giora and the most stubborn among them, the captain of Masada, *Eleazar son of Jairus, the grandson of the revolutionary patriarch Judas the Galilean. But they were no match for the Roman forces of two future emperors, *Vespasian and *Titus. The fight was bloody. Captured Jews were crucified daily in their hundreds. The city was destroyed and the Temple reduced to ashes. Not even the seemingly impregnable stronghold of Masada could stop the men and the war machines of the Roman governor *Silva in 73/4 CE. The discerning defenders preferred self-inflicted death to Roman torture and crucifixion.

According to Jewish tradition, *Yohanan ben Zakkai and *Gamaliel II settled, with Vespasian's permission, in the coastal town of Jamnia or Yavneh and, surrounded by a dedicated group of rabbis, set out to redefine, and thus save, a Jewish religion without Temple, high priest or Sanhedrin.

The state of the Jewish-Christian Church is sketched in the eschatological discourse of Jesus in the Synoptic Gospels. Christian theological tradition, recorded centuries later by the historian Eusebius, interpreted the ruin of Jerusalem as divine punishment visited on the

Jews 'for their abominable crimes against Christ and his apostles'. Eusebius further asserts that the members of the Jerusalem Church, warned by a prophetic oracle before the outbreak of the war, migrated from the capital and settled in the town of Pella in Transjordan. We lack external support for his statement. Nor are we told about the future fate of those who had migrated to Pella, although another Christian legend, referring to the persecution of the Church by the leader of the second Jewish rebellion, *Simeon bar Kosiba or Bar Kokhba, implies that the refugees of Pella recrossed the Jordan after the end of the war and settled again in the land of Israel.

5. From the fall of Jerusalem to the end of the second rebellion under Hadrian – The departure of Christianity from its Jewish social setting (70–135 CE)

The aftermath of the first failed rebellion against Rome brought hardship to both Jews and Christians. The victorious emperor Vespasian treated the entire conquered territory as his private property, and in addition to the loss of the national and religious institutions, all the Jews in Palestine and the Diaspora were subjected to the humiliation of having the annual poll tax, which they willingly paid for the upkeep of the Jerusalem sanctuary, confiscated and converted to a yearly tribute, known as *fiscus Iudaicus* or Jewish tax, which was to support the temple of Jupiter Capitolinus in Rome. It was collected with particular harshness under Domitian (81–96 CE), though apparently the severity was relaxed according to a coin minted by his successor, the emperor Nerva (96–98 CE). Conversion to Judaism, considered as the adoption of atheism, was also strictly prohibited. The rebellion of the Jews in Egypt and Cyrene in 115 CE under *Trajan added further fuel to the virulent anti-Judaism of the Romans and the major conflict of the second war (132–135 CE) was already looming on the horizon.

The causes of the Jewish uprising inspired and led by Simeon bar Kosiba or Bar Kokhba during the reign of Hadrian have long been a subject of debate, but the circumstances of the war and the revolutionary administration of the country have become better known now thanks to the archives of legal documents and letters discovered in the caves of Wadi Murabbaat and Wadi Seiyal in the Judaean desert in the 1950s and early 1960s. The Roman governor of Judaea, *Tinneius Rufus, was unable to stand up to the guerrilla forces of Simeon, the self-proclaimed imperious head of state – he called himself Prince (*Nasi*) of Israel – and it took three years of strenuous struggle with much blood shed on both sides before Julius Severus, the greatest general of Rome, urgently summoned from far-distant Britain, managed to quell the revolt in 135 CE. For years persecution reigned; famous rabbis, among them Akiba, lost their lives, and the practice of the Jewish religion was prohibited under the pain of death. Jews were expelled in droves from Judaea, and their ancient capital, lavishly rebuilt by the emperor as a pagan city, was even deprived of its name and became Aelia in honour of the triumphant Publius Aelius Hadrianus. But outside Judaea, and especially in Galilee, Jewish life continued, and thanks to the zeal and persistence of the rabbinic leaders the Jewish religion, recodified in the Mishnah and the Palestinian or more exactly Galilean Talmud, gained a new lease of life.

The Palestinian Jewish members of the Jesus movement, a small Judaean sect in Roman eyes, continued to exist after the destruction of Jerusalem. Church fathers refer to them as Ebionites or Nazoraeans. They were treated as heretics for resisting the developed Christian doctrines of the divinity of Jesus and his virginal conception, and strictly observing the traditional Jewish way of life. Little evidence has survived concerning them, but occasional anecdotes preserved in rabbinic literature, such as the offer of the Jewish-Christian *Jacob of Kefar Sekhaniah to heal a rabbi in the name of Jesus and the legendary admission of the noted Rabbi Eliezer ben Hyrcanus of having accepted a teaching of Jesus, suggest that the two groups were still on rather unfriendly speaking terms.

If Christian tradition handed down in the fourth century by Eusebius can be trusted, the Roman search for Jewish revolutionaries from the time of Vespasian until Trajan affected also the family of Jesus, suspected of propagating hopes for the return of the Messiah. No doubt the cooling down of the expectation of an imminent Second Coming soon removed the threat of Roman retaliation, though not before the grandsons of *Jude, the grandnephews of Jesus, were put on a political blacklist under Domitian, and *Symeon son of Clopas, the cousin of Jesus and the successor of James the brother of the Lord as bishop of Jerusalem, suffered a martyr's death under Trajan in the first decade of the second century CE.

The outlook for the non-Jewish Christians of the Churches founded by Paul in the Roman world was equally gloomy. Already under Nero they were seen as members of a pernicious superstition; many of them were crucified in Rome and, while membership of the Church was not held to be a sufficient ground for prosecution under Trajan, it carried a *prima facie* suspicion of criminality. In the course of the two centuries following the defeat of Bar Kokhba the situation of the Jews in the Roman empire quietly improved while that of the Christians, subject to successive persecutions, if anything worsened. However, the victory of the emperor Constantine at the Milvian Bridge in 312 CE reversed the process and gave Christianity the upper hand.

This survey of Jewish and Judaeo-Christian history in a nutshell from the annexation of Judaea as a Roman province in 63 BCE to the end of the second Jewish rebellion against Rome in 135 CE, and the *Who's Who* itself, are intended to advance a dynamic understanding of Jesus in his time. He stands in the middle of 200 eventful years: he died roughly 100 years after Pompey's entry into Jerusalem and 100 years before the defeat of Bar Kokhba at the battle of Bether.

It is my sincere hope that the historical perspective opened up through these vignettes will enable the reader to grasp the historical reality of the leading figures of the New Testament and to understand better their link with the Jewish and Roman protagonists of the society of their age.

WHO'S WHO

A

ABBA HILKIAH

Abba Hilkiah, the grandson of *Honi the Circle-drawer and probably an elder contemporary of *Jesus, was a charismatic rainmaker. The rabbinic writings contain no detail about his life, but if he is identical with a certain unnamed Hasid from the village of Kefar Imi, mentioned in the Palestinian Talmud, the locality would suggest that he was a Galilean. Only one anecdote relating to him has survived, but it is very interesting and significant.

Abba Hilkiah was a simple and apparently unsociable countryman, whom the two messengers sent by the rabbis to persuade him to bring rain during a season of drought found in a field busy ploughing. He took no notice of the envoys, finished his work, and walked home barefooted. There he sat down to eat his dinner without inviting the messengers to his table because there was not enough food in the house for the guests. After the meal, still ignoring the two apprentice rabbis, Abba Hilkiah asked his wife to go up to the roof of the house and pray for rain with him. He knew, without being told, the aim of the visit. Husband and wife addressed God at opposite corners of the roof and the clouds arrived from the wife's side, suggesting the greater efficacy of her prayer. Once the miracle was accomplished, Abba Hilkiah inquired about the purpose of the envoys' coming, and when they told him, he modestly replied that his prayer was no longer needed. The student rabbis were not fooled: 'We know well that this rain has come through you,' they declared.

The story marvellously illustrates the psychology of the charismatic. He is self-effacing in his humility and knows in advance what people expect of him. He does not credit himself with performance of the wonder and pretends that either it was due to his wife's prayer or rain was already on its way, so no prayer was necessary. But the envoys, who represent the ordinary Jews of the age, had no doubt that Abba Hilkiah was responsible for the miracle. The anecdote reminds us of many a Gospel passage in which after healing sick persons Jesus attributes the cure not to his charismatic power, but to their faith.

Source: bTaan. 23ab.

AGABUS

Agabus was a Palestinian Jewish-Christian charismatic prophet who is twice mentioned in the company of St *Paul. On the first occasion, in Antioch in Syria, he arrived together with other prophets and announced an approaching worldwide famine which actually came about in the days of the emperor *Claudius. The famine, as far as it affected Judaea, is referred to also by *Josephus who dates it to the time of the procuratorship of Tiberius Julius *Alexander (46–48 CE). The second prophetic performance of Agabus coincided with St Paul's arrival in Caesarea a few days before his arrest in 58 CE. The prophet came down from Judaea and, picking up Paul's girdle, bound himself hands and feet, thus symbolizing the fate of the owner of the girdle, who would be detained by the Jews and delivered by them to the Gentiles. (For the author of the Acts of the Apostles neither Agabus nor Paul counts as a Jew; only their enemies are Jews.)

The case of Agabus is not exceptional. Prophecy and other charismatic activities flourished in the early stages of the Palestinian Jewish Church: healing, speaking with tongues first by the apostles at the Pentecost, and later by the members of the household of the Roman centurion *Cornelius, by the four unmarried prophesying daughters of *Philip the Deacon, and finally by the Gentile-Christian members of the Corinthian Church founded by St Paul (1 Cor. 12:10; 14:1–25). Agabus was a characteristic representative of primitive Christendom.

Sources: Acts 11:28, 21:10. Josephus, *Ant.* 20:101.

AGRIPPA I

Agrippa, or Herod Agrippa, was the son of *Aristobulus, the executed son of *Herod the Great, and *Bernice, daughter of Herod's sister *Salome and her second husband, Costobar, also executed by Herod. Agrippa was born in 10 BCE and at the age of six was sent by his grandfather to Rome to receive a proper education. He remained there for over a quarter of a century.

Before returning to the Levant in 37 CE, first as inheritor of the tetrarchy of *Philip, and later as King of Judaea (41–44 CE), Agrippa led an adventurous existence, living far beyond his means in Roman high society. He befriended Drusus, the son of the emperor *Tiberius, and to keep up with his upper-class milieu incurred enormous debts. When Drusus died, Agrippa lost the imperial patronage, and pressure from moneylenders compelled him to flee. He disappeared from sight for a while in an Idumaean fortress where he contemplated suicide. His sister *Herodias, by then the wife of *Antipas, the tetrarch of Galilee, came to his rescue. Agrippa was provided with a home in the capital, Tiberias, and with a job as supervisor of the markets. The two brothers-in-law soon fell out, however, and the sacked market supervisor found refuge in Antioch with one of his old Roman friends, Flaccus, by then governor of Syria. This arrangement came to an end when Flaccus discovered the dishonesty of Agrippa. With a loan obtained by dubious means, he escaped to Italy in 36 CE. Tiberius welcomed him in his residence in Capri after Agrippa had repaid a large debt to Tiberius with monies borrowed from the mother of the future emperor *Claudius. Meanwhile he ingratiated himself with Gaius *Caligula and carelessly expressed in public his wish that Caligula should quickly succeed Tiberius. The conversation was overheard and reported to the emperor and Agrippa landed in prison.

Six months later, in the spring of 37 CE, Tiberius died. Caligula

King Agrippa I

ascended the throne and Agrippa's prospects suddenly changed for the better. Not only was he freed from gaol, but his close friend, the new emperor, also gave him the tetrarchy of Philip and the title of king. To compensate him for his imprisonment Caligula exchanged Agrippa's iron chains for one of gold of the same weight. Agrippa returned to take charge of his kingdom in the autumn of 38 CE and two years later his imperial friend gave him Galilee and Peraea, the former territories of the disgraced Herod Antipas. In 40 CE Agrippa, again in Rome, dissuaded Caligula for a short time from pursuing his plan to set up his statue in the Temple of Jerusalem. After the murder of the mad emperor, Agrippa successfully manoeuvred at the beginning of 41 CE to secure the imperial throne for his other childhood friend, Claudius. The grateful new emperor added Judaea and Samaria to the former realm of this lucky high-born adventurer. Agrippa I was

King of Judaea from 41 to 44 CE and reigned over a country as large as that of Herod the Great.

As a ruler, Agrippa followed in the footsteps of his grandfather Herod the Great and tried to serve both Judaism and Hellenism. As far as Judaism was concerned, he did better than Herod. On many occasions he showed himself to be a devout Jew. On his first visit to Jerusalem he donated to the Temple the gold chain he was given by Caligula. He also offered sacrifices of thanksgiving and financially assisted devout Jews known as Nazirites to fulfil their sacrificial vows. According to the Mishnah, the earliest rabbinic code, he personally participated in the Temple ritual of first-fruit offering and, at the close of the sabbatical year in 42 CE, read in the Temple the prescribed passage from the Book of Deuteronomy. *Josephus also attests his continuous presence in Jerusalem, his scrupulous observance of the Mosaic Law and his willingness to help Jews who lived outside his realm.

The Pharisees were content with Agrippa's government and recognized him as their brother, despite his Idumaean ancestry. The Romans were less happy. Claudius stopped the completion of a new defensive wall which Agrippa had begun to build in Jerusalem. Also the meeting of five client-kings organized by him in Tiberias was judged prejudicial to Roman interests by Marsus, the Roman governor of Syria, who firmly instructed the potentates to go home at once.

Although he professed Judaism in Judaea, abroad Agrippa, like Herod the Great, was a champion of Hellenism. In Berytus (Beirut) he built baths, colonnades, a theatre and an amphitheatre. He also organized games in Berytus and Caesarea. Greek inscriptions designate him as 'friend of the emperor' and 'friend of the Romans'. His coins, struck in Jerusalem, are devoid of effigy, but others minted outside the Jewish territory carry the image of the emperor and even of Agrippa himself. Both his pro-Jewish and pro-Roman attitudes were sincerely held: Agrippa was a Jewish king who had a Roman education. Nevertheless his Jewish behaviour displeased some of his non-Jewish subjects. At the news of Agrippa's sudden death in 44 CE in his fifty-fourth year, the inhabitants of Caesarea and those of Sebaste (Samaria) shouted obscenities and placed the statues of the king's daughters on the roofs of brothels. Agrippa left three daughters and a son, the seventeen-year-old future Agrippa II. Claudius decided to discontinue the royal succession and the province of Judaea was administered by Roman procurators until the start of the first Jewish war.

A rather different Agrippa, a determined persecutor of the Christian Church, is pictured in the Acts of the Apostles. Without any explanation he is said to have ordered the decapitation of the apostle *James son of Zebedee, and as this move was apparently welcomed by the Jews, he threw *Peter into gaol. According to the Acts, Peter was miraculously rescued by an angel and Agrippa vented his fury by executing the guards. The Acts of the Apostles also presents the death of Agrippa in a typical legendary fashion as a fit punishment for his crime. When, dressed in splendid apparel, he was delivering a speech to a delegation from Tyre and Sidon, the audience, no doubt to flatter him, proclaimed his voice to be that of a god. Thereupon an angel struck him dead and his body was promptly devoured by worms.

In Josephus' account Agrippa was wearing a shiny silvery garment during spectacles in honour of the emperor, which glittered when illuminated by the rising sun. The splendid sight provoked cries from his sycophants that he was a god. Agrippa failed to rebuke them and immediately saw the bad omen of an owl. He suffered terrible abdominal pains and, realizing that he had reached the end of the road, the Agrippa of Josephus devoutly accepted the will of God and died five days later. The passing of the much-loved king was mourned by the whole population.

The portrait of Agrippa sketched in the Acts of the Apostles is hard to reconcile with the man we encounter in Josephus' very detailed account. He was a kind person. On one occasion he is reported by Josephus as having forgiven and dismissed with a present a leading Pharisee who had publicly accused him of transgressing the Law. After the foolishness of his early years, Agrippa turned into a pleasant, good-hearted and generous ruler towards Jews and non-Jews alike. Jews called him their 'brother' (mSot. 7:8) and for Josephus he was a 'great king' (Ant. 20:104).

Sources: Josephus, War 2:178–82, 206–22; Ant. 18:143–239; 19:274–359. Acts 12.

AGRIPPA II

Agrippa II, or Marcus Julius Agrippa, did not inherit his father's kingdom when *Agrippa I died in 44 CE. The advisers of the emperor *Claudius opposed the handing over of full royal powers to a seventeen-year-old who was still continuing his education in Rome until 52 CE. In 50 CE, he received from the emperor the small kingdom previously ruled by *Herod of Chalcis together with the right to supervise the Temple of Jerusalem and appoint or remove high priests. In exchange for his minute territory he was offered by Claudius in 53 CE the former tetrarchy of *Philip, Gaulanitis, Batanaea and Trachonitis, to which the new emperor *Nero added the Galilean and Paraean districts of Tiberias, Tarichaeae and Julias.

Agrippa II was influenced by his sister *Bernice with whom, it was rumoured, he lived in an incestuous relationship. He wholeheartedly devoted himself to promoting the interests of his Roman masters, contributing auxiliaries to the war against the Parthians (54 CE) and solemnly welcoming in 60 CE the procurator Porcius *Festus on his arrival in Judaea. To honour the emperor Nero, he renamed his capital, Caesarea Philippi, Neronias, and placed the effigies of the successive emperors on his coins.

Agrippa II always sought to please his Jewish subjects by looking after their well-being and observing the religious requirements of Judaism. He insisted that the non-Jewish husbands of his sister Bernice should undergo circumcision and is portrayed as familiar with the Mosaic Law, often engaged in discussion with rabbinic teachers. When Herod's Temple was finally completed in the days of the procurator *Albinus, Agrippa re-engaged the 18,000 building workers to keep them in employment and ordered them to pave the streets of Jerusalem with white stones.

At the start of the rebellion against Rome in 66 CE Agrippa supported the peace party among the Jews. The warmongers triumphed, however, and thereafter Agrippa showed himself to be wholly pro-Roman. After initial reverses, the Romans overran Galilee in 67 CE, and Agrippa greeted *Vespasian, the commander-in-chief, in Caesarea

King Agrippa II

Philippi. In the company of *Titus, Vespasian's son, he travelled to Rome after the suicide of Nero in 68 CE, but was summoned home by Bernice when the Roman armies of the east proclaimed Vespasian emperor in the summer of 69 CE.

Agrippa was the constant companion of Titus in the last year of the war and during the siege of Jerusalem. His steadfast support of the Roman cause was rewarded by the granting of further territories in northern Lebanon. In Rome again with his sister in 75 CE, Agrippa was raised to the rank of praetor, while Bernice continued to be the mistress of Titus until under pressure the emperor sent her home. Agrippa died either in the third year of the emperor *Trajan (100 CE) or, more probably, in 92/3 CE.

Agrippa II was in contact with *Josephus and wrote him sixty-two letters. Two of these, in which he praises the historian's account of the Jewish war, are quoted by Josephus: 'You seem to me to have written with much greater care and accuracy than any who have dealt with the subject. Send me the remaining volumes' (*Life* 365). Whether Agrippa actually received the requested complimentary copies is not known. In fact, in *Against Apion* (1:51) we are told that Josephus 'sold' a copy of the work to 'the most admirable King Agrippa'.

The Acts of the Apostles brings Agrippa and Bernice into contact with St *Paul at Caesarea where the new procurator *Festus sought Agrippa's help to make him understand the conflict between Paul and the Jewish authorities. Agrippa willingly agreed and Paul presented his case before them. At the end Festus jocosely told Paul that he must be crazy. Paul then challenged Agrippa to say whether he believed in the prophets. The king evaded the challenge by remarking ironically, 'In a short time you think to make me a Christian!' With all that we know about Agrippa, it is hardly likely that he was seriously on the brink of embracing Christianity. The words, enveloped in polite royal irony, more probably indicated Agrippa's wish to bring Paul's prolonged argument to a close.

Sources: Josephus, *Ant.* 18–20. Acts 25–6.

ALBINUS

Lucceius Albinus was entrusted by the emperor *Nero with the procuratorship of Judaea between 62 and 64 CE. He was a rapacious man who took bribes from all and sundry, from the former high priest *Ananias to the Sicarii, and unscrupulously appropriated public funds as well as private property. Prisoners were released when enough ransom money was paid for them. The whole country was in turmoil and, to make matters worse, when Albinus' governorship came to an end, he emptied the prisons by putting the top criminals to death and letting the rest of the inmates loose on the long-suffering and helpless population.

It was shortly after his arrival in Judaea that Albinus had to deal with the case of *Jesus son of Ananias, a turbulent prophet of doom, whom the Jewish authorities handed over to the procurator as they were unable to control him. Albinus first flogged, then interrogated this Jesus, but when he refused to answer his questions, he declared the man a lunatic and let him go.

Albinus later became governor of Mauritania in North Africa, where he reaped his just deserts. He was murdered by the followers of the emperor *Vitellius, the rival of the emperor Otho, during the conflict for the succession of Nero in 69 CE.

Sources: Josephus, *War* 2:272–7; *Ant.* 20:197–215.

ALEXANDER

Tiberius Julius Alexander was Roman procurator of Judaea from 46 to 48 CE. He came from the wealthy Alexandrian Jewish nobility, being the son of the customs superintendent (*alabarch*) Alexander, who was the brother of the philosopher *Philo. Tiberius Julius Alexander abandoned Judaism. Apparently his uncle Philo discussed religion with him, but without succeeding in convincing the young man to remain within the Jewish fold. Romanized, Alexander entered the imperial civil service and became the only Roman governor of Judaea of Jewish origin.

Political unrest continued during his procuratorship, inspired by Jacob and Simon, the two sons of *Judas the Galilean, the founder of a revolutionary party at the time of the census organized by *Quirinius in 6 CE. Both were caught and Alexander ordered them to be crucified. The great famine, mentioned in connection with the reign of *Claudius, occurred during the procuratorship of Alexander. It is also referred to in the Acts of the Apostles (11:28–30). The Churches of *Paul and *Barnabas sent relief to the Christians of Judaea, while the convert Queen Helena of Adiabene from northern Mesopotamia, who was visiting Jerusalem, bought food in Egypt to assist the needy Jewish inhabitants of Judaea.

The procuratorship of Judaea was only Alexander's first step in a brilliant career. The emperor *Nero appointed him prefect of Egypt and King *Agrippa II hastened to Alexandria to congratulate him. When *Vespasian was proclaimed emperor by his soldiers, Tiberius Julius Alexander obtained for him the full support of both the population and the legions in Egypt. Later he became the most loyal helper, adviser and chief lieutenant of *Titus and was his quartermaster general (*praefectus castrorum* or *magister militum*) during the siege of

Jerusalem in 70 CE. Alexander made a brilliant career for himself and several of his descendants continued to occupy important posts, including consulship, in the Roman administration and in the army.

Sources: Josephus, *Ant.* 20:100–102. Philo, *On the Providence* 2.

ALEXANDRA

Alexandra was a Hasmonaean princess, the daughter of the ethnarch and high priest *Hyrcanus II. She married her first cousin Alexander, the son of *Aristobulus II, the brother of Hyrcanus II. Their daughter, *Mariamme I, became the second wife of *Herod the Great. The proud Alexandra considered the commoner Herod a mismatch for her daughter and as a result a long-lasting feud developed between herself and Mariamme on the one side, and Cyprus and *Salome I, the mother and sister of Herod, on the other. The hostility burst into the open when Herod overlooked the claim of Alexandra's son, *Aristobulus III, to the high priesthood. Alexandra was a friend of *Cleopatra, Queen of Egypt and wife of Herod's Roman patron *Mark Antony, and together the two women induced Antony to compel Herod to dismiss his own nominee, *Anael, and install the seventeen-year-old Aristobulus in the pontifical office. But the stratagem's success was of short duration: a swimming-pool accident contrived by Herod cost the young high priest his life. The distraught Alexandra turned once again to Cleopatra and Antony summoned Herod to appear before him and account for himself. But with the help of a large bribe the crafty Idumaean literally got away with murder. Alexandra courageously stood up to Herod, but her nerve broke when her daughter Mariamme was fighting for her life, charged with adultery with Herod's friend Soemus. To protest her ignorance of Mariamme's conduct Alexandra reprimanded her daughter in public in an undignified manner, shouting at her and pulling her hair. Mariamme was put to death, but Alexandra's own downfall was not far away. While Herod was disintegrating after the execution of his favourite wife, Alexandra planned to seize the throne herself. She was betrayed and was put to death by Herod in 28 BCE. Compared to her father, the kindly and noble Hyrcanus, and her daughter, the dignified Mariamme, Alexandra proved lacking in true royal character.

Source: Josephus, *Ant.* 15:23–252.

ANANEL

Ananel, or possibly Hanamel (37/6 BCE), was the first Jewish high priest appointed by *Herod the Great to replace the Hasmonaean *Hyrcanus II. Hyrcanus was rendered unfit to remain in office when his nephew, the rival high priest-king *Antigonus, maimed him by biting off one or both of his ears. Ananel's origins are disputed. *Josephus describes him first as an obscure priest of Babylonian stock, deliberately chosen by the insecure Herod because his undistinguished character made it unlikely that he would become a leader of opposition. But later Josephus contradicts himself and presents Ananel as a member of a high-priestly family and a valued friend of the king. This Ananel is thought by some to be the high priest Hanamel mentioned in the Mishnah (mPar. 3:5). But Hanamel was an Egyptian, not a Babylonian, Jew. Within a couple of years Herod was forced by his Roman patron *Mark Antony to dismiss Ananel in favour of the grandson of Hyrcanus II, *Aristobulus III, whose mother *Alexandra persuaded her friend *Cleopatra to put in a word to her husband, Antony, in support of the young Hasmonaean prince. The king, having found Aristobulus III a political threat, arranged for his murder in 35 BCE and recalled the demoted Ananel to the high priesthood (34–? BCE).

Josephus describes the deposition of Ananel as unlawful, the office of high priest being by law conferred for life, but during the reigns of the Herodian kings and tetrarchs as well as under the Roman governors of Judaea frequent dismissal and replacement of high priests became common practice. The high priests were more influential under direct Roman administration than during the government of Herod and his successors because in the absence of a Jewish lay ruler the high priest held both the religious and the secular leadership of the nation.

Source: Josephus, *Ant.* 15:22, 40.

ANANIAS SON OF NEDEBAEUS

See under **Ananus son of Sethi**.

ANANUS SON OF ANANUS

Ananus was the fifth son of *Ananus son of Sethi (6–15 CE) to become high priest. This was unprecedented in the history of the Jewish pontificate. He was appointed by King *Agrippa II in 62 CE after the death of the Roman procurator *Festus but before the arrival of *Albinus, who succeeded Festus. Ananus, who was of Sadducean persuasion, occupied the pontifical office for only three months. He had a violent temper and, according to *Josephus, he decided to use the absence of a Roman procurator to get rid of his critics, among them *James the brother of Jesus 'who was called Christ'. They were brought before the Sanhedrin and stoned to death. Josephus notes that the pious and law-abiding Jews of Jerusalem were scandalized by the action of Ananus and reported him to King Agrippa and the new procurator *Albinus. Albinus was furious and Agrippa deprived Ananus of the pontifical office.

After the outbreak of the war against Rome Ananus and Joseph son of Gorion were put in charge of the defence of Jerusalem. During the infighting among Jewish factions Ananus was the leader of the peace party and tried to bring calm to troubled waters. In political matters Josephus calls him 'a man of profound sanity'. Ananus opposed the rebels and with his colleagues he turned against *Simon son of Giora, one of the chief revolutionaries, and forced him to withdraw for a time to the fortress of Masada. However, the Sicarii and their Idumaean allies finally captured Ananus and killed him, leaving his naked body unburied for the dogs and beasts of prey to devour (Josephus).

The contrast between the negative portrait of Ananus in *Antiquities* and the favourable depiction found in the earlier *Jewish War* is striking. The savage character of *Antiquities* contrasts with the picture of a virtuous man. In his obituary of Ananus Josephus described him in flattering terms as a person of the highest integrity, kind towards the humble, a lover of freedom and peace and a leader who always rated public welfare above private interests (*War* 4:325). Whether Josephus' favourable judgement of Ananus in *Jewish War* resulted from his hatred of the Zealots, the mortal enemies of the high priest, or whether the deposition of Ananus from the high priesthood served as a deep shock which actually mollified his savage character, is hard to decide. In judging the issue one must bear in mind that in general the Josephus of *Antiquities* is a harsher critic of Jewish life than the Josephus of the *War*.

Sources: Josephus, *War* 2:563, 648–53; *Ant.* 20:197–203; *Life* 193–6, 216, 309.

ANANUS (OR ANNAS) SON OF SETHI

Ananus or Annas (the Hebrew Hanan or Hanin) son of Sethi (or Seth) was the most influential high priest in the first century CE and the patriarch of a pontifical dynasty. Five of his sons, his son-in-law Joseph *Caiaphas and one of his grandsons held the high priesthood between 16 and 66 CE. The first Ananus was appointed high priest by *Quirinius, the Roman governor of Syria, after the dismissal of *Joazar son of Boethus in 6 CE for being too much under the influence of the populace. Ananus remained in office for nine years until the arrival of *Valerius Gratus, who was Roman prefect of Judaea from 15 to 26 CE.

After his retirement Ananus remained an influential active leader of the Jewish nation. According to *Luke (3:2), at the start of the public activity of *John the Baptist, Annas and Caiaphas jointly held the high priesthood. However, since Jewish religious law recognized only a single ruling high priest at a time the most likely explanation of Luke's misrepresentation is that the power behind the throne during the pontificate of Caiaphas was his father-in-law, the former high priest Ananus or Annas. According to the Gospel of *John, which contains no mention of a trial proper of Jesus, he was first taken for interrogation to the house of Annas (Jn 18:13–24). After completing a preliminary inquiry, Annas dispatched Jesus to Caiaphas. Annas is again mentioned as present with Caiaphas and all the members of the high-priestly family at the inquiry into the apostles *Peter and *John by the Sanhedrin in Jerusalem (Acts 4:6). Deposed high priests often played an important role in Jewish life in the first century CE. So the intervention of Ananus in the story of Jesus and of the leaders of the early Church was nothing out of the ordinary.

After the dismissal of Ananus, Valerius Gratus appointed three high priests in quick succession. *Josephus has nothing to say about any of them. A lament preserved in rabbinic literature criticizes the house of the first, Ismael son of Phiabi (15–16 CE), because of their violence (unless this comment applies to the second *Ismael son of Phiabi, who was high priest from 59 to 61 CE). Eleazar son of Ananus (16–17 CE) remains completely obscure unless the charge of calumnies levelled against the house of Hanin in the same rabbinic passages applies to him. As for the third, Simon son of Kamithus (17–18 CE), he is remembered in the Talmud and the Midrash for having been disqualified from conducting the liturgical service on the Day of Atonement on account of levitical impurity caused by contact with the spittle of an Arab. The pontifical instability was rectified by Valerius Gratus when he appointed to the high priesthood Joseph Caiaphas, who held the office for the record time of eighteen years, from 18 to 36 CE.

Sources: Ananus: Josephus, War 5:506; Ant. 18–26, 34. Ismael: Ant. 18:34. Eleazar: Ant. 18:34. Simon: Ant. 18:34; tNid. 5:3; yYom. 38d, etc.

ANDREW

Andrew was one of the leading members of the circle of twelve apostles whom Jesus entrusted in Galilee with the mission of proclaiming the Kingdom of God and performing exorcisms. He was a fisherman by profession, a native of Bethsaida by the Lake of Gennesaret and the brother of Simon-*Peter. During the ministry of Jesus he resided in Capernaum where he shared a house with Peter. According to the Fourth Gospel the two brothers met Jesus when they were disciples of *John the Baptist. Apart from the lists of the apostles and a couple of insignificant anecdotal references, the Gospels report nothing about Andrew.

The Church historian Eusebius (fourth century) attributes to Andrew the evangelization of Scythia, and Christian legend relates that he died crucified in Achaia in Greece.

Sources: Mk 3:16–19; Mt 10:2–4; Lk 6:14–16; Acts 1:12–14; Jn 1:40, 44; 6:8; 12:22. Eusebius, *Eccl. Hist.* 3:1.

ANNIUS RUFUS

See under **Coponius**.

ANTIGONUS

Antigonus, the son of Judas *Aristobulus II, was the last priest-king of the Hasmonaean dynasty (40–37 BCE). Although *Josephus never calls him by his Jewish name, his coins bear the legend 'Mattathias High Priest' in Hebrew and 'Antigonus King' in Greek. He took the religious and political office from his uncle, *Hyrcanus II, with the help of the Parthians who invaded Palestine in 40 BCE. In the same year *Mark Antony appointed *Herod King of Judaea. Antigonus spent the three years of his ephemeral reign in fighting Herod. In 37 BCE Herod's army, with the helping hand of the Roman legions of *Sosius, governor of Syria, conquered Jerusalem. Sosius took Antigonus, who had surrendered to him, and mockingly called him Antigone, the feminine form of the name Antigonus. Antigonus was brought to Antioch where he was beheaded by order of Mark Antony, whom Herod had encouraged with a bribe to remove his rival. Thus with the first execution by the Romans of a reigning king the century-long rule of the Hasmonaean priests came to an indecorous end.

Sources: Josephus, *War* 1:274–375; *Ant.* 14: 370–491.

ANTIPAS

Antipas, or Herod Antipas, was the second son of *Herod the Great by the Samaritan Malthace, and ruled Galilee and Peraea in Transjordan with the title of tetrarch from 4 BCE to 39 CE. On his coins he simply describes himself as Herod. He was more closely associated than any other Herodian with leading New Testament figures. His name appears some twenty-five times in the Synoptic Gospels and the Acts of the Apostles.

The career of Antipas was profoundly affected by his marital affairs. His first wife was a daughter of Aretas IV, King of the Nabataeans (9 BCE–40 CE). This union was politically useful as it protected Peraea, the Transjordanian territory of Antipas, from marauding Arab nomads. However, things went sour years later when Antipas decided to divorce his wife after falling in love in Rome with the wife of his half-brother *Herod, son of Mariamme II, the high priest's daughter. This *femme fatale* was his niece *Herodias, the daughter of Aristobulus, son of *Mariamme I, the beloved Hasmonaean wife of Herod the Great. From her first husband she had a daughter, *Salome, who subsequently became the wife of Antipas' half-brother, *Philip. Therefore Philip was the son-in-law of Herodias and not her husband as the Gospels imply.

The rumour about Antipas' marital plans reached his wife: gossip-mongering flourished in the Herodian royal courts. The shrewd Nabataean princess obtained permission from her naive husband to leave Galilee and travel to the fortress of Machaerus in southern Transjordan from where she could easily cross the border to Petra, the capital of the Nabataeans. With the rejected and humiliated wife safe with her father, Aretas was free to wage a war of revenge against Antipas.

Machaerus was also the place where *John the Baptist had been imprisoned by Antipas. *Josephus describes John as a 'good man' who encouraged the Jews to practise 'justice' and 'piety' and undergo a 'baptism' of repentance. But his popularity and the power of his eloquence aroused the suspicion of Antipas, which led to John's downfall. Josephus' report on the matter is quite different from the story given in the Gospels. The tetrarch of Galilee is said to have foreseen the possibility of political disturbances resulting from the Baptist's preaching and he took drastic preventive measures. He ordered John's arrest and execution. The defeat of the army of Antipas in 36 CE by the Nabataeans was seen by Jews as the divine punishment of Antipas for the murder of John.

The jealousy of the domineering Herodias finally led to Antipas' undoing. When the new emperor Gaius *Caligula ordered in 37 CE the transfer of the recently deceased *Philip the Tetrarch's territories (Batanaea, Gaulanitis, Auranitis, Trachonitis and Panaias) to *Agrippa I, the brother of Herodias, and decided to grant him the title of king, the ambitious woman kept on badgering her husband until he applied to the emperor for the same promotion to royal status. The move misfired. To bring down Antipas, Agrippa's envoy accused him of treason. He was believed and Caligula removed the unfortunate tetrarch from office and exiled him to Lyons (Lugdunum) in Gaul. Being the sister of the favourite Agrippa, Herodias was exempted from banishment, but she proudly declined Caligula's favour. 'My loyalty to my husband prevents me from accepting your kind gift,' she is quoted as saying before she took the road to Gaul. Antipas died in exile, possibly put to death by the emperor, who had the habit of disposing of banished grandees.

Like his father Herod the Great before him, Antipas loved grandiose architectural projects. Not only did he restore the city of Sepphoris, destroyed during the campaign led by the Roman governor of Syria, *Varus, against the Jewish rebels after the death of Herod the Great in 4 BCE, he also built a magnificent new capital on the shore of the Lake of Galilee and named it Tiberias in honour of the emperor *Tiberius. Since ancient tombs had been uncovered by the workers on the building site, pious Jews refused to settle in the new town. Tiberias, which is never mentioned in the Synoptic Gospels, was constructed and organized as a Greek city. It was governed by a council of 600 men; it had a stadium and a royal palace decorated with images of animals, but it also had a great synagogue. To please his Jewish subjects, Antipas struck no human effigy on his coins, neither the emperor's nor his own, and according to the Gospel of *Luke (23:7) he went on pilgrimage to Jerusalem at the Feast of Passover.

The New Testament references to Herod Antipas, usually called Herod the Tetrarch, are linked to John the Baptist or to *Jesus of Nazareth. The beginning of John's ministry is dated to the time when Herod was tetrarch of Galilee, and more precisely to the fifteenth year of Tiberius, i.e. 29 CE (Lk 3:1). The Gospel account of the death of the Baptist differs from that given in Josephus. According to *Mark and *Matthew he was executed for disapproving of the marriage of Antipas and Herodias. Although at variance with Josephus' explanation, the Gospel story is plausible. John is likely to have condemned Antipas' remarriage since marital union between a man and his sister-in-law is prohibited by the Torah if the brother is still alive. John's interference was bound to provoke furious resentment on the part of Herodias, and it was natural that she should seek revenge. So during the celebration of her husband's birthday she advised her daughter Salome, whose dance had delighted Antipas, to ask for the head of the Baptist. Having solemnly promised in front of all the assembled guests to grant the girl whatever she wished, the weak Antipas reluctantly complied and, despite his fear of the holy man, sent an executioner to the nearby goal to do the deed. The venue of the event is not indicted in the Gospels. Machaerus, specified by Josephus, is definitely not referred to and in Mark at least a Galilean location is implied by the presence of 'the leading men of Galilee' at the birthday party. Strictly speaking, the accounts of Josephus and of the New Testament could be reconciled. Antipas may have planned to rid himself of John because his eloquence was thought to be potentially dangerous if used for revolutionary purposes, and his decisive action could have been triggered by Herodias' machination on the occasion of the birthday festivities. Nevertheless, if Herodias' scheming had been known, and in the Herodian courts few secrets failed to come to light, one would expect the well-informed Josephus to have heard of it. Indeed, this is just the kind of story that he loved to report. So on the whole the political motivation for John's execution is the more likely explanation.

As far as Jesus is concerned, each Synoptic evangelist attributes to Antipas the superstitious fear that Jesus was the reincarnation of John the Baptist. *Luke testifies to two contradictory attitudes. Antipas, we are told, longed to meet him (Lk 9:9), but also wanted to kill him.

When told about the latter, Jesus reacted sharply and called Herod 'that fox' (Lk 13:31–2).

Luke also recounts another episode. During the trial of Jesus, when Pilate learned that Jesus was a Galilean, he dispatched him to Antipas, assuming that the 'Jewish' ruler of Galilee, who was in Jerusalem for the Passover, was better qualified than himself to pronounce sentence on one of his subjects. Antipas was apparently delighted to meet Jesus and expected him to perform a miracle. Jesus refused and the furious Antipas, after allowing his soldiers to mock Jesus, returned him to *Pilate and to the Roman cross.

Sources: Mk 6:14–29; Mt 14:1–12; Lk 9:7–9; 23:6–12. Josephus, *War* 2:167–8, 181–3; *Ant.* 18:27, 36–8, 101–29, 240–56.

ANTIPATER

Antipater, the father of *Herod the Great, was a Palestinian statesman of growing importance during the rule of the Hasmonaean Jewish high priests *Aristobulus II and *Hyrcanus II. He was most likely of Idumaean (Edomite) origin, according to *Josephus, although the Greek historian *Nicolaus of Damascus, chronicler of Herod's reign, claimed that Herod was descended from Jews who returned from Babylonia in the late sixth century BCE. By contrast, according to Julius Africanus (*c.* 200 CE) the father of Antipater (also called Herod) was a servant of the temple of Apollo in Ascalon and the boy Antipater was captured by the Idumaeans and was adopted by them. Josephus in turn writes that the father of Antipater, who bore the same name, was a noble Idumaean who was appointed military governor of that country by Alexander Jannaeus, and his son inherited the same position. At the outbreak in 67 BCE of civil strife between Aristobulus II and Hyrcanus II, the shrewd Antipater, foreseeing greater chances for advancement under the weakling Hyrcanus, embraced his cause and also persuaded the Nabataean king Aretas III to turn against Aristobulus. The joint armies of Hyrcanus, Antipater and Aretas forced Aristobulus to retreat to Jerusalem. On *Pompey's conquest of Judaea in 63 BCE Antipater offered his services to the Romans and after the death of Pompey in 48 BCE, both he and Hyrcanus conveniently switched their allegiance to Julius *Caesar. Caesar granted Roman citizenship to Antipater and appointed him procurator of Judaea with authority to rebuild the fortified walls of Jerusalem. Under Roman tutelage the powers of Antipater continued to increase until he was in a position to appoint his two sons, *Phasael and Herod, military governors of Jerusalem and of Galilee. After the assassination of Julius Caesar in 44 BCE, Antipater and Herod sought to ingratiate themselves with Cassius, one of Caesar's murderers, who had taken possession of Syria. But when Brutus and Cassius were defeated at Philippi in 42 CE by *Mark Antony and Octavian, the future *Augustus, Antipater and his sons found favour with Antony.

Having managed to navigate many troubled waters and secure a strong position for his son Herod, Antipater finally fell foul of political intrigues and was poisoned by the butler during a banquet which he attended in the palace of the high priest Hyrcanus II in 43 BCE. Out of piety and gratitude towards his father, after his elevation to the kingship of Judaea by the Romans, Herod founded a new city northeast of Jaffa and called it Antipatris. St *Paul spent a night there when as a prisoner under armed escort he was taken by the Romans from Jerusalem to Caesarea to appear before *Felix, governor of Judaea (Acts 23:31).

Sources: Josephus, *War* 1; *Ant.* 14–16.

ARCHELAUS

Archelaus, the elder son of *Herod the Great's Samaritan wife Malthace, was the principal successor to his father and ruled over Judaea, Idumaea and Samaria from 4 BCE to 6 CE. He was named as heir in Herod's last will and was meant to inherit the title of king. He set out to Rome at once to obtain the consent of the emperor *Augustus. So did his brother *Antipas, who contested Herod's last-minute change of arrangements since in the previous will he was designated as his father's principal beneficiary. Many other members of Herod's family, opposed to Archelaus, also intervened, as well as a delegation of Jewish notables, hostile to all the Herodians and favouring direct rule by Rome. Because of successive rebellions in Judaea and Galilee, which *Varus, the Roman governor of Syria, was sent to put down, the emperor's decision was delayed. Finally the plea of Herod's minister, the famous *Nicolaus of Damascus, brought partial triumph to the cause of Archelaus. He was allotted Judaea, Samaria and Idumaea, but had to content himself with the title of ethnarch, the royal dignity being denied to him.

Herod's disposition in favour of his other two sons, Antipas and *Philip, was confirmed. The former became tetrarch of Galilee and Peraea, the latter tetrarch of Batanaea, Trachonitis and Auranitis. Their aunt *Salome, one of the chief troublemakers during the life of Herod, inherited a sizeable sum of money (500,000 silver coins), together with the cities of Jamnia, Azotus and Phasaelis and the royal palace in Ashkelon.

Like his father, Archelaus showed himself to be cruel and despotic. He also upset his traditional subjects by marrying, contrary to Mosaic Law, Glaphyra, the former wife of one of his brothers, Alexander, by whom she had sons. He tried to imitate his father in architectural matters, restoring the royal palace in Jericho and building a new town in the same area, which he named Archelais after himself.

Archelaus failed to satisfy either the Jews or the Samaritans and the aristocrats of both groups denounced his lawless rule to Augustus. The emperor summoned Archelaus to Rome, listened to the ethnarch's accusers and allowed him to speak for himself. But his apologia was to no avail and he was deposed by Augustus, who exiled him to Vienne in Gaul and confiscated all his possessions.

Archelaus is alluded to once in the Gospel of *Matthew (2:22). His rule over Judaea is given as the explanation for *Joseph, *Mary and *Jesus settling in Galilee and not in Bethlehem. The evangelist erroneously calls Archelaus a king although he was only an ethnarch.

Sources: Josephus, *War* 2:3–9, 111–17; *Ant.* 17:339–55; 18: 1–108.

ARISTOBULUS II

Judas Aristobulus II, the younger son of Jonathan (Yannai) or Alexander Jannaeus (103–76 BCE), was the penultimate Hasmonaean to hold the office of both high priest and King of the Jews, between 67 and 63 BCE. Jannaeus was succeeded by his wife Alexandra Salome (Shelamzion) as queen from 76 to 67 BCE. As a woman, however, she could not occupy the post of high priest, which was inherited by her elder son, John *Hyrcanus II. The same Hyrcanus took over the royal power too on his mother's death, but his ambitious younger sibling dethroned the weak Hyrcanus after defeating his forces at Jericho. Aristobulus' usurpation of the chief political and religious function gave rise to a protracted civil war between the two brothers. Hyrcanus was supported by the Idumaean *Antipater, the father of *Herod the Great, and the Nabataean king Aretas III. Their combined forces compelled Aristobulus to take refuge on the Temple Mount in Jerusalem. It was in the course of this conflict that the charismatic rainmaker *Honi or Onias the Righteous was stoned to death by Hyrcanus' irate followers for refusing to put a curse on Aristobulus and his supporters. The internecine strife came to an end only when the Roman *Pompey, invited to intervene by the representatives of both Aristobulus and Hyrcanus, conquered Jerusalem in the autumn of 63 BCE. He arrested Aristobulus and reinstated Hyrcanus as high priest but deprived him of the royal title. The disgraced Aristobulus, together with his two sons Alexander and *Antigonus, as well as his two daughters and a great number of Jewish prisoners of war, were taken to Rome, where Aristobulus suffered utmost humiliation when as a defeated leader he was paraded in front of the chariot of the victor during Pompey's triumphal procession in 62 BCE.

Five years later Aristobulus and his son Antigonus managed to escape from Rome and organized an armed uprising in Judaea, but they were forced by the Roman legions to retreat to Transjordan. They finally gave themselves up in the mountain-top fortress of Machaerus, where later *John the Baptist was beheaded, and were sent back to Rome. Aristobulus remained there in prison for six years, but his children were released by the Roman Senate. At the outbreak of the civil war in 49 BCE between Julius *Caesar and Pompey, Caesar decided to free Aristobulus and planned to use him in his fight against Pompey's armies in Syria. However, Pompey's partisans frustrated this project by poisoning Aristobulus before he could leave Rome and also getting rid of his son Alexander, another supporter of Caesar, who was decapitated in Antioch. Aristobulus' other son Antigonus survived and was the last bearer of the Hasmonaean high-priestly office from 40 to 37 BCE. Thus came to a sad conclusion the story of the penultimate priest-king of the Maccabaean-Hasmonaean dynasty who, like his predecessors, was more deeply engaged in politics and military ventures than in religious matters or the divine service in the Temple of Jerusalem.

In addition to *Josephus, who is the principal source of the history of Aristobulus II (and Hyrcanus II), the Psalms of Solomon from the Pseudepigrapha and some of the Dead Sea Scrolls appear to contain further information. The rulers of Jerusalem mentioned in Psalms of Solomon 8:15–17, who went to greet the ruthless conqueror (Pompey), are unquestionably Aristobulus II and Hyrcanus II. The same two leaders are identified by A. Dupont-Sommer as the Wicked Priests of the Qumran Bible commentaries on Habakkuk and Nahum. Also the revolutionary chief Peitholaus, named in Josephus, who continued the anti-Roman struggle after the recapture of Aristobulus II in 56 BCE, is probably the person referred to as Ptolaus in a historical fragment among the Scrolls (4Q468e 3).

Sources: Josephus, *War* 1:120–58; *Ant.* 14:1–79. mTaan. 3:8.

ARISTOBULUS III

Aristobulus III was the last Hasmonaean high priest. His appointment to the office was the result of the plotting of his mother *Alexandra and the Egyptian queen *Cleopatra against *Ananel, installed as high priest by *Herod the Great. *Mark Antony, Cleopatra's husband and Herod's patron, put pressure on the king, and the seventeen-year-old Aristobulus was allowed to don the high-priestly vestments in 35 BCE. However, the popularity of the young Jewish prince aroused Herod's suspicion and he arranged for a swimming-pool 'accident' which resulted in the death of Aristobulus in 35/4 BCE.

Sources: Josephus, *War* 1:437; *Ant.* 15:23–64; 20:247–8.

ATHRONGES

Athronges or Athrongaeus was an obscure poor shepherd of remarkable stature and physical strength, who in the company of four equally powerful brothers started an uprising in the political chaos that followed the death of *Herod the Great in 4 BCE. Athronges proclaimed himself king, wore a royal diadem, and attacked Herod's army and the Romans. The violence against the armed forces, Jewish and Roman, not to mention the long-suffering civilian population of Judaea, went on for a long time. However, at the end the ringleaders were captured by the ethnarch *Archelaus and his men and the guerrilla war was brought to an end.

Sources: Josephus, *War* 2:60–65; *Ant.* 17:278–84.

ATTICUS

Atticus, probably Titus Claudius Herodes Atticus, was the Roman governor of Judaea from 99/100 to 102/3 CE. His notoriety in early Christianity stems from Eusebius' statement that it was under his administration during the reign of the emperor *Trajan that the cousin of *Jesus of Nazareth, Symeon son of Clopas, the second bishop of Jerusalem, successor to *James the brother of Jesus, suffered martyrdom at the age of 120 years (*Eccl. Hist.* 3:32). According to Hegesippus, who was Eusebius' source, Cleopas or Clopas was the brother of *Joseph, i.e. the uncle of Jesus.

Source: Eusebius quoting Hegesippus, *Eccl. Hist.* 3:32.

AUGUSTUS

Augustus, formerly Caius Julius Caesar Octavianus (63 BCE–14 CE), was the first emperor of Rome, from 31 BCE to 14 CE. In general, Augustus as a ruler continued Julius *Caesar's favourable policy towards the Jews, granting them freedom to practise their religion, autonomy to administer their affairs and permission to send monetary contributions to the Temple of Jerusalem. In return for Augustus' respect for Judaism daily sacrifices were offered for the emperor in the Jerusalem Sanctuary, a custom that continued under his successors until the beginning of the first war against Rome in 66 CE. The expenses for the sacrifices were borne by the Jewish people according to *Josephus, but *Philo maintains that Augustus himself provided sums for the purchase of two lambs and an ox per day.

The direct involvement of Augustus in Jewish matters began after his victory over *Mark Antony in 31 BCE. He recognized *Herod the Great as a friendly client-king, despite his former allegiance to Antony, and granted him important new territories such as the northern districts of Trachonitis, Batanea and Auranitis. In gratitude, Herod renamed various cities after the emperor (Caesar). Panaias in the north, where *Peter was to acknowledge Jesus as Messiah, was restyled Caesarea Philippi; the former Strato's Tower on the Mediterranean coast Caesarea Maritima; and the old city of Samaria, which was rebuilt by Herod, was known thereafter as Sebaste in the Greek (Latin *Augusta*).

Herod frequently visited the emperor, who treated him as a close friend. Augustus also took an active part in sorting out the turbulent marital and family affairs of the King of Judaea and acted as an arbiter in the matter of Herod's succession. Before his death Herod wrote several wills, the terms of which varied, and the confusion was further increased when a delegation of Judaeans requested Augustus not to allow the sons of Herod to rule over them. The emperor finally refused to acknowledge as king any of the three surviving sons of Herod. Instead he decided to redraw the political and administrative map of the Herodian realm. As a result, during the early years of the life of *Jesus, *Archelaus, the son designated by Herod as his successor, was

Bronze head of the Emperor Augustus found in the Sudan

refused the royal title and was downgraded to be the ethnarch of Judaea, Samaria and Idumaea. *Antipas and *Philip were named tetrarchs, the former of Galilee and Peraea (Transjordan) and the latter of Batanea, Auranitis, Gaulanitis, Panaias and Trachonitis north-east of Galilee.

Augustus directly intervened again in the government of Judaea when he deposed and exiled Archelaus as ethnarch, and ordered the governor of Syria, *Quirinius, to organize the tax registration of the inhabitants of Judaea, Samaria and Idumaea when Archelaus' former territories were annexed in 6 CE and became the new directly adminis- tered Roman province of Judaea.

The account of *Luke referring to a universal census in the Roman empire ordered by Augustus and executed in Judaea by Quirinius at the time of the birth of Jesus during the reign of Herod the Great is historically unlikely (see the articles on Quirinius and Herod the Great). Luke antedated the census of Quirinius from 6 CE to the last years of the life of Herod.

Sources: Philo, *Legatio* 156–7, 311–20. Josephus, *Ant.* 16:162–73; *War* 2, 197, 408–21. Lk 2:1–2.

B

BANNUS

Bannus was a hermit living in the Judaean desert in the mid-first century CE. The meagre information we possess regarding him comes from Flavius *Josephus. In his *Life* he reports that having experi- mented with the way of life according to the philosophy of the Phar- isees, Sadducees and Essenes, he became for a while the pupil of this ascetic. Josephus describes him as a man living in the wilderness, clothed with leaves or tree bark and eating the natural produce of the land. To ensure continuous ritual cleanness, he underwent frequent ablutions in cold water. His way of existence was not unlike that of *John the Baptist, who lived on locusts and wild honey and practised baptism (Mk 1:6). Another possible similar feature is that like the Baptist, Bannus also had disciples. The repeated purifications attributed to Bannus recall the ceremonial baths of the Essenes. However, since he did not live within an organized community, it is unlikely that he belonged to the Essene movement proper.

Source: Josephus, Life 11.

BARNABAS

Barnabas was the Aramaic surname of a Cypriot Levite called Joseph, who was for a time the principal companion of St *Paul. The name Barnabas is mistakenly translated in the Acts of the Apostles as 'Son of Encouragement'; its more likely meaning is 'Son of Prophecy'. Barnabas introduced his acquaintance, Saul of Tarsus, the future Paul, to the apostles in Jerusalem after Saul's mystical experience outside Damascus. When Barnabas was dispatched from Jerusalem to organize the Church in Antioch, he travelled to Tarsus and persuaded Saul-Paul to join him as his deputy. The two men were sent to Jerusalem with the relief money collected in Antioch for the Judaean brethren during the great famine under the emperor *Claudius, which was foretold by the prophet *Agabus. On their return to Antioch they were accompanied by John surnamed *Mark, the cousin of Barnabas. The three of them departed on the first missionary journey, by which time the leadership passed from Barnabas to Paul. At the council of the apostles in Jerusalem Paul and Barnabas jointly defended their Gentile mission and were sent back to Syria to continue the evangelization. In Antioch the friendship between Barnabas and Paul broke down when *Peter and Barnabas withdrew from table companionship with Gentile Christians under the moral pressure of the Jewish Christian visitors from Jerusalem, for which they were publicly rebuked by Paul. Before the second journey another clash occurred and their ways parted. Barnabas sailed with John Mark to Cyprus while Paul together with *Silas travelled by land through Syria and Cilicia. Thereafter

Barnabas is totally eclipsed by Paul and the Acts no longer refers to him.

The pseudonymous Epistle of Barnabas, an early Christian document written between 70 and 135 CE, with a strong anti-Jewish bias, has nothing to do with the Barnabas of the Acts.

Sources: Acts 4:36; 9:27; 11:21, 30; 12:25; 13–15; 1 Cor. 9:6; Gal. 2:1, 9; Col. 4:10.

BARTHOLOMEW

Bartholomew was one of the twelve apostles of Jesus according to the lists contained in the Synoptic Gospels and the Acts of the Apostles (Mk 3:16–19; Mt 10:2–4; Lk 6:14–16; Acts 1:12–14). His name never figures in the Gospel of *John, however, and it is often thought that Bartholomew and John's Nathanael, brought by *Philip the Apostle to Jesus (Jn 1:45–6), were one and the same person. We learn nothing about Bartholomew from the New Testament or anything historically reliable in later sources.

The Church historian Eusebius (fourth century) knew of a legendary tradition according to which Bartholomew preached the Christian message in India and left there a copy of the Aramaic Gospel of *Matthew.

Source: Eusebius, *Eccl. Hist.* 10:3.

BERNICE

Bernice or Berenice, the daughter of King *Agrippa I and the sister of King *Agrippa II, was one of the favourite subjects of the gossipmongers of the ancient world, Jewish and Roman. She was three times married. Her first husband was Marcus Julius Alexander, the son of the Alexandrian Jewish financier Alexander the Alabarch, and brother of Tiberius Julius *Alexander, Roman procurator of Judaea from 46 to 48 CE and nephew of *Philo of Alexandria. After Alexander's death, like many of the Herodian princesses, Bernice was given in marriage to an uncle, King *Herod of Chalcis. She was widowed a second time in 48 CE and thereafter we find her constantly in the company of her brother Agrippa II: rumour spread in both Palestine and in Roman high society that the two were lovers. To give the lie to the story, Bernice persuaded Polemon, King of Cilicia, to go through a marriage ceremony with her, but divorce soon followed and she returned to live with Agrippa. *Josephus expressly alludes to the liaison, as does the Latin poet Juvenal. The renowned satirist refers to a precious diamond ring which was made very famous by the finger of Bernice, a ring given by the barbarian Agrippa to his incestuous sister ('*adamas notissimus et Beronices/ in digito factus pretiosior. Hunc dedit olim/ barbarus incestae dedit hunc Agrippa sorori*').

Bernice's greatest conquest was *Titus, the son of *Vespasian, to whom his father, the newly proclaimed emperor, entrusted in 69 CE the conclusion of the war against the Jews. According to Roman chatterers the affair started before 69 CE in Palestine. The Roman historian Tacitus ascribed to Titus' 'passionate longing' for Queen Bernice his prompt return to Judaea from his mission to Rome, where he was sent by his father after the suicide of Nero to spy out the political lie of the land. In 75 CE, after the end of the Jewish war, we find Bernice in Rome living openly with Titus as his mistress. According to the small talk of the city Titus was so enamoured of her that the wedding bells were almost ringing ('*propterque insignem reginae Berenices amorem, cui etiam nuptias pollicitus ferebatur*'; 'on account of his notorious passion for Queen Berenice, to whom, it was said, he even proposed marriage' (Suetonius, *Divus Titus* 7:1)). In fact, he allowed her to behave as his wife (Cassius Dio). However, when in 79 CE on the death of Vespasian Titus ascended the imperial throne, he realized that marriage with Bernice would be unacceptable to the Roman people. Thereupon he forced himself to send her away from Rome 'against her will and his own' ('*invitus invitam*', *ibid.*, 7:2).

Her enjoyment of complete sexual freedom did not stop Bernice observing Jewish religious practices such as the fulfilment of a Nazirite vow in the Temple. As far as New Testament connections are concerned, the Acts of the Apostles recounts that she attended the famous meeting of 60 CE in Caesarea where St *Paul explained his religious ideas to Bernice's brother, Agrippa II, in the palace of the Roman procurator Porcius *Festus.

She is the eponymous heroine of *Bérénice*, the tragedy in verse written in 1670 by the great French dramatist Jean Racine.

Sources: Acts 25:13, 23; 26:30. Josephus, *War* 2; *Ant.* 18–20. Tacitus, *Histories* 2:2. Suetonius, *Divus Titus* 7:1–2. Dio 66:15, 4. Juvenal, *Saturae (Satires)* 6:156–8.

C

CAESAR

Caius Julius Caesar (100–44 BCE) was a Roman general and statesman. Apart from those trained in Roman history, few readers of the New Testament are aware of the considerable part played by Julius Caesar in the history of the Palestinian and Diaspora Jews during the last years of his life (49–44 BCE). The *Jewish Antiquities* of the historian Flavius *Josephus include extracts from a series of the relevant official documents dealing with Caesar's policy towards the Jews. Despite their fragmentary condition, they allow us to perceive the essentials.

To understand the situation, it is to be recalled that Judaea was conquered by *Pompey in 63 BCE. Pompey deposed and imprisoned the ruling Jewish high priest *Aristobulus II and replaced him with his brother *Hyrcanus II. Thus, to begin with, Hyrcanus as well as the emerging Palestinian political leader, the Idumaean *Antipater, the father of *Herod the Great, were supporters of Pompey. In 49 CE, at the outbreak of hostilities between Caesar and Pompey, Caesar and his party sought the support of the Jewish leaders. So he ordered the release from gaol in Rome of Aristobulus II, deposed by Pompey, and put at his disposal two legions to attack Pompey in Syria. This first plan misfired when Pompey's supporters poisoned Aristobulus in Rome before he was able to set off for Syria. Nevertheless, after Pompey's death, which soon followed his defeat by Caesar's forces in

Julius Caesar

the battle of Pharsalus (48 BCE), the high priest Hyrcanus II and Antipater switched allegiance and sided with the victor. Antipater, at the head of 3,000 Jewish soldiers, actively intervened in the battle and Hyrcanus ingratiated himself with Caesar by encouraging the Egyptian Jews to back him. As a reward, Caesar confirmed Hyrcanus as high priest and ethnarch of the Jews, and conferred on Antipater Roman citizenship and the title of procurator of Judaea, and exempted him from paying taxes. He thus ensured the rise of the Herodian dynasty, which was to rule in Palestine for the next 100 years or so.

Caesar's further favours to Hyrcanus included transferring to his territory the port of Ioppa/Jaffa and other cities, which Pompey had taken away from the Jews. He also authorized him to rebuild the walls of Jerusalem and exempted the Jews living in the land ruled by him from military service. Diaspora Jews also enjoyed Caesar's good will. The Alexandrian Jewish community saw its citizenship rights confirmed and Jews in Asia Minor were assured religious freedom.

Not surprisingly, Caesar became the hero of Jews all over the Roman world, and when he was assassinated on the Ides of March in 44 BCE, he is said to have been mourned more by the Jews than by the other nations. 'At the height of the public grief,' writes Suetonius, 'a throng of foreigners went about lamenting each after the fashion of his country, *above all the Jews, who even flocked to the funeral-pyre for several successive nights.*'

In 42 BCE Caesar was deified and from then on he was venerated as *divus Iulius.*

Sources: Josephus, *Ant.* 14. Suetonius, *Divus Iulius*, 84:5.

CAIAPHAS

Caiaphas, or Joseph Caiaphas according to *Josephus, was the longest-serving high priest of the Jews in the first century (18–36 CE). He played a very important part in the drama leading to the death of *Jesus of Nazareth. The most reliable elements of the evidence relating to him come from Josephus; some of the data contained in the Gospels are more questionable. Caiaphas was appointed high priest by *Valerius Gratus in 18 CE and remained in office under this prefect of Judaea and under his successor *Pontius Pilate. In 36/7 CE, both Caiaphas and Pilate were deposed by *Vitellius, the Roman governor of Syria. The Gospel of *John describes him as the son-in-law of the former high priest, *Ananus (or Annas), though Josephus remains silent on the matter.

In the Gospels of *Mark and *Luke the trial of Jesus is conducted in the house of an unnamed high priest, but *Matthew specifies that this high priest was Caiaphas. In the Gospel of John there is no mention of a trial proper, but rather of an interrogation of Jesus by the former high priest Annas, who then dispatches Jesus to Caiaphas. The latter, apparently without further questioning, hands him over to the Roman governor, Pilate (Jn 18:13–14, 19–24, 28). Matthew and Mark, but not Luke, who alludes to no court session at night, a practice which in fact was prohibited by Jewish law, speak of a nocturnal meeting of the council in the house of Caiaphas during which several witnesses proffered various accusations against Jesus, including his threat to destroy the Temple of Jerusalem. However, since their testimony did not fully tally, their evidence was not of the requisite quality to satisfy the court (Mt 26:59–61; Mk 14:55–9). The evangelists imply, however, that the high priest and the council were determined in advance to condemn Jesus to death. Therefore, in the absence of conclusive evidence supplied by witnesses, Caiaphas decided directly to confront Jesus with the question of whether he was 'the Christ' (Lk 22:67) or 'the Christ the son of God' (Mt 26:63) or 'the Christ, the son of the Blessed' (Mk 14:61).

Matthew and Luke furnish Jesus' customary evasive answer to such a question. 'You have said so' (Mt 26:64), he declares, or 'You say that I am' (Lk 22:70); either reply can be completed by the tacit 'but not I'. Mark (14:62) departs from Jesus' usual style with a plain 'I am', although variant readings in manuscripts reproduce the indecisive reply found in Matthew and Luke. Thereupon, the high priest without hesitation declares Jesus guilty and the council condemns him to death on the religious charge of blasphemy. As a matter of fact, there is no known Jewish law which would declare blasphemous the claim of being the Messiah or son of God. In fact, in the strict sense to blaspheme means to curse the name of God, which Jesus obviously did not do.

Once this dubious charge carrying the death sentence had been made, the religious line of criminal proceedings was not pursued any further. There is no question of applying to the condemned person the legally prescribed form of execution, which was stoning. Instead, the case of Jesus was abruptly transferred to the tribunal of the Roman governor under the politically motivated indictment of fomenting rebellion against the emperor. Mark, Matthew and Luke made no attempt to explain this switch. John, however, justifies it by asserting that the Jewish authorities were legally incompetent to carry out capital sentences stipulated by biblical law. In fact, they were impertinent

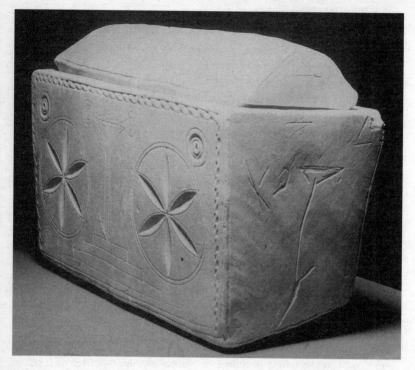

The ossuary thought to be that of the High Priest Caiaphas

enough to remind Pilate of the Roman law, which denied to Jews the right to put any man to death (Jn 18:31).

Opinions on the validity of this statement vary. Those who hold that the Sanhedrin had no power to carry out death sentences imposed on Jews for grave religious offences justify their view by claiming that the imperial legislation enacted in 6/7 CE reserved for the governor of the newly created Roman province of Judaea the power to execute criminals. For them this means that no capital sentence decreed by a Jewish court could be implemented without Roman consent. But the opposite view, which maintains that the Sanhedrin continued to enjoy capital jurisdiction in the field of biblical criminal law, can marshal equally strong, if not even stronger, support from literary and epigraphic evidence. Josephus states, and an inscription proclaims, that a non-Jew, even a Roman citizen, was to be put to death if caught in the inner court of the Temple. There is no mention of the need of Roman approval. *Philo also asserts that entry into the Holy of Holies, that is, the innermost area of the sanctuary, by a Jew or even by a priest, was automatically punishable by death (*Legatio* 307). Furthermore, the trial of *Paul before the Sanhedrin, referred to in the Acts of the Apostles (23–6), also assumes that the Jewish high court possessed capital jurisdiction. In brief, while Joseph Caiaphas by delivering Jesus to Pilate was instrumental in his crucifixion, the ultimate responsibility for this miscarriage of justice belonged to Pontius Pilate and to the Roman empire, which he represented.

The Gospel accounts concerning Caiaphas need to be corrected on three additional points. According to Luke (3:2), Annas and Caiaphas *jointly* held the high priesthood during and after the public career of *John the Baptist. However, such a state of affairs would have conflicted with Jewish religious law, which recognized only a single ruling high priest at a time. The most likely explanation of Luke's misrepresentation is that the power behind the throne during the pontificate of Caiaphas was his father-in-law, the former high priest Annas. His considerable influence is obvious from the fact that he not only managed to make his son-in-law his immediate successor (Jn 18:13), but also secured the high-priestly office for five of his sons and for a grandson. John (11:49; 18:13) twice describes Caiaphas as the high priest of 'that year', thus implying that the appointment was annual. This assumption is not backed by any historical evidence, however. In biblical times the hereditary high priest remained in office for life. Under Herod and his successors as well as under the Roman governors the choice of the high priest was in the hands of the civil authority. It is true that many of them officiated for relatively short periods, but Annas and Caiaphas constituted notable exceptions and held their posts for nine and eighteen years respectively. John (11:50) makes Caiaphas proclaim an important Jewish legal principle, namely that the welfare of the community is more valuable than the life of an individual. The issue was repeatedly discussed by the rabbis of the Mishnaic and Talmudic age in connection with cases when the Roman authorities demanded the extradition of a Jewish revolutionary under the threat of general retaliation against the population for harbouring the fugitive. The rabbis were generally unwilling directly to hand over a Jew to Gentiles, but in the interest of the larger community they attempted to persuade the fugitive to give himself up voluntarily. In this context, it is easy to assume that the readiness of the high priest and the council to deliver Jesus to Pilate was motivated by their belief, based on the riot caused by Jesus in the merchants' quarter of the Temple, that he was a potential troublemaker and that it was their duty as guardians of law and order to protect the population from Roman violence, even if that entailed the handing over of an irresponsible individual to the Gentile state. Passing the buck is not a modern invention.

As far as material relics relating to Caiaphas are concerned, an unverifiable early Christian tradition recorded by the so-called Bordeaux Pilgrim in 333 CE locates his house in the neighbourhood of today's Armenian Monastery of St Saviour next to the Benedictine Abbey of the Dormition. More sensationally, in the course of building works performed in 1990 in the Peace Forest on the southern edge of Jerusalem, a Jewish burial cave was discovered which yielded four ossuaries among other relics. On one of these the name Qapha or Caiaphas figures, and on another, a splendidly decorated bone-box, we read Yehoseph bar Qayapha, or Joseph son of Caiaphas. The letters are clearly legible and represent an unaesthetic cursive script of the first century CE. The most likely conclusion is that the ossuaries come from the tomb of the Caiaphas family. The most ornate of them contained the bones of six individuals: two infants, a two- to five-year-old child, a teenage boy, an adult woman and a man aged about sixty years. There is a chance that this older man was the high priest who presided over the case of Jesus.

Sources: Josephus, *Ant.* 18:35, 95. Ossuary of Caiaphas: W. Horbury, *Palestine Exploration Quarterly* 126 (1994), 32–48.

CALIGULA

Gaius Julius Caesar Germanicus, surnamed Caligula (12–41 CE), sat on the imperial throne from 37 to 41 CE. He was the son of the nephew of *Tiberius and succeeded him at the age of twenty-five. The Jews, we are told, were the first among the nations of the Roman empire to welcome his accession and offered sacrifice for his well-being in the Temple of Jerusalem (*Philo, *Legatio* 231–2). During his short reign Caligula repeatedly interfered with the political and religious affairs of the Jews in Judaea and Alexandria. To begin with politics: he deposed Herod *Antipas from the tetrarchy of Galilee, exiled him to Lyons in Gaul, and assigned his territory, together with the tetrarchy of *Philip, to his friend *Agrippa I, the grandson of *Herod the Great, to whom he granted the title of king.

Caligula's religious conflict with the Jews resulted from his belief that as a Roman emperor he was truly divine. Consequently, refusal to worship him was treated as lese-majesty. In this connection violent riots broke out against the Jews in Alexandria in 38 CE, apparently encouraged by the emperor himself. The governor of Egypt, Flaccus (Philo, *Against Flaccus* 8–24), not only did not stop the disturbances, but created further trouble by allowing images of the emperor to be set up in Jewish synagogues. He also unlawfully stripped the Alexandrian Jews of their civic rights (*ibid.*, 40–57), and even ordered the elders of the Jewish council to be flogged publicly. The persecution continued for several months until the autumn of 38 CE, when Flaccus was first banished from his post and later executed by order of Caligula (*ibid.*, 97–191). Both the Greeks and the Jews of Alexandria sent delegations to Rome to plead their cases. The Greeks were headed by the controversialist Apion, known from *Josephus' polemical work, *Against Apion*, and the Jews by the famous philosopher Philo of Alexandria. However, neither of them made much impact on Caligula. He castigated them both for their disbelief in his divinity (*Legatio*, 349–73).

In the following year, 39 CE, further unrest occurred in Judaea when Caligula decided to set up his image in the Temple of Jerusalem. To achieve his aim, he instructed *Petronius, the governor of Syria, to use half of the Roman legions under his command to enforce his

The Emperor Gaius Caligula

order. Petronius, who was a sensible man, attempted to negotiate a compromise solution with the Jewish representatives but to no effect. He then tried to gain time, but his lack of alacrity to implement the imperial decree enraged Caligula, who instructed him in a letter to commit suicide. Caligula was murdered in January 41 CE, and since news of the emperor's assassination travelled faster than the letter carrying Petronius' death sentence, the governor of Syria abstained from committing suicide and shelved for good the idea of erecting Caligula's statue in Jerusalem.

Sources: Philo, *Legatio* 231–2, 349–73. Josephus, *War* 2:178–208; *Ant.* 18–19.

CLAUDIUS

Claudius Tiberius Drusus (10 BCE–54 CE), grandson of *Mark Antony, step-grandson and great-nephew of *Augustus, was the fourth emperor of Rome. He was raised to the throne by the praetorian guard after the murder of *Caligula and reigned from 41 to 54 CE.

As far as Judaean matters were concerned, the only direct intervention by Claudius consisted in his granting permission for the high priest's vestments to be kept under Jewish, not Roman, custody, thus enlarging the high priest's freedom of action. By contrast, he played a significant part in resolving the conflict between Alexandrian Greeks and Jews, which flared up during the reign of his predecessor, Caligula. Claudius restored religious freedom to the Jews and condemned to death the two Egyptian leaders of the anti-Jewish riots. In a letter dated October 41 CE, the emperor enjoined both parties to keep the peace and ordered them not to interfere with each other's business. At the same time he reminded the Jews of their privileges in a city which was not their own (Papyrus London 19:2). The terms of this settlement differ from those given by *Josephus, who speaks of equal rights enjoyed by the Greek and Jewish citizens of Alexandria (*Ant.* 19:279–85).

Claudius is mentioned twice in the New Testament. The first reference is associated with the great famine which devastated Palestine

The Emperor Claudius

during his rule. According to the Christian prophet *Agabus the famine afflicted the whole world (Acts 11:28–30), but Josephus restricts it only to Judaea (*Ant.* 20:101). The second mention of Claudius is linked to his expulsion of the Jews from Rome, among whom were Aquila and Priscilla, *Paul's associates in Corinth (Acts 18:2). The silence of Josephus on this expulsion is surprising. On the other hand, the Roman historian Suetonius speaks of disturbances among Roman Jews, which he blames on a certain 'Chrestus'. Although Chrestus was a common name, it is quite possible that it is a distortion of 'Christus' and that the allusion concerns upheavals among Jews and Jewish Christians in Rome. Suetonius may imply that this 'Chrestus' was personally the instigator of the troubles. He lacks the precision of Tacitus, who knew that the 'Chrestiani'

(Christians) were the followers of someone called 'Christus' (Christ), who was executed by Pontius *Pilate during the reign of *Tiberius.

Sources: Josephus, War 2:204–48; Ant. 19–20. Suetonius, Divus Claudius 25:4. Tacitus, Annals 15:44, 2–3.

CLEOPATRA

Cleopatra VII (69–30 BCE), the last queen of Egypt, was deeply involved in both Roman and Jewish history. She was the lover of Julius *Caesar to whom she bore a son, Caesarion. Next she bewitched *Mark Antony. They had an affair and married in 36 BCE. They had three children. One of them had a daughter who later became the wife of *Felix, procurator of Judaea from 52 to 60 CE.

Cleopatra had an eye on the territory of *Herod the Great and through her influence on Mark Antony, Herod's Roman patron, she obtained possession of the district of Jericho. She was a close friend of *Alexandra, the Hasmonaean princess and mother-in-law of Herod. The two women persuaded Mark Antony to order Herod to appoint *Aristobulus III, Alexandra's son, as high priest and to compel him, after Aristobulus' suspicious death, to account for the swimming-pool 'accident'. Cleopatra paid a royal visit to Herod and *Josephus mentions her plan to start an affair with the king of Judaea. 'Being in Herod's company very often, Cleopatra attempted to have sexual intercourse with the king, for she was by nature used to enjoying this kind of pleasure without disguise' (Ant. 15:97). She was motivated, Josephus tells us, by 'some measure of passion' as well as by cold political calculation: she knew that an affair would compromise Herod before Mark Antony. Herod, on the other hand, imagined that this might provide him with an opportunity to get rid of the dangerous woman, but foreseeing the danger of upsetting his political master, he dropped the idea. Cleopatra unintentionally saved Herod's neck when during the conflict with Octavian, the future *Augustus, she induced her husband to employ Herod's forces in an attack against the King of the Nabataeans, who owed her a large sum of money, instead of assisting Antony against Octavian.

*The Portland Vase of cameo glass thought to
represent Cleopatra seducing Mark Antony*

Cleopatra, whom the Latin poet Horace depicts as a 'fatal monster'
(*fatale monstrum*), was used by Octavian to discredit his fellow triumvir Mark Antony. After his defeat in the battle of Actium in 31 BCE,
both Antony and Cleopatra committed suicide in 30 BCE.

Sources: Josephus, *War* 1; *Ant.* 14–15. Horace, *Odes* 1:37, 21.

COPONIUS

Coponius was the first Roman governor of Judaea (6–8 CE), appointed
by *Augustus after the deposition of the ethnarch of Judaea,

*Archelaus son of *Herod the Great. Coponius was a Roman knight who was granted full administrative and judicial authority including the right to impose the death penalty. It was during the governorship of Coponius that *Quirinius performed the census of Judaea; *Judas the Galilean or Judas of Gamala, together with a Pharisee called Zadok, launched the revolutionary party of the Zealots-Sicarii, and a desecration of the Temple occurred when a group of Samaritans surreptitiously entered the sanctuary and threw human bones into the holy precincts. On completing his office, Coponius returned to Rome.

He was followed by Marcus Ambivulus or Ambibulus (9–12 CE), about whose administration *Josephus tells us nothing, and Annius Rufus (12–15 CE), under whose governorship Augustus died and *Tiberius inherited the imperial throne in 14 CE.

Sources: Josephus, *War* 2:117–8; *Ant.* 18:2, 29, 31.

CORNELIUS

Cornelius was a Roman centurion garrisoned in Caesarea. The author of the Acts of the Apostles describes him as a God-fearer, that is, a Gentile sympathizer of the Jewish religion. Whether historically attested or not, Cornelius is one of the leading characters in the drama of the reception of non-Jews in the primitive Judaeo-Christian community. The episode is prepared by two visions: the apostle *Peter is instructed in a dream to discard the distinction between clean and unclean food, and Cornelius, while reciting the Jewish prayer of the ninth hour, is commanded by an angel to invite Peter to his house. Peter came and told the centurion and his family and friends that God had revealed to him that Jews could mix with Gentiles. Peter conveyed to them the essentials of the gospel: the baptism of John, the healing, exorcizing and preaching activity of Jesus in Galilee, his death and resurrection and his expected return as the final judge, and forgiveness of sins through faith. Then suddenly Cornelius and his entourage were seized by the Spirit and praised God, speaking in tongues.

The lesson drawn from the story was that Gentile God-fearers could receive baptism and enter the Church without full initiation into

Judaism, that is to say, the substance of *Paul's missionary message. The anecdote has a political bias. Bearing in mind the conflict between Peter and Paul vis-à-vis the treatment of the Gentiles, it was in the interest of Peter's party to credit this fundamental liberal innovation to Peter before the apostolic council attended by Paul. Nevertheless, in favour of some historical reality underlying the Cornelius episode one may point to such concrete details as the address of Peter in Ioppa (the house of Simon the Tanner) or Cornelius' attachment as a centurion to the *Cohors Italica* in Caesarea. So it is likely that a Roman officer was admitted into the Caesarean Christian community without being first obliged to undergo complete initiation into Judaism.

Source: Acts 10.

CUMANUS

Ventidius Cumanus held the office of Roman procurator of Judaea from 48 to 52 CE. While revolution simmered under his two predecessors, it came to the boil from the mid-first century onwards.

The first disorder was provoked during the feast of Passover when one of the Roman guards posted on the roof of the portico of the Temple turned his bare bottom towards the assembled Jews and accompanied the gesture with an appropriate rude noise. Loud protest and stone-throwing ensued and more troops were brought in, forcing the protesters to flee, with a large number of them losing their lives in the stampede. The figure of 20,000 or 30,000 given by *Josephus seems an exaggeration, however.

The next upheaval occurred during a punishing raid by Roman soldiers on Jewish villages in the proximity of which an imperial slave was robbed by Jews. One of the legionaries, having tumbled upon a scroll of the Law, tore it up and burned it. Enraged crowds rushed to Caesarea to ask Cumanus to punish the culprit. To pacify the Jews, the procurator ordered the public execution of the soldier.

The third disturbance was more serious and led to Cumanus' loss of his governorship. The source of the troubles was the murder of a Galilean pilgrim on his way to Jerusalem through Samaria. Cumanus, having been bribed by the Samaritans, remained inactive, and the Jews, from both Galilee and Judaea, decided to take revenge into their own hands. Cumanus then intervened and attacked the Jews, killing many of them and taking others to Caesarea as prisoners. Both the Jews and the Samaritans sought the help of the Roman governor of Syria, Ummidius Quadratus. He decided to investigate the matter, executed the Jewish rebels imprisoned by Cumanus, and sent the Jewish and the Samaritan chief agitators as well as Cumanus to Rome. The emperor *Claudius, advised by the Jewish king *Agrippa II, found in favour of the Jews and executed the Samaritan leaders. He also relieved Cumanus from office and sent him into exile. The storm clouds of the great rebellion were gathering.

Sources: Josephus, War 2:223–46; Ant. 103–36.

D

DOMITIAN

Titus Flavius Domitianus (51–96 CE), younger son of *Vespasian, was Roman emperor from 81 to 96 CE. During his reign anti-Jewish, and apparently also anti-Christian, sentiments rumbled on in Rome. The main channel through which these hostile feelings were expressed was the tax for Jupiter Capitolinus. The tax of two drachmas paid by every adult male Jew for the upkeep of the Temple of Jerusalem was transferred into the treasury of this Roman temple. First introduced by Vespasian, this taxation, the notorious *fiscus Iudaicus*, was more stringently collected under Domitian, though slightly relaxed under his successor Nerva (96–98 CE). Suetonius offers a vivid account of these changes. 'The Jewish tax', he writes,

was levied with the utmost vigour, and those were prosecuted who without publicly acknowledging that faith yet lived as Jews, as well as those who

The Emperor Domitian

concealed their origin and did not pay the tribute imposed upon their people. I recall being present in my youth when the person of a man ninety years old was examined before the procurator and a very crowded court, to see whether he was circumcised.

Conversion to Judaism, identified as atheism, was also severely prohibited. The consul Flavius Clemens, the emperor's cousin, and many others were put to death under this charge. Those who escaped with their lives had to forfeit their property (Cassius Dio). Eusebius, echoing the second-century writer Hegesippus, speaks of Domitian's persecution of Christians who, like the grandsons of *Jesus' brother Jude, were thought in Christian circles to be the descendants of King David. The historicity of this account is questionable, however.

Domitian was suspected, probably unjustly, of the murder of his brother and predecessor *Titus (Suetonius, Dio). It is beyond doubt, however, that he met with violent death in 96 CE.

Sources: Suetonius, *Domitianus* 12:2. Dio 66:17; 67:14, 1–2. Eusebius, *Eccl. Hist.* 3:19.

DRUSILLA

Drusilla was a Jewish Herodian princess who, according to the Acts of the Apostles (24:24), was present at a conversation between her husband *Felix, the Roman procurator of Judaea (58–60 CE), and St *Paul, who was kept in detention in Caesarea.

Drusilla was the daughter of the Jewish king *Agrippa I and his wife Cyprus, and the sister of *Agrippa II and of Queen *Bernice, who made her younger sibling's life unpleasant because she resented her great beauty. Drusilla's troubled marital history gives an interesting insight into the social rules governing Jewish royalty in the first century CE. She was first engaged to Epiphanes, son of the non-Jewish king Antiochus of Commagene, but the engagement was broken by the bridegroom, who refused to undergo circumcision, as was demanded by Drusilla's family. The Herodians considered themselves and behaved publicly as Jews. A second marriage was arranged for Drusilla by her brother Agrippa II to Azizus, King of Emesa, another Gentile who had no objection to becoming a Jew. This union broke down, however, when the Roman procurator Antonius Felix, with the collaboration of a Jewish magician, persuaded the beautiful Drusilla to disregard the demands of Judaism and marry an uncircumcised Roman freed slave who, as the historian Suetonius observed, became the husband of three queens. They had a son called Agrippa who was among the victims of the eruption of the Vesuvius, which destroyed Pompeii and Herculaneum in 79 CE.

Sources: Josephus, *War* 2:220; *Ant.* 19:354–5. Suetonius, *Divus Claudius* 28.

E

EGYPTIAN, THE

'The Egyptian' was the nickname of a Jewish rebel leader who belonged to the group called by *Josephus 'deceivers and impostors' and who pretended to be divine envoys commissioned to instigate revolution. The Egyptian burst on to the public scene probably in 58 CE under the procuratorship of *Felix (52–60 CE) and attracted a large following in the desert – about 30,000 men according to Josephus in the *Jewish War*. From there he took them to the Mount of Olives outside Jerusalem and promised the misguided crowd the renewal of Joshua's miracle at Jericho: at his command the walls of Jerusalem would collapse and as King of the Jews he would annihilate the Roman forces stationed in the city. The governor Felix anticipated this move. He attacked the insurgents with a large force, and according to *Jewish Antiquities* killed 400 men and captured another 200. The rest, including their Egyptian leader, escaped. In the version included in the *Jewish War* most of the 30,000 were struck down or taken prisoner and only a few managed to slip away with the Egyptian.

The story has a New Testament dimension. When in 58 CE the apostle *Paul was taken into custody by the Roman guard in the Temple, the arresting officer, Claudius Lysias, mistook him for the Egyptian (Acts 21:38). According to the author of the Acts the size of the rebel forces amounted to 4,000, a much smaller number than the 30,000 mentioned in Josephus' *Jewish War*, but larger than the 400 killed and 200 captured in his *Jewish Antiquities*.

Sources: Josephus, *War*, 2:261; *Ant.* 20:171.

ELEAZAR SON OF ANANUS

See under **Ananus (or Annas) son of Sethi.**

ELEAZAR SON OF BOETHUS

See under **Joazar son of Boethus**.

ELEAZAR SON OF JAIRUS

Eleazar son of Jairus, a member of the revolutionary family of *Judas the Galilean, possibly his grandson, and a relative of the leader of the Sicarii, *Menahem, was the captain of the last group of Jewish resistance fighters who continued the war against the Romans in the fortress of Masada after the destruction of Jerusalem in 70 CE. The apparently impregnable stronghold, built by *Herod the Great, was besieged by the Romans under Flavius *Silva. Before its fall, probably in 74 CE, Eleazar exhorted the defenders and their families to choose death rather than servitude. In a long speech, no doubt penned by *Josephus, he persuaded his followers to sacrifice themselves. The men killed their families and then one another, down to the last ten. Nine of these were slaughtered by the last who finally committed suicide. Altogether 960 persons died. Only two women and five children, hidden in underground passages, survived to tell the tragic and heroic tale.

Josephus dates the event to the fifteenth day of Xanthicus (Nisan), that is, to the feast of Passover. The death of Eleazar, the fall of Masada and the end of the first war against Rome used to be dated to 73 CE. However, two Roman inscriptions prove that Flavius Silva did not become governor of Judaea before 73 CE and that consequently the siege of Masada could not have been completed before the spring of 74 CE.

The name 'son of Jairus' (*ben Yair*) appears on a potsherd found at Masada during the excavation of the site by Yigael Yadin in the 1960s. Nevertheless Yadin admits that the same two words could be read as 'sons of light' (*beney 'ôr*), a title used by the members of the community of the Dead Sea Scrolls.

Sources: Josephus, *War* 7: 250–406. Y. Yadin and J. Naveh, *Masada I* (Jerusalem, 1989), no. 437, p. 28.

The Fortress of Masada, defended by Eleazar son of Jairus

ELEAZAR SON OF SIMON

Eleazar son of Simon was the leader of one of the Jewish factions fighting the Romans, and to an even greater extent the other Jewish groups in Jerusalem, during the first anti-Roman rebellion between 66 and 70 CE. At the start of the uprising Eleazar and his men attacked the party led by *Menahem son of *Judas the Galilean, and murdered him and his lieutenant Absalom. The same thugs were also responsible for the killing of the former high priest *Ananias son of Nedebaeus and his brother Ezechias. Eleazar appears again in 70 CE as one of the three Jewish captains hostile to one another, the other two being *John of Gischala and *Simon son of Giora. Eleazar was holding the inner forecourt of the Temple with his 2,400 men, John the Temple Mount and Simon the upper city and much of the lower city. Eleazar was eliminated by a ruse when at Passover in 70 CE he allowed pilgrims into the Sanctuary. The fighters of John of Gischala used the opportunity to enter the Temple forecourt with their weapons concealed and launch a surprise attack on Eleazar's forces, which forced them to withdraw. Eleazar's end has not been recorded by *Josephus, but it is unlikely that he survived the final stages of the siege.

Source: Josephus, *War* 2:564–5; 5:5–21, 99, 250.

ELEAZAR THE EXORCIST

Eleazar, possibly an Essene, was a renowned exorcist during the first Jewish war against Rome (66–70 CE). *Josephus was the eye-witness of a master class in exorcism given by Eleazar in the presence of *Vespasian, his sons, officers and soldiers, in the course of which he delivered several men of demonic possession. He put to the nose of the possessed a ring, which contained roots prescribed by King Solomon, the greatest expert in the secret properties of nature and author of healing incantations. The smell of the roots made the possessed sneeze and the exorcistic formula caused the evil spirit to depart through the nostrils. In his fit the man fell down and in the name of

Solomon Eleazar forbade the demon to return. To make things more dramatic, before the exorcism Eleazar placed a cup filled with water close to the patient and ordered the demon to spill the water as he left the agitated possessed.

Eleazar's performance has definite similarities to the exorcism practised by *Jesus of Nazareth. He too commanded the demon to depart and never to return (Mk 1:25; 9:25), but he did not make use of incantations or histrionics.

Later Jewish magical literature also refers to Solomon's signet ring with a precious stone (Testament of Solomon 1:6) or to a ring on which the sacrosanct name of God was engraved (bGit. 68b).

Source: Josephus, *Ant.* 8:46–8.

ELIONAEUS SON OF KANTHERAS

See under Simon Kantheras son of Boethus.

ELYMAS

Elymas, known also as Bar Jesus, was a Jewish magician-prophet attached to the personnel of the Roman proconsul Sergius Paulus in Cyprus. At the city of Paphos he met St *Paul who, in the company of *Barnabas, himself a Cypriot, was invited by the proconsul to address him about his religious ideas. Elymas stood up to Paul whom he no doubt considered as a rival. According to the author of the Acts of the Apostles, Paul, using his own charismatic power, inflicted blindness on the magician. Sergius Paulus, having witnessed Paul's superior power, believed in his preaching.

The anecdote may be apocryphal, but it testifies to the charismatic atmosphere of primitive Christianity not only in Palestine but in a Graeco-Roman and Pauline setting as well.

Source: Acts 13:8.

EXORCIST, ANONYMOUS

An unnamed exorcist who did not belong to the circle of the apostles is reported to have expelled demons in the name of *Jesus. The quick-tempered apostle *John son of Zebedee and his colleagues attempted to stop him. Having failed to do so they reported the matter to Jesus, who however poured cold water on their enthusiasm. Anyone successfully working for the Kingdom of God and fighting Satan was an ally of Jesus (Mk 9:38–40; Lk 9:49–50).

The story indicates that charismatic exorcism was a not uncommon phenomenon in first-century CE Palestine. On the other hand, it appears from the episode of the seven Jewish itinerant exorcists, sons of the otherwise unknown high priest Sceva, that professional exorcists plagiarized their rivals' successful formulae. According to the Acts of the Apostles the sons of Sceva employed the name of Jesus in Ephesus, but the demon made fun of them, saying, 'Jesus I know . . . but who are you?' (Acts 19:13–15).

Sources: New Testament.

EZECHIAS

Ezechias the robber captain was the leader of a band of irregulars who were roaming Galilee when the future King *Herod the Great, then aged about twenty-five, was its governor in the mid-first century BCE. All we know for certain is that Ezechias was caught and put to death by the young Herod. Yet instead of being congratulated for freeing the province of bandits, Herod was arraigned before the Jewish Sanhedrin and tried for summary executions after the complaints of the mothers of the executed men were heard by *Hyrcanus II, the high priest and ethnarch. It would seem therefore that Ezechias and his companions were not common criminals but quasi-political insurgents protesting against the growing importance of Herod and his family. The term 'robber' (*lêstês*) is often used as a synonym for a revolutionary in *Josephus, for whom the foundation of the Zealot party amounted to the proliferation of acts of brigandry.

It is reasonable to assume that the events which took place in Galilee in 47 BCE marked the beginning of clandestine nationalist resistance to the Romans and their agents, the Herodians. The identification of the robber captain Ezechias with Ezechias the father of *Judas the Galilean, the great rebel leader who appeared on the public scene after the death of Herod, cannot be definitively proved, but it carries a serious degree of probability. If so, with the events in Galilee in the mid-first century BCE we witness here the birth of the Zealot movement, which played a major role in Jewish history during the following 100 years before climaxing in the great Jewish uprising against Rome in 66 CE.

Sources: Josephus, *War* 1:204, 256; *Ant.* 14:159, 167.

F

FADUS

Cuspius Fadus was the first procurator of Judaea under the emperor *Claudius and held office from 44 to 46 CE. Of his two predecessors in the post of governor, Marcellus (36/7 CE) and Marullus (37–41 CE), nothing is known apart from their names. Between 41 and 44 CE *Agrippa I was made King of Judaea, Samaria and Galilee by Claudius, in whose succession as emperor Agrippa played a notable part. The restoration of the Judaean kingship meant that for three years there was no need for Roman governors. The responsibility for the government of the country lay on the shoulders of Agrippa I.

Fadus' period of office was characterized by political and religious turmoil. The people of Peraea (Transjordan) were in open conflict with the inhabitants of the Hellenistic city of Philadelphia (present-day Amman) about their respective frontiers. Fadus intervened on behalf of the Philadelphians, but as soon as peace was established he upset the Jews by reclaiming the right to the custody of their high priest's vestments. The dispute was settled by Claudius in favour of the status quo.

A further upheaval, which links Fadus to the New Testament, soon followed when a self-proclaimed prophet by the name of *Theudas led a crowd of credulous Jews to the Jordan with the promise of repeating the miracle of crossing the river performed by Joshua at the time of the conquest of Canaan. The division of the waters of the Jordan allowing free passage would prove that Theudas was a God-chosen leader of the Jews against the Romans. The cavalry unit sent by Fadus surprised the rebels and put an end to the Theudas party. The leader himself was captured and killed, and his severed head was carried to Jerusalem. The Acts of the Apostles (5:36) refers to the episode in the speech of *Gamaliel the Elder, who quoted the case of Theudas to prove before the Sanhedrin of Jerusalem that religious movements unsupported by God always come to nothing.

Sources: Josephus, *War* 2:220; *Ant.* 19:363; 20:97–9.

FALCO

Quintus Roscius Caelius Pompeius Falco followed the otherwise little-known Caius Julius Quadratus Bassus (102/3–104/5 CE) as the Roman governor of Judaea between 105 and 107 CE. There are no records about his dealing with Jewish matters during his governorship. However, a letter of recommendation addressed to him by the Younger Pliny from Rome, where he was a top civil servant in charge of the maintenance of the bed and banks of the Tiber and the sewers of the city, marvellously illustrates the genre of epistolary literature practised in highly literate Roman circles. This was a few years before *Trajan appointed Pliny governor of Pontus and Bithynia in Asia Minor. (On Pliny's correspondence with the emperor about the treatment of Christians, see the article on Trajan.) Pliny's letter implies that there was an earlier communication between him and Falco. In it, while sympathetic to Pliny's request to grant a position in the

Roman army under his command in Judaea to an unnamed friend of Pliny, Falco had asked for more information, which he was given in this second letter.

You may have felt that I was rather pressing in my request for you to confer a military tribunate [temporary command of a legion] on a friend of mine, but you will be less surprised when you know who and what he is. Now that I have your promise I can give you his name and full description. He is Cornelius Minucianus, in rank and character the pride of my native district [Pliny was born in Comum, that is to say in Como in North Italy]. He is well born and rich, but cares for literature as a poor professional might; and he is remarkable too for his justice on the bench, courage at the bar, and loyalty in friendship. You will feel that it is you who are receiving the favour when you come to know him more intimately and find that he is equal to any official position or distinction. I don't want to say more in praise of the most modest of men.

We cannot be sure whether Cornelius Minucianus had been offered the tribunate, but on the basis of Pliny's letter he should have been. The great ancient historian Sir Ronald Syme expressed doubts about Minucianus ever taking up the position brokered for him by Pliny in Judaea, as there is inscriptional evidence of a Cornelius Minucianus serving at the relevant time as military tribune in the third (Augusta) legion in North Africa. Did he opt for a better or safer job even at the cost of letting his patron Pliny down?

Source: Pliny the Younger, *Letters* 7:22.

FELIX

Antonius Felix, a favourite of the emperor *Claudius and of the Jewish high priest *Jonathan son of Ananus, succeeded the dismissed *Cumanus in the procuratorship of Judaea in 52 CE and held it for the relatively long period of eight years until 60 CE. He and his brother Pallas were very influential freedmen in the Claudian court. Felix was a successful social climber who married three royal princesses in succession. One of these was the granddaughter of *Cleopatra and *Mark Antony. With the help of a Jewish magician he persuaded another, *Drusilla, the daughter of the Jewish king *Agrippa I, to marry him in complete disregard of the Mosaic prohibition of matrimony with a non-Jewish person.

Felix, despite his high rank, revealed himself as the true progeny of his lowly ancestors. The Roman historian Tacitus describes him as a man who 'practised every kind of cruelty and lust, wielding the power of a king with all the instincts of a slave' (*Histories*). Tacitus also judges scathingly Felix's administration: 'He thought he could perform all criminal acts with impunity' (*Annals*).

Lawlessness reigned in the country and this was to a large extent provoked by Felix's harsh treatment of dissatisfied Jews. He captured the leader of the Zealots, Eleazar son of Dinaeus, by ruse and dispatched him to Rome for trial. He took advantage of the insurrectionists, known as 'daggermen' or Sicarii, and bribed them to murder his constant critic, the high priest Jonathan. These Sicarii terrorized the population by stealthily assassinating their political opponents with small daggers easily concealed under their cloaks. Political and religious disturbances continued simultaneously. Deceivers and impostors fooled many gullible Jews who followed them to the desert to witness the fulfilment of the promised liberation from the Romans, only to be cut down savagely by the swords of Felix's legionaries. The best known of the rogues was nicknamed 'the *Egyptian'. He paraded as a prophet and persuaded a multitude of Jews to follow him to the Mount of Olives from where he planned to force his way into Jerusalem. Felix's heavy infantry made minced meat of the Egyptian's followers but their leader managed to escape. The figures regarding the size of the rebellion vary. *Josephus speaks of 30,000 followers of the Egyptian, most of whom were killed (*War* 2:261–3), but the Acts of the Apostles (21:38) gives their number as 4,000, and Josephus in the *Antiquities* (20:171), without giving the grand total of the rebels, notes more realistically that the Roman cavalry and infantry slaughtered 400 men and captured another 200 prisoners. Terror continued to escalate, with political and religious fanatics banding together and venting their fury against the hated Felix.

The episode of the Egyptian establishes a link between Antonius

Felix and the New Testament, and more specifically between Felix and St *Paul. According to the Acts of the Apostles (21:38), the Roman tribune who arrested Paul in the Temple of Jerusalem in the midst of a fracas triggered off by the false rumour that Paul had brought a non-Jew into the Temple area forbidden to Gentiles, mistook the Greek-speaking Paul for the fugitive Egyptian. He was sent to Caesarea to appear before the procurator and face his Jewish accusers. At the end of the legal exchanges Felix postponed judgement and kept Paul in prison in Caesarea. One day apparently he summoned Paul to address himself and his Jewish wife Drusilla about his beliefs. Although Paul's views on justice, self-control and judgement were not to Felix's liking, he is nevertheless said to have often conversed with the apostle during the two years of his Caesarean imprisonment.

Sources: Acts 21:38. Josephus, *War* 2:247–70; *Ant.* 20:137–81. Tacitus, *Histories* 5: 9, 3; *Annals* 12:54.

FESTUS

Porcius Festus was dispatched by the emperor *Nero as Roman procurator of Judaea in succession to *Felix. He held the office from 60 to 62 CE. Festus inherited the troubles in Caesarea about civic rights between the Syrian Greek inhabitants and the Jews, which began during the procuratorship of his predecessor. Both parties claimed the city for themselves, the Syrians on the ground that they formed the majority of the population, while the Jews based their entitlement on the fact that the founder of the city, King *Herod the Great, was a Jew! Felix first decided against the Jews, but finally sent the case to Rome for imperial decision. Jewish delegates criticized the procurator's handling of the matter, but Felix's brother Pallas, still enjoying imperial favour, arranged with the help of Nero's secretary for Greek correspondence that an imperial decree be issued giving Caesarea to the Hellenized Syrians. As a result, the strife festered on and became one of the chief causes of the outbreak of the Jewish war against Rome in 66 CE.

The outrages due to the Sicarii worsened. Festus tried to stop them but only with ephemeral success. Exhausted by his efforts, he died in office in 62 CE. The temporary absence of the representative of Roman power allowed extreme anarchy to develop. It also gave an opportunity to the Jewish high priest *Ananus son of Ananus to get rid of his opponents, including *James the brother of the Lord whom he ordered to be stoned.

Shortly after his arrival in Judaea, Festus was faced with the case of the imprisoned St *Paul, left undecided by his predecessor Felix. Paul refused to appear before a Jewish court and used his right as a Roman citizen to appeal to the tribunal of the emperor, an appeal that the governor was legally bound to grant. The Acts of the Apostles reports that Festus presented Paul to the visiting King *Agrippa II and his sister *Bernice before whom Paul made a powerful apology of himself and of his beliefs. 'Paul, you are mad,' commented the uncomprehending Festus, and Agrippa sarcastically remarked, 'In a short time you think to make me a Christian.'

Sources: Acts 24:27; 25, 26. Josephus, War 2:271–2; Ant. 20:182–200.

FLORUS

Gessius Florus (64–66 CE) was the last Roman procurator of Judaea, whose office ended with the outbreak of the great war of the Jews against Rome. He was a Greek from Asia Minor and owed his appointment to the friendship between his intriguing wife Cleopatra and the empress Poppaea, the spouse of *Nero. Florus was far the most corrupt of all the Roman governors of Judaea. Indeed, *Josephus notes that compared to him, even the crooked *Albinus was a paragon of virtue whom the Jews might have considered their benefactor! Whereas Albinus attempted to conceal his dishonesty, Florus openly flaunted his villainy. The great rebellion exploded in the second year of his governorship.

The final outburst was provoked by two particularly heinous acts of Florus. Josephus reports that in May 66 CE the procurator initiated the massacre of 3,600 men, women and children, among them Jews of equestrian rank who were Roman citizens. The bloodshed, which

not even the repeated intervention of Queen *Bernice, sister of King
*Agrippa II, could prevent, represented Florus' revenge on a group of
Jews who had organized a mock collection of small change to support
the penniless procurator after he had unlawfully removed a substantial
sum of money from the Temple treasury. Agrippa II endeavoured to
calm the situation, but without success, and Florus' provocative cruelty
and disregard for the law inevitably led to the chaos of the first war of
the Jews against Rome. According to Josephus, even the governor of
Syria, *Cestius Gallus, laid the blame for the hostilities on Florus'
shoulders, and the Roman historian Tacitus summarized the situation
in his characteristic laconic style: 'Still the Jews' patience lasted until
Gessius Florus became governor; in his time war began' ('*Duravit
tamen patientia Iudaeis usque ad Gessium Florum procuratorem: sub
eo bellum ortum*').

Sources: Josephus, War II: 277; Ant. 20:252–3. Tacitus, Histories
5:10, 1.

G

GABINIUS

Aulus Gabinius was the Roman governor of Syria from 57 to 55 BCE.
While the principal agent of the conquest of Judaea under Pompey
was *Scaurus, the first governor of Syria, the quelling of the rebellion
fomented by *Aristobulus II and his son *Alexander, and the administrative reorganization of the new province were the work of Scaurus'
third successor, Gabinius. He divided the territory assigned to his
administration into five councils or *synedria*. These were centres of
government of which Jerusalem and Jericho lay in Judaea, Sepphoris in
Galilee, and the remaining two, Gadara and Amathus, in Transjordan,
unless Gadara is an error for Adora in Idumaea. The non-Jewish
inhabitants of the cities which the Romans had taken away from

*Hyrcanus II, the Hasmonaean ruler – among them Scythopolis, Samaria, Jamnia and Gamala – owed a deep debt of gratitude to Gabinius for restoring them to their former independent glory. In his campaign against Egypt Gabinius received military assistance from Hyrcanus and *Antipater, the father of *Herod the Great. Gabinius was found not guilty of the crime of conspiracy on his return to Rome in 55 CE, but he was later condemned on the charge of extortion, even though *Pompey testified on his behalf and Cicero was his defence counsel.

Sources: Josephus, *Ant.* 14:92–104; *War* 1:60–178. Dio 39:59–63.

GALLIO

Lucius Iunius Annaeus Gallio was the Roman proconsul of Achaia between 51/2 and 52/3 CE. Before he was adopted by the wealthy Lucius Junius Gallio, from whom he received his name, he had been called Annaeus Novatus. He was the son of the rhetorician Marcus Annaeus Seneca. Gallio's elder brother, the famous philosopher Seneca, was tutor to the emperor *Nero. Gallio enters the New Testament as the head of the Roman administration in Corinth before whom St *Paul had to appear. The encounter was brought about by the apostle's attempt to persuade Corinthian Jews to join the Jesus movement. Paul was largely unsuccessful and the local Jews accused him before Gallio of disturbing the communal peace by promoting a type of religion which in their eyes was contrary to the Law. The proconsul, however, refused to investigate the charges, because in his opinion they did not amount *prima facie* to a criminal offence. Gallio declared himself incompetent to judge the issue and for this reason did not invite Paul to present his defence. As the matter pertained to their religion, he advised the Jewish complainants to resolve the dispute among themselves. Such a policy of non-involvement with the peculiarities of Jewish law appears in general to have been adopted by Roman magistrates. Gallio proved a fair and perspicacious judge. Soon after this accidental meeting with Paul he returned to Rome, where he became consul in 58 CE. His life ended in tragedy. Both he and his more famous brother, Seneca, had to face charges of conspiracy against Nero and were compelled to commit suicide.

Sources: Acts 18:12–16. Dio 62:25.

GALLUS

Cestius Gallus was the Roman governor of Syria from 63 to 66/7 CE and played a significant role in the early stages of the Jewish rebellion, which began in May 66 CE. Several months later Gallus led a substantial force from Alexandria to Judaea. From Lydda, where he arrived at the Feast of Tabernacle (September/October), he launched an attack on Jerusalem, but realizing that he had not enough strength to capture the city, he decided to withdraw. His retreat was turned into a rout when he was surprised by Jewish fighters near Beth-Horon. With depleted Roman forces relinquishing all their equipment, Cestius Gallus returned to Antioch. He died in 67 CE, either naturally or out of vexation in Tacitus' words, having met defeat more often than he gained victory.

Sources: Josephus, *War* 2:499–555. Tacitus, *Histories* 5:10, 1.

GAMALIEL THE ELDER

Gamaliel the Elder, the grandson or possibly the son of *Hillel, was a leading Pharisee in the first half of the first century CE. Little is known about his life or teaching. Rabbinic literature credits him with letters, dictated on the Temple Mount and sent to the Jews in Galilee, the South and Babylonia and Media, instructing them about the intricacies of the times of tithing and of the leap year. He had a reputation for kindness and concern for women, authorizing for example the remarriage of a widow on the evidence of a single witness of her husband's death.

Gamaliel the Elder has a good press in the New Testament. Not only is he referred to as the teacher at whose feet St *Paul studied the Torah in Jerusalem (Acts 22:3), but he also spoke up in favour of the apostles when they were examined by the Sanhedrin. He cited the failure of *Theudas and *Judas the Galilean to prove that movements unsupported by God always collapse, and persuaded the court to let the apostles go and leave Providence to decide the fate of the new religious party (Acts 5:34–9).

Sources: Enc. Jud. 7, 295–6. HJP II, 367–8.

GAMALIEL II

Gamaliel II or Rabban Gamaliel was the son of *Simeon son of Gamaliel and presided over the academy of Yavneh (Jamnia) from *c.* 90 to 110 CE. He was an autocrat and a strict interpreter of the Torah, but he was not a bigot. He had no scruples about frequenting the bath dedicated to Aphrodite in Acco, and when challenged by a Gentile philosopher, he is said to have retorted that he had visited the bath-house and not the decorative statue of the goddess (bAZ 44b). Once he is reported to have travelled to Rome in the company of other rabbis.

According to the Talmud it was during the presidency of Rabban Gamaliel that the so-called *Birkhat ha-minim* (the benediction, or rather the curse, of the heretics) was added to the thrice-daily recitation of the Eighteen Benedictions, one of the principal statutory prayers of Judaism. Gamaliel asked for a volunteer to compose the blessing, or rather the curse, and Samuel the Small invented the formula praying for the quick eradication of the Nazarenes and all heretics and the deletion of their names from the Book of Life (bBer. 28b). This wording is attested in the early medieval version of the prayer found in the Cairo Geniza, where the Nazarenes are surely Judaeo-Christians. It is thought however that in the earlier wording of the benediction only the generic term 'heretics' (*minim*) figured. This would mean that the often asserted thesis that the introduction of the *Birkhat ha-Minim* under Gamaliel II in the 90s CE marked the parting of the ways between Jews and Jewish Christians is unfounded, or at least debatable.

Sources: Enc. Jud. 7, 296–8. HJP II, 372–3.

H

HADRIAN

Publius Aelius Hadrianus (76–138 CE), the successor of *Trajan, ruled the Roman world from 117 to 138 CE. He acquired renown for his fortification of the boundaries of the empire, which in Britain consisted of the building of a defensive wall, roughly 75 miles long, still known as Hadrian's Wall, between Newcastle and Carlisle. As the ruler who put down the second rebellion of the Jews against Rome, Hadrian left a profound mark on Jewish history. He entertained no hostile sentiments towards the Jews during the best part of his reign. The conflict under the leadership of Bar Kokhba (see the article on *Simeon bar Kosiba), known as the second war of the Jews against Rome, did not occur until 132 and lasted until 135 CE. How it came about is the subject of much debate.

The least likely explanation is the Jewish legend according to which Hadrian first approved the request of Jews to rebuild the Temple but later withdrew his consent because the Samaritans objected. His refusal resulted in an armed uprising developing into a three-year war. The story is reported in the rabbinic midrash called Genesis Rabbah, probably compiled in the fifth century, but is not confirmed by any Roman source. A reconstruction of the Jewish Temple would have clashed with Hadrian's own building programme.

A more likely, yet still questionable, cause of the war was the prohibition of circumcision imposed by Hadrian. According to the Roman historian Spartianus, the uprising was sparked off by the ban forbidding Jews to 'mutilate their genitals' ('*vetabantur mutilare genitalia*'). In fact the legislation outlawing circumcision was not specifically directed against the Jews, but against all the nations which practised this rite, including the Nabataean Arabs, the Samaritans and the priestly caste in Egypt. This decree derived from the assumption that circumcision was a sub-category of castration, which by virtue of the Roman law known as *lex Cornelia* was punishable by exile or

The Emperor Hadrian

the death penalty. It is no surprise that the Jews saw in it a head-on attack on their religion, which they felt they had to resist at all costs. In fact the more tolerant Antoninus Pius, Hadrian's successor (138–161 CE), while keeping the general interdiction, exempted the Jews from it as far as the circumcision of their own male children was concerned. A third reason for the war may be seen in Hadrian's decision to erect a Roman city to be called Aelia, after his own family name of Aelius, on the site of the ruins of Jerusalem (Cassius Dio). Bearing in mind the general historical context, this explanation appears to be the most likely. Cassius Dio reports that the construction of the city of Colonia Aelia Capitolina – Aelia for short – started during Hadrian's stay in Egypt, Judaea and Syria around 130 CE, and we know that the war, inspired and led by Simeon bar Kosiba, broke out in 132 CE. It is quite conceivable that hostile sentiments provoked by the building of the new city were combined with the outrage felt in face of the anti-circumcision legislation, but it is equally likely that the latter was forcefully imposed on the Jews as a measure of punishment after the quelling of the rebellion.

The suppression of the revolt was first entrusted to the governor of Judaea, *Tinneius Rufus, but when he was unable to cope Hadrian summoned from Britain one of his best generals, Julius Severus, who brought the war to an end in 135 CE with the capture of Bether, the last stronghold of the Jewish rebels south of Jerusalem.

The new city erected on the ruins of Jerusalem was totally paganized and Jews were forbidden to enter it. The Jewish Temple was replaced by one dedicated to Jupiter Capitolinus and an equestrian statue of Hadrian dominated the landscape. Jewish political independence came to an end for the next 1,800 years.

Christians fared better at Hadrian's hand than Jews did. He continued Trajan's relatively liberal policy. In a response to a letter addressed to the emperor by Quintus Licinius Silvanus Granianus, proconsul of Asia in 121/2 CE, which was received in 122/3 by his successor, Minucius Fundanus, Hadrian insisted that charges against Christians must be made, not by petitions and shouts, but in the proconsul's tribunal. If Christians were proved to be guilty of breaking the law, they had to be sentenced according to the gravity of the offence. But the emperor added: 'By Hercules, if anyone takes this course in order to make a mischievous accusation, take cognisance of his wickedness and consider how to punish him' (Justin, Eusebius).

Sources: Spartianus, *Historia Augusta*: *Life of Hadrian* 14:2. Dio 69:12, 1–2. Justin, *Apology* 1:68. Eusebius, *Eccl. Hist.* 4:9. Genesis Rabbah 64:8.

HANAN

Hanan or Hanin, nicknamed *ha-Nehba* ('the hidden', probably 'the shy'), and addressed as *Abba* (Father), like his first cousin, *Abba Hilkiah, was the grandson of *Honi the Circle-drawer. He was probably an elder contemporary of *Jesus of Nazareth. It was believed that the supplication of Hanan, like that of Honi and Abba Hilkiah, infallibly produced rain in periods of drought. Only a single anecdote relating to him has survived, without further biographical details. According to the Talmud, in times of famine the rabbis regularly sent schoolchildren to Hanan to obtain his intercession for rain. Like children of all ages, they enjoyed their extra-curricular activity and, running after the man of God, they grabbed the lower edge of his cloak and shouted the rhythmic words, 'Father, Father, give us rain!' ('*Abba, Abba, hav lan mitra*'). While the immediate fulfilment of the prayer was attributed to him by the grateful beneficiaries, Hanan in his humility begged God to send rain for the sake of the children, who confused in their plea the Abba (Hanan), who could not bring down rain, with the Abba (God), who could. The saying, in which God is addressed as Father, is in line with the style of praying regularly attributed to Jesus in the Gospels.

Source: bTaan. 23b.

HANINA BEN DOSA

Hanina ben Dosa was a first-century CE Galilean charismatic who lived in the town of Arav/Araba or Gabara, some 12 miles north of Nazareth. He was a younger contemporary of *Jesus of Nazareth and rabbinic literature presents him as a pupil of *Yohanan ben Zakkai, the spiritual leader of Arav for eighteen years according to the Talmudic tradition.

Nothing is known of Hanina's family background. His father's Greek name, Dosa, short for Dositheus, was commonly borne by rabbis, so it does not necessarily point to Hellenic culture. Hanina is not connected with any datable historical event, but we have enough circumstantial evidence to place him to the first century CE, and probably to the pre-70 period. He is associated with three important figures: Yohanan ben Zakkai during the Galilean stage of his career, Nehuniah, a Temple official, so by definition a pre-70 figure, and Gamaliel. If this Gamaliel is *Gamaliel the Elder, the teacher of St *Paul, we are again before the fall of Jerusalem. In any case, nothing is recorded about Hanina that would require a date after the destruction of the Temple.

While in the later Talmudic tradition Hanina is portrayed as a wholesale performer of miracles, the primary depiction of the rabbis represents him as a man of outstanding piety, a Hasid, with an extraordinary talent for healing. His piety was based on an absolute concentration on prayer. It was said that neither the arrival of a king nor the threatening presence of a snake could disturb his devotion. According to a story told about him, he continued his prayer unharmed even after a snake had bitten him. In fact, it was the snake that died. This anecdote produced the proverb, 'Woe to the man who has been bitten by a snake, but woe to the snake, which has bitten Hanina ben Dosa' (mBer. 5:1; tBer. 2:20; yBer. 9a; bBer. 33a).

His reputation as a spiritual healer was so high that even the leaders of first-century CE Pharisaism reportedly solicited his help. He cured the son of his former master, Yohanan ben Zakkai, by conveying his request to God in a mystical praying position with his head pressed between his knees in imitation of the miracle-working prophet Elijah. In another story, Gamaliel, probably the Elder, dispatched two of his disciples from Jerusalem to distant Galilee to beg for Hanina's intercession on behalf of his sick son. Hanina achieved the cure *in absentia* even before he had heard the request of Gamaliel conveyed by the envoys:

It happened that when Gamaliel's son fell ill, he sent two pupils to Hanina ben Dosa that he might pray for him. When he saw them, he went to the upper room and prayed. When he came down, he said to them, 'Go, for the fever has left him.' They said to him, 'Are you a prophet?' He said to them, 'I am no prophet, nor am I a prophet's son, but this is how I am favoured. If my prayer is fluent in my mouth, I know that the sick man is favoured; if not, I know that his disease is fatal.' They sat down and noted the hour. When they returned to Gamaliel, he said to them, 'By heaven, you have neither detracted from it nor added to it, but this is how it happened. It was in that hour that the fever left him and he asked us for water to drink' (bBer. 34b; yBer. 9d).

Hanina was also renowned as a man in control of demons, including the queen of the evil spirits, Agrath daughter of Mahlath, and like *Honi and his grandsons, *Hanan and *Abba Hilkiah, he had the reputation of being a rainmaker. His contemporaries believed that he had thus restored nature to fertility, and honoured him as a rescuer of mankind. According to rabbinic legend, he was celebrated as a 'son of God' with a heavenly voice, daily proclaiming: 'The whole universe is sustained on account of *my son* Hanina' (bTaan. 24b). Religious speculation went even further and asserted that the world, and even the future world, the world-to-come, was created for the sake of Hanina ben Dosa (bBer. 61b) and that because of his merits God's favour was granted to all his contemporaries (bHag. 14a).

A man living in utmost poverty, Hanina was more of a miracle-worker than a teacher, and when he died, the 'men of [marvellous] works' ceased according to the Mishnah (mSot. 9:15). Only a few of his sayings have survived. He extolled fear of sin and pious deeds over the words of wisdom and commended kindness towards people, for 'Any man with whom men are pleased, God is pleased with him' (mAb. 3:9–12).

Many of the features of Hanina ben Dosa recall those of Jesus, albeit on a minor scale. In particular the healing of Gamaliel's son reminds us of the cure from a distance of the servant of the centurion from Capernaum. Hanina's superiority over demons parallels the picture of Jesus as an exorcist. The story of Hanina and the snake reminds one of the saying of Jesus, 'Those who believe may take up snakes . . . and nothing will harm them' (Lk 10:19). Most interestingly, the heavenly voice calling Jesus, Hanina and others, such as Rabbi Meir, 'my son', gives an excellent insight into the original metaphorical use of the concept 'son of God' in Palestinian Jewish religious thinking.

On the negative side, representatives of conventional Judaism tried to find fault with the unorthodox behaviour of a charismatic. Hanina was criticized for his neglect of ritual obligations, for conduct unseemly for a man of God like walking alone in the street by night. His announcement of a cure from a distance provoked the sarcastic question, 'Are you a prophet?' and the miraculous efficacy of his prayer was attributed to the merits of Abraham, Isaac and Jacob.

All in all, the picture of Hanina ben Dosa sheds valuable light on the portrait of Jesus in the Gospels and on the lines of the early theological developments in Palestinian Judaeo-Christianity.

Sources: mBer. 5:1; tBer. 2:20; yBer. 9a; bBer. 33a; bBer. 34b; yBer. 9d; bTaan. 24b; bBer. 61b; bHag. 14a; mSot. 9:15; mAb. 3:9–12. See G. Vermes, *Jesus the Jew*, 53–60.

HEROD OF CHALCIS

Herod of Chalcis, the brother of *Agrippa I, was the grandson of *Herod the Great through his murdered son *Aristobulus. The emperor *Claudius made him rule as king from 41 to 48 CE over Ituraea and Abilene, north of Galilee. In gratitude to the emperor Herod named himself 'friend of Claudius' on his coins. Like most Herodian princes he married close relations. His first wife was Mariamme, a granddaughter of Herod the Great, and his second his niece *Bernice, the daughter of Agrippa I. Herod was one of the five client-kings who attended the meeting summoned by Agrippa in Tiberias, which was promptly disbanded by Marsus, governor of Syria. On the death of Agrippa I in 44 CE Claudius placed Herod of Chalcis in charge of the supervision of the Temple of Jerusalem and empowered him to appoint Jewish high priests. Shortly after his death his nephew *Agrippa II inherited his kingdom.

Sources: Josephus, *War* 2:221–2; *Ant.* 20:103–4.

HEROD THE GREAT

Herod the Great, son of the Idumaean parvenu *Antipater, was appointed King of the Jews by Rome and reigned from 40 (or 37) to 4 BCE. Idumaea, the biblical Edom, lay in the south of Palestine, in the region known today as the Negev. Herod's lasting fame is principally due to his rebuilding of the sanctuary in Jerusalem (known as Herod's Temple) and to the fact that the birth of *Jesus of Nazareth occurred during the final years of his rule.

The Idumaeans counted as Jews since the Hasmonaean ruler John *Hyrcanus I (134–104 BCE) converted them to Judaism, imposing on them circumcision and the observance of the Law of Moses. Though legally they counted as Jewish, in the eyes of the Judaean aristocracy the Idumaeans were only second-class Jews. Herod himself was called a 'half-Jew' by his haughty rival, the Hasmonaean priest-king *Antigonus. Rabbinic sources downgrade him to the status of a slave (bBB 3b; bSanh. 19a).

Herod claimed to be Jewish when he was among Jews. He maintained good relations with the Pharisees, but did not fully satisfy all their demands. As a result, they twice refused to swear an oath of allegiance to Herod and to his master the emperor *Augustus, yet on account of Herod's respect for some of the Pharisee leaders they remained unpunished. The Essenes also received preferential treatment because Herod had remembered with gratitude the Essene prophet *Menahem's prediction that he would one day occupy the royal throne.

Years before his appointment first as tetrarch and in 40 BCE as king by his Roman patron, *Mark Antony, the office of governor of Galilee had already been conferred on Herod by his father *Antipater. He defeated, captured and put to death *Ezechias, the revolutionary Galilean robber captain, and some of his followers. He was summoned before the Sanhedrin for illegal executions, but thanks to the intervention of the high priest *Hyrcanus II, he escaped punishment. After his appointment as king a three-year struggle was necessary for Herod to overcome the last Hasmonaean priest-king *Antigonus, even with the substantial help offered him by *Sosius, Roman governor of Syria.

Victory was finally achieved when, by order of Mark Antony, who had been bribed by Herod, the last Hasmonaean ruler was decapitated in 37 BCE. Herod decided to strengthen his entitlement to the throne by marrying the Hasmonaean princess *Mariamme, the granddaughter of Hyrcanus II. This matrimonial bond with Jewish royalty helped to enhance Herod's status but did the Hasmonaeans little good. Within less than ten years of her marriage to Herod, not only Mariamme, but also her mother *Alexandra (Herod's mother-in-law), her grandfather, the former high priest Hyrcanus, and her younger brother, the high priest *Aristobulus III (Herod's brother-in-law), were all put to death by decree of the King of Judaea.

Herod spent the first dozen years of his reign securing his position by winning friends and eliminating opponents. He gained the support of two influential Pharisees, *Pollion (possibly Abtalion) and *Samaias (Shemaiah or Shammai), who not only spoke up for him during his trial in c. 47 BC for the unlawful killing of Galilean rebels by the Jewish Sanhedrin during his governorship of Galilee, but also later persuaded the common people of Judaea to accept Herod as their ruler. The Judaean upper classes, attached to the Hasmonaeans, resisted him, but they were brought to their knees when Herod put to death forty-five of the most eminent and wealthy citizens of Jerusalem. The appropriation of their possessions made Herod exceedingly rich.

The elderly Hasmonaean Hyrcanus II, having become unfit to function as high priest after his usurping nephew Antigonus bit off one or both of his ears, was replaced by Herod, who appointed an obscure Babylonian Jewish priest by the name of Ananel. However, Herod's mother-in-law, Alexandra, Hyrcanus' daughter, found this appointment unacceptable as she wanted the high priesthood for her seventeen-year-old son *Aristobulus III. She used the good offices of her friend the Egyptian queen *Cleopatra to ensure that Cleopatra's husband Mark Antony, Herod's patron, should demand the post for the young Aristobulus. Initially successful, the manoeuvre ended in tragedy. The popularity of the youthful high priest aroused Herod's suspicion, and when Aristobulus was enjoying himself with his companions in a swimming pool at Jericho, Herod arranged for the 'accidental' drowning of the new high priest. Accused of murder by the victim's mother Alexandra, who was backed by Cleopatra, Herod

The Fortress of Herodium where King Herod the Great was buried

none the less managed to bribe his way out of trouble and was acquitted by Mark Antony when he was summoned to appear before him in Egypt and account for himself.

The chief threat to Herod came from the Queen of Egypt, Cleopatra. She was not only the friend of Alexandra, the mother-in-law who disliked and despised Herod, but a monarch in her own right, intent on seizing Herod's territory. She was also the wife of Mark Antony, Herod's Roman patron. Through her influence on her husband she obtained the transfer to her domain of most of the Palestinian and Phoenician littoral and the fertile region of Jericho. Herod was duty-bound to extend lavish hospitality to Cleopatra when she was travelling through Judaea. The sex-mad queen tried to seduce Herod, possibly with a view to compromising him before Mark Antony. Herod in turn was toying with the idea of using the bedroom to get rid of Cleopatra for good. However his friends persuaded him to distance himself from her and thus maintain his good relations with his patron.

With the start of the Roman civil war between Antony and Octavian, the future Augustus, Herod's diplomatic skills were put to a tough test. He owed loyalty to Antony, and this might have been the end of his career. But as usual he was lucky. Antony, pressed by Cleopatra, instructed Herod to attack the Nabataeans instead of employing his forces against Octavian. Even so, Antony's defeat in the battle of Actium in 31 BCE might have exposed Herod to the fury of the victor. The clever and calculating Herod therefore took a risk and visited Augustus in Rhodes, but before doing so he ordered the harmless, aged Hyrcanus II, whom he still considered a potential claimant of the Judaean royal title, to be put to death on a trumped-up charge.

The perilous trip to Rhodes also precipitated the end of Mariamme, Herod's favourite wife. Finding intolerable the idea that she might remarry should Augustus decide to eliminate him, Herod renewed the secret orders, already given at the time of his visit to Mark Antony, that Mariamme should be put to death if Herod failed to return. In both cases the men instructed to murder the queen disclosed Herod's instruction to her and paid for it with their lives. On the first occasion Joseph, the uncle and brother-in-law of Herod, accused by the king's sister *Salome of having had an affair with Mariamme, was promptly executed without a hearing. The second protector of Mariamme at the time of Herod's visit to Augustus, a certain Soaemus, was also accused by Cyprus and Salome, mother and sister of Herod, of having committed adultery with Mariamme. They further charged Mariamme with plotting to poison her husband. Both Mariamme and her mother, Alexandra, were condemned to death by Herod, the former in 29 and the latter in 28 BCE. Mariamme went to her death 'with a wholly calm demeanour and without changing of colour', according to *Josephus, thus demonstrating her true Hasmonaean royal grit. Her mother Alexandra, on the other hand, behaved disgracefully in an attempt to save her neck. She reproached her daughter with shameful behaviour towards her husband and humiliated her by grabbing and pulling her hair in public. Alexandra escaped the executioner for a short while. The following year she planned to remove Herod and seize the throne herself. As usual, no secret could be kept for any time in Herod's court, and the mother-in-law joined the already long, but far from complete, list of the members of the royal family who were executed by Herod.

The loss of his passionately loved wife truly unhinged the king. He tried unsuccessfully to drown his sorrow in banquets and hunting – he was an outstanding horseman, and a champion archer and javelin-thrower – but fell seriously ill, displaying signs of temporary madness.

Herod's family relations were rather complicated. He had ten wives. The first was the Idumaean Doris who bore him his first son, *Antipater. The second was the Hasmonaean Mariamme by whom he had three sons, Alexander, Aristobulus and a third who died in Rome, and two daughters. His third wife, also called Mariamme, was the daughter of a high priest and the mother of another son, Herod. Among his further wives, the Samaritan Malthace gave birth to *Archelaus and *Antipas, both named in the Gospels, who were successors of Herod. As for *Philip, also mentioned in the New Testament, he was the son of Cleopatra of Jerusalem. The three eldest sons, Antipater, Alexander and Aristobulus, spent years in Rome; the last two were educated there and enjoyed the hospitality of the Roman statesman Asinius Pollio or possibly of Vedius Pollio, a friend of Augustus. The royal court of Herod was a hotbed of intrigue and the jealousy between the Idumaean branch of the family (Cyprus, the king's mother, Pheroras and Salome, his brother and sister, and Antipater, his eldest son) and the Hasmonaean side resulted in the execution by strangulation of Alexander and Aristobulus in 7 BCE. Finally, even the Idumaean Antipater was to share the fate of his half-Hasmonaean brothers: he was executed by Herod five days before the king's own death in 4 BCE.

Herod's handling of his family affairs does not justify the title 'the Great' which he is often granted in modern literature. It is interesting to note that the relevant epithet (*ho megas*) is used only once in *Josephus. It would seem that 'the Great' is primarily meant to distinguish him from his lesser successors. Nevertheless, certain aspects of his reign are distinguished. His middle period (25–13 BCE) was characterized by the splendour of his remarkable building activity, both at home and abroad. In Jerusalem and its vicinity Herod erected a theatre, an amphitheatre and a new royal palace as well as the fortress Antonia, which he named after his erstwhile patron Mark Antony. He reconstructed the city of Samaria and called it Sebaste in honour of Augustus (*Sebastos* in Greek). In 22 BCE he started to construct a new city with an excellent harbour on the site of the ancient town of Straton's Tower, and on its completion twelve years later he dedicated it to Caesar Augustus and named it Caesarea. Another temple in honour of the emperor was built at Caesarea Philippi, north-east of the Lake of Galilee, the place where *Peter was to proclaim *Jesus of Nazareth as the Christ. The cities of Antipatris and Phasaelis commemorated Herod's father Antipater and his brother Phasael. He built a fortress and named it Herodium after himself, and fortified others, chief among them Machaerus, where *John the Baptist was later decapitated, and Masada, the last stronghold of the Jewish rebels in the first war against Rome. Both Machaerus and Masada were turned into royal residences. His palaces were surrounded by parks, pools and statuary and he provided dovecotes for his specially bred 'Herodian' doves.

Without any doubt, Herod's most famous architectural enterprise was the reconstruction of the Jerusalem Temple, which he started in 20 BCE. The work continued during the rest of his reign and long after his death. It was only finished during the procuratorship of *Albinus (62–64 CE), shortly before its destruction by the Romans in

70 CE. Some parts of Herod's Temple, in particular the Western or Wailing Wall, still exist today. In the rebuilding of the Temple Herod was careful to please his Jewish subjects and entrusted the supervision of the work to Jewish priests. No images were displayed in it and Herod never entered the area of the sanctuary. None of his existing coins bears an effigy. No statue of him exists, although according to a Greek inscription engraved on its surviving pedestal, a statue of Herod once stood at Fia in the Auranitis, south of Damascus. However, Herod instituted athletic games not only in Caesarea but also in Jerusalem, which upset conservative Jews.

Herod was responsible for the appointment of eight Jewish high priests. In addition to Ananel and Aristobulus, already mentioned, the list includes the names of *Jesus son of Phiabi, *Simon son of Boethus, *Matthias son of Theophilus, Joseph son of Ellem and *Joazar son of Boethus.

Outside his own territory Herod financed luxurious temples and public buildings in Rhodes, Antioch and even Athens. Closer to home, Tyre, Sidon, Byblos, Berytus and Damascus witnessed his generosity.

While he considered himself a Jewish monarch, he was principally concerned with the promotion of Greek culture. In the non-Jewish cities of his realm Herod behaved like a Gentile ruler and went so far as sponsoring pagan places of worship. He surrounded himself with learned Hellenists, the most famous of whom was the polymath *Nicolaus of Damascus, who was Herod's tutor in philosophy, rhetoric and history, and was also employed as his ambassador to the emperor. Nicolaus' great historical work served as the principal source of Josephus' lengthy account of Herod's story in *Antiquities*, 15–17.

Herod's foreign policy was wholly successful. He was a Roman citizen, like his father Antipater before him, and Augustus always treated him with favour. Herod enjoyed the privileged status of a client king (*rex socius*), a friend and ally of the Roman people. His territory was almost doubled during his reign by the annexation of the non-Jewish cities of Palestine and of the territories north-east of Galilee, Trachonitis, Batanaea, Auranitis and the districts of Ulatha and Panaias. According to Josephus, Augustus' esteem for Herod came second only to his regard for his best friend, Marcus Agrippa.

However, at the end even Augustus lost his respect for the King of the Jews.

Although a despot protected by mercenaries from Gaul, Germany and Thrace, Herod was able to show care and even magnanimity towards his Jewish subjects. The harbour built by him in Caesarea improved the nation's commerce, and he supported the poor during the famine in 25 BCE. To help the revival of the economy he reduced taxes in 20 and 14 BCE by 33 per cent and 25 per cent. Life was not unpleasant in his kingdom despite the iron fist of the Hellenized Idumaean who was playing the Jew.

Gravely ill and having killed three of his older sons, the seventy-year-old Herod ended up by naming Antipas as his heir, but a few days before he died, he redrafted his will in favour of Archelaus. Augustus, however, did not confirm the nomination of Archelaus as king and downgraded him to the rank of ethnarch. Antipas was named tetrarch of Galilee, and Philip tetrarch of Gaulanitis, Trachonitis, Batanea, Panaias and Auranitis. To ensure that his subjects would mourn when he was buried, Herod instructed his brother-in-law Alexas and his sister Salome to arrange on the day of his death for the murder of many distinguished Jews who were kept imprisoned in the hippodrome of Jericho. Fortunately his last horrible wish was not carried out. Herod died in Jericho in 4 BCE, unlamented by his family and the Jewish people, and was buried in Herodium.

Herod had a profoundly split personality. On the one hand he was very generous and beneficent, but on the other he was barbarous and viciously vengeful towards both his subjects and his close family. In Josephus' view both his generosity and his cruelty sprang from his insatiable craving for honour. His liberality towards his subjects and his family was aimed at generating respect and adulation. However, his failure to achieve this unleashed his bitter revenge. In consequence he was hated by the Jews despite his munificence, and through his barbarous behaviour towards his family alienated even his Roman patrons. It is enough to quote the sarcastic epigram attributed to Augustus, 'It is better to be Herod's pig than Herod's son' (Macrobius, *Saturnalia* 2:4, 11). Herod believed that he had always enjoyed good fortune. Josephus begged to differ: 'In my opinion he was very unfortunate indeed.'

Herod's worldwide notoriety is to a large extent due to the historical accident that Jesus of Nazareth was born at the end of his reign, and his name is recorded in the New Testament Gospels of *Matthew (2:1–22) and *Luke (1:5). The birth of Jesus is erroneously connected with the census of *Quirinius, which took place in AD 6, ten years after the death of Herod (see the articles on Quirinius, Mary and Joseph). The story of the massacre of the male infants ordered by Herod in the region of Bethlehem is patterned on the account of the murder of the newly born Israelite boys by Pharaoh, King of Egypt, according to the Book of Exodus. Herod's well-known cruelty towards his own children supplied the legend with considerable verisimilitude. As a parting reference to Herod, Matthew notes that Joseph and his family returned from their exile and settled in Galilee when the news of the death of Herod the Great had reached them in Egypt.

Sources: Josephus, *War* 1:347–673; *Ant.* 15–17.

HERODIAS

Herodias was the second wife of Herod *Antipas. She was the daughter of Aristobulus, son of *Herod the Great by *Mariamme I, and was a strange mixture of brutality and pride, inheriting the former from her grandfather and the latter from her royal Hasmonaean grandmother. Herodias was the sister of King *Agrippa I and was married first to her uncle, also called Herod, son of Mariamme II, the high priest *Simon son of Boethus' daughter. Antipas met Herodias when he was visiting his half-brother (Herod). Antipas promptly fell in love with her, and after quickly divorcing his then wife, the daughter of the Nabataean king Aretas IV, married Herodias. The repudiation of the Nabataean princess brought about a war between her father Aretas and her ex-husband Antipas, which the latter lost. Herodias' ambition brought ruin to Antipas. Annoyed by the elevation of her brother Agrippa I to the royal dignity by the emperor *Caligula in 37 CE, Herodias urged her husband to petition the emperor for the same preferment. The move failed. Antipas was deposed by Caligula in 39 CE and banished to Lyons in Gaul. Herodias was permitted to stay in

Galilee, but the proud woman spurned the imperial favour and joined her husband in exile.

According to the New Testament Herodias was responsible for the execution of *John the Baptist. John, already imprisoned by Antipas for criticizing his marriage to Herodias, was beheaded at the request of *Salome, whose dance at the king's birthday party so pleased Antipas that he promised the girl whatever she requested. At her vengeful mother's suggestion Salome asked for the head of the Baptist on a silver salver. *Josephus offers a different explanation for the execution of John: his eloquence made him politically dangerous in the revolutionary atmosphere of the age. He locates the event in the hilltop fortress of Machaerus in Transjordan, whereas the Gospels do not specify where the murder of John the Baptist occurred and give the impression that it took place in Galilee.

Sources: Mk 6:17–29; Mt 14:3–12. Josephus, *Ant.* 18:116–19.

HILLEL

Hillel the Elder was the leading Jewish teacher in the last decades of the first century BCE and the first decades of the first century CE. He is known as 'the Elder' (*ha-Zaken*) as the technical title 'Rabbi', applying to experts in the Bible and traditional law, was not adopted until the latter part of the first century CE. This very famous master who, according to Talmudic tradition, shaped the future teaching of rabbinic Judaism, was a contemporary of *Jesus of Nazareth.

As is the case with most early rabbinic masters, very little is known about Hillel's background. Not even the name of his father is recorded. We are told, without solid evidence, that he originated from Babylonia and belonged, like Jesus according to the genealogies of *Matthew and *Luke, to the royal family of David. Apparently he kept body and soul together by earning his living as a day labourer, probably taking home one denarius per day like the hired hands of the Gospel parable. In the Mishnah tractate 'Sayings of the Fathers', he and *Shammai form the last of the 'pairs', or *zuggot*, in the series of Jewish teachers, which starts in the early second century BCE and continues through the age of *Herod the Great to the beginning of the Christian era. Hillel's fame notwithstanding, *Josephus does not mention him although the 'pair', *Shemaiah and Abtalion, which immediately preceded Hillel and Shammai, is alluded to as *Samaias and Pollion in *Jewish Antiquities* (14:175; 15:3). These were the only two teachers whom Herod spared in 37 BCE, when he took revenge on the members of the Sanhedrin who in 47 BCE had criticized his lawless conduct in Galilee.

According to rabbinic tradition Hillel's influence on the subsequent development of traditional law or *halakhah* was enormous. In particular, three significant innovations are attached to his name. The Talmud maintains that he first acquired fame when he argued in the name of his masters Shemaiah and Abtalion that the slaughter of the Passover lamb had to be performed even when the feast of Passover fell on a Sabbath (bPes 66a).

Hillel further introduced the judicial proviso called *prozbul* (*prosbolê*), a legal fiction made necessary by the economic circumstances of the age. Biblical law cancelled all existing debts in every seventh or sabbatical year (Dt 15:1–11). This escape clause in favour of the debtor made it very difficult to raise a loan towards the end of the sabbatical cycle, as the creditor had no guarantee that he would have enough time to collect his due. Hillel rescued the system and the creditor by authorizing him to include in the loan agreement entered into before judges that he could collect his debt 'at any time', even in a sabbatical year (mSheb 10:4). An Aramaic legal document dating to the second year of Nero (55/6 CE), discovered in a cave in the Judaean desert, exemplifies a legal custom similar to the *prozbul*. Here it is the borrower who undertakes to repay his debt even if he is requested to do so in a sabbatical year.

In the more theoretical domain, the creation of the seven legal principles (*middot*) through which new rules could be deduced from existing legislation is attributed to Hillel. His seven *middot*, and their expansion by Rabbi Ishmael to thirteen, form the basis of most of the later rabbinic legal development.

As a moralist Hillel was renowned for his kindness and gentleness towards people. 'Be a disciple of Aaron, a peace lover and a peace maker; love men and draw them near to the Torah' (mAb 1:12) is quoted as his favourite saying. It is often suggested that Jesus, who put the love of God and the love of one's neighbour at the very top of his moral requirements, was influenced by Hillel. This hypothesis would make sense if it could be proved that Jesus in general shared the doctrinal and religious outlook of the Pharisees. However, such a theory clashes with two major facts. First, Jesus lived and exercised his itinerant ministry in Galilee where there is no evidence of a demonstrable Pharisee presence before 70 CE. Second, the nature of Pharisaic Judaism was essentially legal (*halakhic*), whereas the religion of Jesus primarily belonged to the moral and charismatic category.

The ethical principle known as the Golden Rule is another topic that links Hillel to Jesus as well as to *Philo, the Alexandrian Hellenistic Jewish philosopher. Hillel and Philo formulated the rule in the traditional negative form, in which it was handed down in Jewish literature. 'What someone would hate to suffer, he must not do to others,' wrote Philo (*Hypothetica* 7:6). Similar words are assigned to Hillel: 'What is hateful to you, do not do to your fellow', but with the additional comment, 'This is the whole Torah' (bShab 31a). Jesus turned the negative counsel into a positive one: 'Whatever you wish that men would do to you, do so to them', and in words strikingly reminiscent of those ascribed to Hillel, he declared, 'This is the Law and the Prophets' (Mt 7:12; Lk 6:31). The anecdotal context surrounding Hillel's saying, namely, that it was his response to a request by a tiresome Gentile who wanted to learn the whole Torah while standing on one leg, can safely be ignored.

Another doctrine of Hillel sheds light on a question formulated by Pharisees in the Gospel of Matthew concerning the right of a husband to dismiss his wife 'for any cause' (Mt 19:3). Hillel had a very lax attitude in this regard and declared that any kind of marital breakdown, even one caused by the incompetence of the wife as a cook, could serve as a valid justification for divorce (mGit. 9:10). Josephus' nonchalant explanation of his own divorce has a similar basis: he was displeased with his wife's behaviour (*Life* 426). While Jesus himself absolutely outlawed divorce in the age leading to the imminent arrival of the Kingdom of God (Mk 10:2–9), Matthew inserted an exception clause permitting the dissolution of the union in the case of the wife's 'unchastity' (Mt 5:32; 19:9). In doing this, he reflects the more stringent doctrine of Shammai, Hillel's opponent, for whom divorce was permissible only as the result of some kind of sexual misbehaviour on the part of the wife (mGit. 9:10).

Debate between the schools of Hillel and Shammai dominated the development of Jewish law and Bible interpretation throughout the first century CE. The teachings of both schools were held to be authoritative and treated as 'the words of the living God' (yBer. 3b). However, the views of the school of Hillel in general prevailed because, according to a later rabbinic legend, a heavenly voice (*bat qol*), like that reported by the Gospels to have been heard at the baptism of Jesus, proclaimed that the true doctrine was 'according to the words of the school of Hillel' (yBer. 3b).

Although Hillel was probably the greatest and most influential Jewish teacher in antiquity, his life and death remain in the shadows. The fact that Josephus failed to allude to a character of the stature of Hillel, or of *Yohanan ben Zakkai, shows what a fortunate accident it is that he mentioned, however briefly, *John the Baptist, Jesus and his brother *James.

Sources: Enc. Jud. 8:482–5. HJP II, 363–7.

HONI

Honi the Circle-drawer, or Onias the Righteous, was a famous Palestinian charismatic in the first century BCE. The gist of his story, obtained from a combination of the rabbinic sources and the *Jewish Antiquities* of Flavius *Josephus, is that by means of his all-powerful prayer he brought a long period of drought to an end. Honi thus acquired nationwide renown and was celebrated as a famous charismatic holy man or Hasid.

Chronologically, both the rabbis and Josephus place Honi's achievement in the early sixties BCE. The rabbis do this by associating him with *Simeon ben Shetah, the brother of Queen Alexandra Salome (76–67 BCE). Josephus in turn inserts the Onias episode in the story of the civil war between the two sons of Alexandra, *Aristobulus II and *Hyrcanus II. The events referred to followed the death of

Alexandra (67 BCE), and probably took place close to the feast of Passover in 65 BCE, two years before the conquest of Jerusalem by *Pompey. The younger Aristobulus, who sought to seize the high priesthood from Hyrcanus, was besieged in the Temple by his brother and his ally, the Nabatean Arab king Aretas III. To bring about instant victory, the partisans of Hyrcanus urged the renowned Onias to destroy Aristobulus and his party by putting a curse on them. The saintly Onias refused to employ charismatic power to help one Jewish political party against another and his unwillingness to intervene cost him his life: the fanatical supporters of Hyrcanus stoned him to death (*Ant.* 14:22–4). Josephus implies that the murderers were punished for their crime by a substantial shortage of food resulting from the destruction of the crops all over the country (*Ant.* 14:25–8), which nullified Honi's previous rain miracle.

The fact that the story of Honi/Onias is preserved in both rabbinic literature and Josephus makes it possible to compare the theologically embellished Jewish mode of presentation with the more sober Hellenistic style of Josephus. Both he and the rabbis consider the fame of Honi/Onias as resulting from the popular belief that he was a miraculous rainmaker. Since biblical antiquity the power of bringing rain was held to be the privilege of men of God like the great prophet Elijah who announced: 'There shall be neither dew nor rain these years except by my words' (1 Kings 17:1).

Josephus, for whom Onias is a 'righteous man' and the 'beloved of God', reports in a prosaic manner that at the end of a prolonged drought 'God had heard his [Onias'] prayer and sent rain' (*Ant.* 14:22). The event is not strictly depicted as miraculous; nevertheless Onias is seen as the object of popular veneration. The rabbinic account, preserved in the Mishnah (mTaan 3:8), tells basically the same story, but in it the natural merges with the supernatural. God is pictured as playing a game with Honi and goes on teasing him until finally he fulfils his request. First the charismatic prays, but no rain comes. Then, like a spoiled child, Honi draws a circle around himself and threatens God that he will not step out of it until his prayer is granted. God tantalizingly replies with a slight drizzle. Honi then insists on a decent rain, but is given a devastating cloudburst instead.

Finally, he couches his supplication in humble words and along comes a 'rain of grace' truly beneficial to nature.

As usual, Josephus shies away from acknowledging the supernatural character of an event. The rabbis are less reticent. For them Honi's achievement shows that the relationship between him and God is that of son and father. In fact, Honi's capricious behaviour makes him appear like a spoilt child. Rabbinic tradition nicknames him the 'circle-drawer', a phrase that possesses magical connotations. Simeon ben Shetah, the leader of the Pharisees in the age of Honi, is presented as shocked by the rainmaker's familiarity in addressing God. But having witnessed the efficacy of his words, Simeon could only sigh and relent: 'If you hadn't been Honi, I would have excommunicated you! But what can I do? You importune God, yet he does your will as in the case of the son who importunes his father, yet the father does his will' (mTaan 3:8). Here, as in other rabbinic tales, the charismatic bears the title of 'son of God' as does *Jesus of Nazareth, too, in the Gospels.

Honi also became the head of a charismatic dynasty. Two of his grandsons, *Hanan and *Abba Hilkiah, also belonged to the class of the ancient Hasidim.

The charismatic power of Honi, revealing a particular closeness to God, led the rabbis to speculate on his role in the religious history of the Jews and of mankind. Simeon ben Shetah, even though he criticized Honi for improperly addressing God, still recognized that he was a 'son of God' in whom the words of Scripture, 'Let your father . . . be glad' (Prov 23:25) were fulfilled. Another ancient Jewish source states that the members of the great Sanhedrin applied to Honi a verse from Job (22:28), 'Whatever you command will come to pass' [and interpreted]: 'You have commanded on earth and God has fulfilled your word in heaven' (bTaan 23a). Strict correspondence between heavenly and earthly worship is stressed in the Qumran community and the Gospels speak of simultaneous forgiveness of sins on earth and in heaven. Even more significantly, Honi is presented as an imitator of the prophet Elijah, the special model of the Hasid, as far as bringing about repentance was concerned: 'No man has existed comparable to Elijah and Honi the Circle-drawer causing mankind to serve God' (Genesis Rabbah 13:7).

It should be emphasized that rabbinic theology invests Honi with extensive, and possibly universal, influence on the fate of all Jews and perhaps even of all mankind. Many of the characteristics of Honi reappear in the personality of another renowned Galilean Hasid, *Hanina ben Dosa, in the first century CE. Both Honi and Hanina provide significant parallels to Jesus, the most famous of the ancient Jewish charismatic holy men.

Sources: Josephus, *Ant.* 14:22–9. mTaan. 3:8; bTaan. 23a; Genesis Rabbah 13:7. See G. Vermes, *Jesus the Jew*, 51–3.

HYRCANUS II

John Hyrcanus II (111–30 BCE) was the most pathetic, indeed tragic, of all the Hasmonaean Jewish high priests and ethnarchs (63–40 BCE). The elder son of Alexander Jannaeus and his wife Shelamzion Alexandra Salome, he inherited the high priestly office on the death of his father in 76 BCE and held it during the reign of his mother which ended in 67 BCE. He was to combine the priestly and the royal dignity when his mother died, but was deprived of both by his aggressive younger brother Judas *Aristobulus II. Having been defeated by Aristobulus, the weak and malleable Hyrcanus became a puppet in the hands of the ambitious Idumaean *Antipater, the father of *Herod the Great, and the Nabataean Arab king Aretas III who, playing the role of protectors of Hyrcanus, expected to dominate the political scene. Their combined forces obliged Aristobulus to retreat to the Temple Mount in Jerusalem, where he was besieged. It was in the course of this conflict that the charismatic rainmaker, *Honi or Onias the Righteous, was stoned to death by Hyrcanus' irate followers for refusing to put a curse on Aristobulus and his supporters. In 63 BCE the Roman *Pompey conquered Jerusalem; he removed Aristobulus from office and gave his support to Hyrcanus, whom he reappointed as high priest, but deprived him of the royal title. Indeed, administrative power was taken away from him and remained in the hands of the Romans until Julius *Caesar restored Hyrcanus' political status by confirming him as ethnarch of Judaea, with Antipater holding the office of procurator. In fact the reins of government were held by the family of Antipater whose two sons, *Phasael and *Herod, were in charge of Jerusalem and Galilee. Herod's unrestrained violence in Galilee brought him into conflict with the Jewish Sanhedrin, but with Hyrcanus' connivance and with the backing of the Romans Herod escaped conviction. The appointment of Phasael and Herod as tetrarchs of Judaea by *Mark Antony simply reaffirmed the status quo: Hyrcanus was ruler only in name.

In 40 BCE the Parthians invaded Judaea and using *Antigonus, the son of Aristobulus II and nephew of Hyrcanus, as their puppet, they appointed him king and high priest. Herod fled to Petra in Arabia, but Hyrcanus and Phasael were handed over to the new ruler. To disqualify his uncle from acting again as high priest, Antigonus mutilated him. According to one version of the story, one high priest bit off one or both ears of another high priest!

Hyrcanus' end was as tragic as his life. Herod, although he was the husband of Hyrcanus' granddaughter Mariamme, decided to rid himself of his last potential rival and, on the false charge of conspiracy with the Nabataean king, ordered the execution by strangulation of the eighty-one-year-old last Hasmonaean ruler.

The Psalms of Solomon from the Pseudepigrapha and some of the Dead Sea Scrolls appear to contain some additional information about Hyrcanus II (and Aristobulus II). They are unquestionably the rulers of Jerusalem mentioned in Psalms of Solomon 8:15–17, who went to greet the ruthless conqueror (Pompey). The same two leaders are identified by A. Dupont-Sommer as the Wicked Priests of the Qumran Bible commentaries on Habakkuk and Nahum.

Sources: Josephus, *War* 1:159–273; *Ant.* 14:80–369.

I

ISMAEL SON OF PHIABI

See under **Ananus (or Annas) son of Sethi.**

ISMAEL SON OF PHIABI II

Ismael son of Phiabi (59–61 CE), not to be confused with the pontiff bearing the same name and belonging to the same family who functioned in 15–16 CE, was the first appointee of King *Agrippa II (50–92/3 CE). He took office in tempestuous times. The high-priestly families clashed with the ordinary priests and the people and resorted to stoning one another. They also came into conflict with Agrippa II when they ordered a wall to be built in the Temple to prevent the king from watching the ceremonies from his palace and the Roman garrison from keeping an eye on the happenings in the sacred precincts. The king expressed his displeasure and *Festus, the Roman procurator (60–62 CE), issued an order to demolish the wall. The high priest Ismael led a delegation to Rome to obtain the revocation of Festus' directive. The emperor *Nero accepted their plea after the intercession of his wife Poppaea who, however, detained the high priest as a hostage in Rome. *Josephus reports without any explanation that Ismael was condemned to decapitation in Cyrene (*War* 6:114).

The consequence of the act of the empress was the removal by King Agrippa of Ismael son of Phiabi from the high priesthood and his replacement by Joseph Kabi son of the high priest *Simon Kantheras son of Boethus (41 CE). Of this Joseph no information has survived except that he was one of the Jewish leaders who gave themselves up to the Romans during the siege of Jerusalem.

Rabbinic literature has preserved several anecdotes about Ismael son of Phiabi. He was one of the few high priests who sacrificed the red heifer (see article on Simon Kantheras son of Boethus). He, or his house, is accused of violent behaviour towards the people (mPar. 3:5;

mSot. 9:15; bPes. 57a). We are also told that his mother gave him an expensive tunic, which may underlie the saying that when Ismael son of Phiabi died, the splendour of the priesthood ceased.

Sources: Ismael: Josephus, *Ant.* 20:179, 194–5. Joseph Kabi: Josephus, *War* 6:114; *Ant.* 20:196.

IZATES AND HELENA OF ADIABENE

Izates was the ruler in the mid-first century CE of the small kingdom of Adiabene, situated on the eastern shore of the River Tigris adjacent to the kingdom of Parthia in Iran. *Josephus reports that during the reign of the emperor *Claudius (41–54 CE) a Jewish merchant by the name of Ananias persuaded Izates to embrace the Jewish faith. Izates' mother Helena was also converted to Judaism by another Jew. Both Ananias and Helena advised Izates against circumcision, which looked to them politically unwise, indeed dangerous, and emphasized that a person could worship God even without undergoing this rite. However, Izates, urged by another missionary, a strictly observant Galilean Jew, got himself circumcised and brought the whole royal family within the Jewish fold. Five of his sons received Jewish education in Jerusalem. Following the famine which devastated Judaea in the days of Claudius, mentioned by Josephus and the Acts of the Apostles (11:28), Queen Helena travelled to Jerusalem and arranged for food to be imported from Egypt and Cyprus for the Jerusalemites; her son Izates also contributed a large sum of money for the relief of the starving Jews.

This case of converting Gentiles to the Jewish religion is of considerable interest for the understanding of the parallel Christian evangelizing activity conducted by St *Paul and his colleagues among the peoples of the Graeco-Roman countries, especially with reference to the problem of circumcision on which, if the example of Ananias is typical, liberal Jewish missionaries did not insist.

Helena and her other son Monobazus, the successor of Izates, owned palaces in Jerusalem and according to the Mishnah (mYom. 3:10) they donated precious gifts to the Temple. Helena built a splendid mausoleum in the city and she and Izates were buried there by Mono-bazus. It is thought that the so-called 'Tombs of the Kings' in Jerusa-lem are the burial places of the royal family of Adiabene, and the inscription 'Queen Zadda' or 'Queen Zaddan' engraved on her sar-cophagus preserves the Aramaic name of Queen Helena.

Source: Josephus, Ant. 20:17–96.

J

JACOB OF KEFAR SEKHANIAH

Jacob of Kefar Sekhaniah (or Kefar Sama) was a charismatic Judaeo-Christian healer referred to several times in rabbinic literature. The personalities with whom he is associated suggest that this Jacob func-tioned at the turn of the first to second century CE. He promised to perform cures in the name of *Jesus of Nazareth and transmitted his teaching.

An anecdote associates him with Rabbi Eleazar ben Dama and his uncle Rabbi Ishmael ben Elisha. Jacob proposed to heal in the name of Jesus Eleazar, who had been bitten by a venomous snake. Rabbi Ishmael vetoed the offer. Eleazar, longing to be cured, wanted to argue with his uncle, but died before he could do so. A second anecdote brings Jacob into contact with Rabbi Eliezer ben Hyrcanus, a disciple of *Yohanan ben Zakkai. Eliezer was arrested for heresy but was subsequently released. Nevertheless he was perturbed by the idea of the arrest and wondered whether he had done wrong. Rabbi Akiba came up with the idea that Eliezer might have been pleased by some-thing a heretic had told him. He then remembered that one day in the Galilean city of Sepphoris Jacob of Kefar Sekhaniah had conveyed to him the interpretation of a biblical verse advanced by Jesus and Eliezer had gladly agreed with it.

These stories indicate that a Galilean Jewish Christian of the late first century CE was engaged, like the apostles and their immediate followers in the Acts of the Apostles, in healing and teaching in the name of Jesus. The rabbinic texts show that officialdom frowned on these practices, but that Jews and even rabbis were not necessarily opposed to them in the Palestinian Jewish society of the late first century CE.

Sources: tHul. 2:22–24; yShab. 14d; bAZ 27b; bAZ 16b–17a.

JAMES SON OF ALPHAEUS

Practically nothing is known of James son of Alphaeus, Thaddaeus, Simon the Zealot and Matthias, the four apostles of *Jesus of Nazareth who figure in the lists found in the Synoptic Gospels and in the Acts.

James son of Alphaeus may have been the brother of the tax collector Levi son of Alphaeus who is thought to be identical with the apostle *Matthew. James is distinguished by his patronymic (son of Alphaeus) from the apostle *James son of Zebedee, the brother of *John.

Thaddaeus or, according to manuscript variants, Lebbaeus, is listed in Matthew and *Mark. *Luke (6:16) has Judas son of James instead. A legend reported by the Church historian Eusebius ascribes to Thaddaeus the evangelization of northern Mesopotamia and makes him instrumental in arranging a fictional exchange of letters between Abgar, King of Edessa (4 BCE–50 CE), and Jesus. According to the legend, when struck by illness, Abgar asked Jesus to cure him and received a written promise that a disciple of Jesus, Thaddeus, would do so and preach the gospel to the people of Edessa.

Simon the Cananaean or Zealot (the Aramaic *qanna'an* or *qannay*) may have been a member of the Jewish revolutionary movement of the Zealots.

Matthias was chosen by casting of lots to replace *Judas Iscariot in the college of the apostles. His election was no doubt due more to the need to restore the symbolical community of twelve, corresponding to the tribes of Israel, than to any practical necessity. Eusebius suggests that Matthias was one of the seventy disciples of Jesus promoted to apostleship.

In short, apart from their names the New Testament contains no evidence whatever about one third of the apostles of Jesus.

Sources: Mk 3:16–19; Mt 10:2–4; Lk 6:14–16; Acts 1:12–14. Eusebius, *Eccl. Hist.* 1:12.

JAMES SON OF ZEBEDEE

James son of Zebedee was a fisherman who became an apostle of *Jesus of Nazareth. With his brother *John and possibly their father Zebedee, he formed a partnership with *Peter and *Andrew (Lk 5:10; Mt 4:21). James was one of the first apostles to be called by Jesus, and James and John, together with Simon-*Peter, were the leaders of the group. James was among the three apostles who witnessed the raising of Jairus' daughter (Mk 5:37; Lk 8:51) and he belonged to the trio who attended the 'transfiguration' of Jesus (Mk 9:2; Mt 17:1; Lk 9:28). Despite the obviously important position occupied by James in the circle of the apostles, the Gospels say very little about him and even the few statements that have survived are not always flattering. According to *Mark (10:35–7), James and his brother John asked Jesus to permit them to take the best seats on either side of the Master at the great banquet in the heavenly Kingdom. (*Matthew (Mt 20:20–21) attributes the request to the mother of James and John.) James and his brother also wished to bring down fire from heaven on a Samaritan village for refusing hospitality to Jesus and his company but were rebuked by Jesus (Lk 9:54–5), who called them 'sons of thunder' (Aramaic *Boanerges*) on account of their irascibility (Mk 3:17).

The dearth of information regarding one of the closest associates of Jesus is quite remarkable. Nevertheless, on one point James does better than the other apostles: he has his death recorded in the New Testament. According to the Acts of the Apostles Herod the King, that is to say Herod *Agrippa I (41–4 CE), ordered his decapitation. *Josephus is silent on the event, which does not tally well with Agrippa's generous and amiable nature.

Early Christian tradition further transmits the legendary story that the man who denounced James to Agrippa for being a member of the Church at once repented, became a Christian and was executed together with James by the Herodian monarch (Eusebius). According to a later legend James travelled to Spain and died there. His body is said to have been buried in Santiago de Compostela, which became one of the great places of pilgrimage in medieval Christendom.

Sources: Acts 12:1–2. Eusebius, *Eccl. Hist.* 2:9:3.

JAMES THE BROTHER OF THE LORD

James the brother of the Lord plays no part in the Gospels during the lifetime of *Jesus of Nazareth apart from being simply named on one occasion. According to the evangelists Jesus was not supported during his Galilean ministry by any of his brothers. The brothers and *Mary, Jesus' mother, first appear in the company of the apostles only in the opening chapter of the Acts of the Apostles (1:14). St *Paul also reports that the brothers of the Lord, accompanied by their wives, were later active in Christian missionary work (1 Cor. 9:5). Yet the Acts of the Apostles and later Christian tradition assert that the previously unremarkable James became one of the leading figures, if not *the* leading figure, in the early Church. Significantly, James is the only New Testament personality, after *John the Baptist and Jesus himself, whom the historian *Josephus mentions in his *Jewish Antiquities*.

James, with the epithet of 'the brother of the Lord' or of Jesus, appears in St Paul (Gal. 1:19) and Josephus (*Ant.* 20:200). In the Acts of the Apostles, where he is clearly the head of the Jerusalem Church and the president of the council of the apostles, he is simply James, without reference to his relation to Jesus, despite the fact that two other men of the same name, *James son of Zebedee and *James son of Alpheus, figure on the list of the twelve apostles. In the title of the New Testament letter of James he is described as the 'servant [not the brother] of the Lord Jesus Christ' (Jas. 1:1). The author of the letter of Jude, on the other hand, is 'a servant of Jesus Christ, and *brother* of James', revealing the importance of the latter.

It is possible to follow the progressive rise of James in the hierarchy of Jerusalem during the first decades of nascent Christianity. The principal source is Paul's letter to the Galatians. When Saul of Tarsus, after his so-called conversion, decided to visit the leaders of the Jesus movement in Jerusalem, he first made contact with Cephas (*Peter), the leader of the community, and with James 'the brother of the Lord' (Gal. 1:19). Yet fourteen years after the Damascus event (Gal. 2:1), on the occasion of the council of the apostles in Jerusalem (49 CE), Peter was still the first speaker at the meeting to favour the acceptance of uncircumcised Gentiles into the Church, but the formal decision was made by James, the president of the council. It was he who issued a judgement to the effect that if certain conditions were fulfilled, pagans could be accepted into the Church without becoming Jews in the first instance (Acts 15:6–20).

The superiority of James over Peter is suggested also by Paul when he names him as the first of the three pillars of the Church, James, Cephas and *John (Gal. 2:9). This new order of precedence is further confirmed by Peter's hypocritical behaviour in Antioch after the arrival of the envoys of James, a strict enforcer of the Law: in their presence Peter stopped eating with Gentile Christians, whose table he had previously been sharing (Gal. 2:11–13). On the occasion of Paul's last visit to Jerusalem (58 CE), the sole leader of the Church to whom he paid his respects was James, though the non-mention of Cephas may perhaps be due to Peter's absence by then from the Holy City (Acts 21:18).

The New Testament contains no explanation of the meteoric rise of James. There are two likely motives: his personal holiness, attested indirectly by Josephus and directly by Christian tradition, and the importance of his family connection with Jesus.

Josephus' opinion concerning the brother of Jesus is given in his account of James's execution, an event unmentioned in the New Testament. It happened in 62 CE in the interval between the death of the procurator *Festus and the arrival of his successor *Albinus. The reckless *Ananus, recently appointed high priest by King *Agrippa II, was flexing his political muscles during the procuratorial absence, and brought before a Jewish court 'James, the brother of Jesus called the Christ', declared him and others guilty of transgressing the Law and condemned them to death by stoning. The most fair-minded and

The ossuary (of questionable authenticity) of James the brother of Jesus

religiously observant citizens of Jerusalem firmly disapproved of Ananus' conduct, we learn from Josephus, and they persuaded King Agrippa to sack the high priest. Early Christian tradition represented by the Church historian Eusebius (third to fourth century), quoting the second-century writer Hegesippus, recounts James's execution in detail. He was first thrown down from the pinnacle of the Temple, but miraculously survived both the fall and the subsequent stoning. He was then put to death by a fuller who smashed his skull with his club.

Hegesippus portrays James as an outstanding holy man called 'the Righteous', an ascetic bound by the multiple vows of abstinence of the Nazirites. 'This [James]', he writes,

was holy from his birth; he drank no wine or intoxicating liquor and ate no animal food; no razor came near his head; he did not smear himself with oil, and took no baths . . . He used to enter the Sanctuary alone, and was often found on his knees beseeching forgiveness for the people, so that his knees grew hard like a camel's from his continually bending them in worship of God . . . (Eusebius)

It was because of his 'outstanding virtue' that Peter, James and John would choose James the Righteous, rather than one of themselves, for the most honourable post of bishop of Jerusalem. Moreover, Eusebius declares that even the Jewish Josephus presented the conquest of Jerusalem by *Vespasian as divine punishment for the murder of James. Origen, too, attributes the same view to Josephus (cf. Against Celsus i. 47; ii. 13), but none of the surviving manuscripts of the Jewish Antiquities includes such a statement.

The second apparent reason for the rise of James on the hierarchical ladder of the Church was his kinship with Jesus. Neither Paul nor the rest of the New Testament includes a hint of this sort, but early Christian tradition displays such pointers. The already cited Hegesippus describes the choice of James's successor to the bishopric of Jerusalem in quasi-dynastic terms. 'When James the Righteous had suffered martyrdom . . . *Symeon the son of his uncle Clopas was appointed bishop. He being a cousin of the Lord, it was the universal demand that he should be the second' (Eusebius, Eccl. Hist. 4:22). Eusebius through Hegesippus further reports that in the days of the emperor *Domitian the relatively impoverished grandsons of *Jude brother of James (Jude 1:1), that is to say, the great-nephews of Jesus, were placed by the Romans on the political blacklist because, as descendants of David, they were considered potential messianic rebels (Eccl. Hist. 3:20). So it would seem that during the sixty or seventy years after the death of Jesus, a family link with the Master was a significant asset when the leadership of the Church was at issue. However, by the early second century, with the bulk of the Jesus movement having by then moved away from the Holy Land, such connections ceased to play a significant role in the primitive Church.

Whether the Letter of James in the New Testament is the work of 'the brother of the Lord' is highly disputed. It is worth noting that some authorities, including St Jerome, attribute it to the apostle *James son of Alphaeus. In its present form, displaying a mastery of the

Greek language and a great familiarity with the style of the Greek (Septuagint) Bible, it is hard to imagine that it was written by an uncultured Galilean fisherman. Also, bearing in mind James's reputation of heading the party of the Judaizers in the Church, one would expect to find some allusion to the compulsory observance of the Mosaic Law by Jewish Christians in the letter. Yet there is none.

On the other hand, even though direct derivation from James cannot be proved, the contents of the epistle reflect a genuinely Jewish cultural and religious background. The message is theocentric rather than christocentric. Apart from the numerous biblical allusions and citations, the letter reproduces the main tenet of the Jewish profession of faith, 'God is one' (2:19), and insists that faith is inseparable from the doing of the Law (1:19–25). The writer of the Letter addresses himself to 'the twelve tribes of the Dispersion' (1:1) and calls the Christian cult assembly a 'synagogue' (2:2). He testifies to a prolonged expectation of the return of Christ: the Second Coming has been long delayed but is now at hand (5:7–9). Elements of the Hasidic piety of Jesus resurface in James, with the kingdom of God being promised to the poor (2:5) and with a recommendation to Church elders to use charismatic prayer and oil to heal the sick and obtain the forgiveness of sins (5:14–15; cf. Mk 6:13). They should imitate the miraculously efficient supplication of the prophet Elijah, the model of the charismatic Hasid (5:17–18). So, while James is unlikely to be responsible for the Greek style of the letter, the ideas contained in it may at least in part have come from him.

Two archaeological items of a dubious kind are associated with James. Tourist guides show pilgrims in Jerusalem the Tomb of James, located between the so-called Tomb of Absalom and the Tomb of Zechariah, in the cemetery lying on the eastern side of the Kidron Valley below the Temple Mount. In fact, a Hebrew inscription engraved on the monument and dating to the second century BCE declares that the burial place belonged not to James, but to the Jewish priestly family of Bene Hezir.

The second artefact linked to James is a privately owned stone ossuary, which in 2002 gained public notoriety. The Aramaic inscription engraved on it purports to identify the person whose long-vanished bones originally lay in the box. He is a certain YA'AQÔB

BAR YÔSEPH 'AHÔY DEYESHÛA' or James [=Jacob] son of Joseph, brother of Jesus. The script itself is thought by some experts to belong to the first century CE, but the mention of a brother is uncommon, though not wholly unprecedented, on Jewish ossuary inscriptions. Nevertheless the uncertainty surrounding the provenance of the bone-box, the chemical composition of the patina covering the engraving and a forger's kit discovered in the house of the owner weigh heavily against its authenticity. Should this 'James son of Joseph, brother of Jesus' none the less turn out to be the brother of the Lord, the humble 'coffin' would bring us marvellously near to the real world of Jesus, and even to a member of his family.

Sources: Josephus, *Ant.* 20:200–201. Eusebius, *Eccl. Hist.* 2:1, 23. André Lemaire, 'Burial Box of James the Brother of Jesus', *BAR* 28/6, Nov.–Dec. 2002, 24–33.

JESUS OF NAZARETH

Jesus of Nazareth (*c.* 6/5 BCE–30 CE) was a Jewish charismatic prophet, healer, exorcist and teacher whose message was centred on the imminent coming of the Kingdom of God. His life is recounted with substantial variations in the four Gospels of the New Testament. A small amount of additional early evidence is supplied by *Josephus and the Roman historian Tacitus. Only a few details are firmly established. Jesus was crucified under the governorship of Pontius *Pilate, the Roman prefect of Judaea between 26 and 36 CE. The Gospels portray him as a Galilean whose centre of ministry was in the area of the lake of Gennesaret. The Infancy Gospel of *Matthew (2:1) places his birth at the end of the reign of King *Herod the Great who died in 4 BCE (see also Lk 1:5). Apart from a doubtless fictional anecdote relating to the twelve-year-old Jesus (Lk 2:41–52), the evangelists report nothing of his childhood and youth.

The start of the public life of Jesus, which is also the starting point of the Gospel of *Mark, the oldest of the Gospels, coincided with the ministry of the hermit preacher *John the Baptist, dated to the fifteenth year of the emperor *Tiberius (29 CE) according to the chronology of

*Luke (3:1). While undergoing the baptism of repentance administered by John, Jesus himself had a vision and heard a heavenly voice, which declared him to be the son with whom God was well pleased (so Mk 1:10–11 and Lk 3:21–2). But according to Matthew (3:16–17) and *John (1:32–4), the subject of the supernatural experience was not Jesus but the Baptist, who afterwards proclaimed to all those present the divine election of Jesus.

Jesus began his own preaching mission in Galilee after the imprisonment of John by the tetrarch Herod *Antipas. The precise length of the teaching activity of Jesus is nowhere stated. If we follow the chronology of the earlier Synoptic Gospels in which only one Passover is mentioned, which coincides with the crucifixion, Jesus' public career is confined to a maximum of twelve months, and possibly no more than half a year (autumn 29 to spring 30 CE). The Gospel of John, mentioning two or three Passovers, allows for a duration of between two and three years for the preaching of Jesus.

Before joining John the Baptist who was baptizing in the Jordan valley, Jesus had lived in the small Galilean town of Nazareth with his family, that is, his parents *Joseph and *Mary, his brothers *James, *Jude, Joses and Simon, and at least two sisters. He was, according to Mark and Matthew, a carpenter or builder, yet hardly anything in the imagery of his teaching confirms that he was an artisan. The language of his parables would rather suggest a smallholder. The oldest Gospel of Mark, echoed by Matthew, leads one to believe that the family of Jesus objected to his new vocation and endeavoured to stop his charismatic activity. A complete gulf appears to have opened between Jesus and his near kin, including his mother, and no member of the family plays any further role in the Gospel story told by the Synoptics. The oddity of the situation speaks in favour of the authenticity of the account. However, the author of the Fourth Gospel proposes a partly different scenario. Soon after the start of his public life Jesus with his mother and brothers attended a wedding in the Galilean village of Cana, and at the end of the same Gospel his mother reappears at the foot of the cross.

From the outset, Jesus was aware of his duty to proclaim and prepare the imminent arrival of the Kingdom of Heaven, and to bring his contemporaries into it through repentance and through surrendering themselves to God. He chose a group of associates, an inner circle of twelve apostles and a larger body of seventy disciples, to assist him in the execution of his task. Only Jews, 'the lost sheep of the house of Israel', were the addressees. His envoys were explicitly ordered not to approach Gentiles or Samaritans. Throughout the ministry of Jesus, as described in the Gospels, this exclusively Jewish orientation remained firm. He hardly ever crossed the border of the Jewish territory. On the two or three occasions when Jesus ventures into the neighbouring regions of Tyre and Sidon in Lebanon, into Caesarea Philippi in the Golan, and into the Decapolis in Transjordan, he is represented as healing or exorcizing, but never as announcing the coming of God's Kingdom. The Fourth Gospel takes Jesus to Samaria on his way to Jerusalem, but Luke (17:11), with greater historical verisimilitude, indicates that Jesus preferred to bypass the country of the Samaritans on his pilgrimage to the Temple, and chose the longer but safer route through the valley of the Jordan.

Jesus was an itinerant preacher and delivered his message in synagogues, streets and squares, in the wilderness, or sometimes from a boat on the lake shore. He addressed large gatherings, small groups of passers-by or single individuals. His appeal was magnetic, mostly taking the form of pithy wisdom sayings or colourful and poetic parables. His religious message was genuinely Jewish, centred on the Law of Moses, with particular insistence on the internal meaning of the commandments and on their inner spirituality. Unlike the traditional Jewish scribes, he did not regularly rely on biblical proof texts; instead he taught 'with authority', this authority being manifested in charismatic deeds, in spiritual healing, usually by means of bodily contact, and in exorcism by simple command. He abstained from the recitation of set formulae. Jews in those days believed that sickness and demonic possession were the consequences of sin. Hence cure and the expulsion of evil spirits preceded by repentance revealed divine forgiveness and salvation. Their recurrence day after day persuaded people that the messianic age of redemption was approaching or had already begun.

The religious activity of Jesus followed the line established by biblical prophets, especially Elijah and Elisha, who had been active some 800 years earlier in the northern provinces far away from the centre

Remains of the synagogue of Capernaum probably built on the site of an earlier place of worship frequented by Jesus

of Jerusalem. Josephus and the authors of rabbinic literature know of some other Jewish charismatics from the first century BCE and CE: *Honi, his grandsons *Abba Hilkiah and *Hanan, and the Galilean *Hanina ben Dosa, a younger contemporary of Jesus. They were all celebrated as miraculous rainmakers, but Hanina was also a renowned healer. His curing from a distance of the son of the Pharisee leader Gamaliel furnishes a striking parallel to Jesus healing the servant of the Roman centurion in Capernaum. Josephus in his famous passage known as the *Testimonium Flavianum* describes Jesus as a 'wise man' and a 'performer of astonishing deeds', that is to say, as a teacher and a miracle worker. Josephus thus furnishes an external confirmation of the mainstream portrait of Jesus in the Gospels.

The preaching and healing of Jesus were given a twofold reception in Galilee. Not counting his disgruntled family, and with the one exception in Luke where the inhabitants of Nazareth quite unreasonably intended to stone Jesus for curing the sick outside his town (Lk 4:25–9), the only hostility shown to Jesus in Galilee came from petty-minded synagogue officials and village scribes. They objected to his healing activity on the Sabbath, which in their eyes broke the law regarding sabbatical rest, and considered as a blasphemy his declaration that the sins of a paralysed man were pardoned, forgiveness of sins being held to be a divine prerogative. Both charges are false. Healing of the sick in principle overrode the Sabbath law and since sickness was believed to be the consequence of sin, when someone was restored to health his sins, the cause of his illness, were implicitly forgiven. The healing charisma of a prophet or a man of God ultimately signified deliverance from sin.

The grievances of the self-important local leaders were insignificant compared with the enthusiastic approval of Jesus' ministry by the ordinary Galileans. Crowds gathered to listen to his teaching, and the sick were brought out on stretchers and laid down in the street wherever he was expected to pass. Even his shadow was deemed to possess a therapeutic effect. He was hailed as 'the prophet Jesus from Nazareth'. It is only in the Gospel of John that either the Jews, a derogatory collective term for Jesus' opponents, or the chief priests sought his death before his only – or, in John, before his last – visit to Jerusalem. Their main charge against him was that he broke the Sabbath and called God his Father (Jn 5:18). In fact neither accusation can be upheld: Jesus' style of healing by speech and touch did not amount to work, and all the Jews in his day and since prayed to God as their Father, implicitly proclaiming themselves as his sons, without committing blasphemy. The Synoptic Gospels, which are historically more reliable than John, include no advance explanation for Jesus' sudden loss of popularity in Jerusalem during the week of his final Passover.

Even his visit to the holy city began auspiciously. The evangelists depict Jesus' entry into Jerusalem as triumphal (though in Luke the welcoming 'crowds' consist of Jesus' Galilean disciples). Even more telling, the Temple authorities were unwilling to arrest Jesus openly because of his popularity (Mk 11:18; 14:1–2; Mt 26:3–5; Lk 19:47–8; 22:2). Without hindrance he was preaching daily in the Temple during the days preceding the feast, and when the authorities decided to detain him, they thought it best to do so stealthily in the depth of night. The disappearance of sympathizers in the account of the trial and crucifixion of Jesus and their replacement by an inimical mob lack explanation in the Gospels.

The only event that can possibly account for the suspicion and hostility of officialdom towards Jesus is the upheaval created by him in the Temple a day or two after his arrival in Jerusalem. The fiery rural prophet appears to have been profoundly shocked by the sight of the merchants' quarter in the forecourt of the Sanctuary and in his anger he overturned the stalls of the vendors of sacrificial animals and the tables of the money-changers. Although he was not a revolutionary himself, Jesus thus created a tumult in a revolutionary age. Jerusalem, filled to capacity with pilgrims at the approach of Passover, was a dangerous powder keg. The nerves of the Jewish authorities responsible for the maintenance of law and order were stretched to the limit and the Romans, present with increased strength, were at the ready to retaliate and quash the slightest breach of the peace. The leaders of the Temple felt duty-bound to intervene.

The party consisting of chief priests, scribes and elders which inquired of Jesus with what kind of authority he acted as he did in the Temple incident, was no doubt sent to cool down the atmosphere. But Jesus' provocative rejoinder – 'I will answer you if you tell me what you think of John the Baptist' – was not exactly helpful. So two days before Passover the chief priests and elders (interestingly, the Pharisees are never mentioned in the Passion story) decided to apprehend Jesus quietly. A good opportunity arose one night when they had received information from *Judas Iscariot, a member of the Galilean inner circle, that Jesus would retire to a garden outside the city. They sent a group of Temple policemen to capture him there and bring him before the chief priests.

The four Gospels contain three different and irreconcilable accounts of the events. The first divergence, separating John from the Synoptics, relates to the date. In the Synoptics the arrest of Jesus happens after the Passover meal, that is to say, after the start of the feast of Passover in the night of 15 Nisan. In this version, the trial and execution of Jesus took place during the festival itself, a most unlikely eventuality as Jewish courts did not sit, investigate or pronounce sentence on a feast-day or a Sabbath. In John, with greater probability, everything is dated twenty-four hours earlier: the Last Supper of Jesus with his apostles is not described as a Passover meal and it is specifically stated that Jesus was delivered by the chief priests to Pilate in the morning of the day *before* the feast, on 14 Nisan.

The four Gospels agree on the final stage of the trial of Jesus. On the morning after his arrest the chief priests handed Jesus over to the Roman governor of Judaea on the charge of sedition, and an unenthusiastic Pilate ordered him to be crucified. For all the rest, there is general disagreement.

In John Jesus is first brought by the police to the house of the former high priest *Ananus or Annas. He was interrogated there at night but was not sentenced. Annas sent him to *Caiaphas, the high priest of the day, who with no further investigation delivered Jesus to Pilate to be judged as a revolutionary.

The three Synoptic evangelists place a Jewish court case before the Roman trial. According to Mark and Matthew, the tribunal headed by the high priest was convened at night and Jesus was charged with some religious offence against the Temple. However, the testimony of the witnesses did not comply with the legal requirements for a verdict of guilty. Caiaphas, wishing to complete the case, confronted Jesus with a direct question: was he or was he not the Messiah?, and taking his evasive reply as an admission, condemned him to death for blasphemy. The following morning the court met again and decided to hand Jesus over to the Romans as an enemy of the emperor. In Luke there is no nocturnal trial; the Sanhedrin meets only in the morning; no witnesses are called, and Jesus is sentenced for not denying his Messiahship. The Synoptic account of the religious trial is intrinsically flawed. No Jewish law would equate a claim of someone to be the Messiah with blasphemy, nor is there any reference in the Gospels to a death sentence by stoning, the punishment prescribed by the Bible for blasphemers. Finally, the change of the indictment from blasphemy to fomenting rebellion against Rome remains unexplained. Jesus was transferred to the Romans as a potential revolutionary. John's attempted explanation that no Jewish court could execute a death sentence is highly questionable (see the article on Pilate). Jesus was crucified for a crime he did not commit. The Aramaic phrase *'Eloi, Eloi, lama sabachthani?'* ('My God, my God, why hast thou forsaken me?'), which Jesus utters on the cross, is the prayer of a person who cannot understand what is happening to him (Mk 15:34; Mt 27:46).

Because of the closeness of the Sabbath, Jesus was buried in a hurry in a rock tomb. At dawn on the third day three Galilean women went to the tomb to complete the funeral ceremonies, but found that the body of Jesus had disappeared. According to Mark, they all ran away terrified and said nothing to anyone. In Luke they informed the apostles only to be rebuffed by them: women's silly tales, the male chauvinists said. In Matthew they were instructed by a person in the tomb to tell the apostles to go to Galilee where Jesus would meet them. In John *Mary Magdalene inquired of a man she thought was the gardener, but who apparently was the unrecognized risen Jesus, whether he had transferred the body to some other tomb. The testimony of the unreliable female witnesses about the empty tomb was checked and confirmed by two men, one of them *Peter.

However, for the evangelists the main corroboration of the resurrection came from personal experience. It consisted of a series of visions. Two disciples travelling to Emmaus encountered a stranger who told them he was Jesus. The eleven apostles had a similar experience in Jerusalem; the ghost they saw declared himself to be Jesus. According to Matthew, an apparition took place on a Galilean mountain. The last word was *Paul's, who claimed that Jesus had appeared to no fewer than 500 brethren before he showed himself to Paul. The Church's conviction that Jesus rose from the dead relies on the cumulative effect of these repeated visions.

For the disciples, who had all lost courage and disappeared after the arrest of their Master, the practical proof that Jesus did not remain dead and buried but continued to be with them and act through them was the persistence of charisma in the primitive Church. It first reappeared with the manifestation of the Spirit at Pentecost and afterwards in the renewal in the name of Jesus of the effective healing and exorcism by the apostles. The Jesus who supplied them with such miracle-working powers was not dead. He was alive and active in and through his disciples in the Church. It was with the help of the thus resurrected Jesus that they went on performing their charismatic mission.

The teaching associated with Jesus is twofold. Part of it consists of his actual preaching, his authentic message prior to the accretions attached to it in the New Testament and since. The other part, quite different from the first, relates to doctrines expounding what Jesus has done for mankind, doctrines primarily deriving from the letters of Paul and the Gospel of John. They provide the basis of the Christian religion.

Five major themes summarize Jesus' religious message. They relate to the Kingdom of God; to the observance of the Torah in the final age; to eschatological piety; to Jesus' teaching on prayer; and to his view of God.

The Kingdom of God alludes to a new reality in which God's rule over Israel and the world becomes truly effective. As in the rest of Jewish literature of the period, the description of the Kingdom always proceeds by means of comparison. It is regularly likened by Jesus to this-worldly realities, though significantly never to something of a political or military character. The Kingdom resembles a rich harvest, or a particularly tall mustard shrub grown from the tiniest of seeds. It is likened to a small lump of leaven, to a treasure hidden in the field, or to a precious pearl the acquisition of which is worth every sacrifice. The details do not matter: Jesus is only interested in the action leading to the goal. The Kingdom is the ultimate spiritual value and Jesus' true concern is to show the means by which admittance into the Kingdom can be secured.

The piety of Jesus was centred on the Torah, the lifeblood of the Jewish religion. Having adopted a feverish eschatological stance and expected the imminent arrival of the Kingdom, he perceived and practised the Law in his own characteristic fashion, which from time to time brought him into conflict with his more conventional co-religionists. From his eschatological perspective even the pedestrian rules of the Torah regulating everyday life possessed an inner spiritual significance. Therefore Jesus insisted on the necessity of obeying all the details of the Mosaic rules.

Jesus' conviction that the advent of the Kingdom was looming on the horizon created a sense of extreme urgency. He hated procrastination and demanded total devotion to the cause. In his view an arduous path led to the narrow gate of the Kingdom and progress towards it required continuous sacrifice. The renunciation of material wealth had to go hand in hand with a willingness to cut all ties of kinship for the sake of the Kingdom. The spirit of sacrifice and the sentiment of extreme pressure inspired the positive virtue of generosity. The munificent donor was promised extra recompense. Hate-filled enemies were to be disarmed with love.

Prayer was at the centre of Jesus' religion. It was characterized by three essential features: trust, readiness to forgive and absence of ostentation. To receive divine absolution from sin, the penitent had to be prepared to pardon those who had offended him. The requirement to pray in seclusion was typical of the private religion taught by Jesus. He insisted that his disciples should speak to God, give alms and fast in secret, without being seen by men.

It would be pointless to expect from Jesus a theoretical definition of the Deity; he was not a philosopher or even a theologian. For him, God is what God does. In other words, God reveals himself in what Jesus and his followers acknowledge as divine interventions in their own lives during the present era, soon to become the age of the Kingdom.

Jesus' image of God is uncomplicated. Contrary to Jewish tradition the royal title is applied to God only in parables which may not be authentic. For Jesus God is 'Abba' or 'Father', someone who cares for wild flowers, birds and foxes and for those humans who pin their faith on him. In Jesus' eyes, worry and anxiety count as a denial of God. For the flock of his children God is like a loving shepherd, who spares no effort to find them if they stray, and rejoices when they are brought safely back into the sheepfold (Mt 18:12–14; Lk 15:4–7). The God of Jesus is a solicitous paterfamilias, aware of the needs of all the members of the family. But this God is also superior to Jesus and to all creatures. He is above all the Master who alone determines the moment of the advent of the Kingdom.

Ultimately the God of Jesus is a loving Father. He makes the sun rise and the rain fall for the benefit of all; he gives his children their daily bread. He protects the little ones from temptation and delivers them from evil. He forgives them all, even the publicans and harlots, and welcomes them to his Kingdom. In short, harshness or severity is alien to this portrait of the God of Jesus. This would imply that he felt optimistic about the successful outcome of his mission. He expected the children of God to find their own salvation in the Kingdom of their heavenly Father.

The religion taught by Jesus was positive and hopeful; those embracing it were to steam ahead at top speed. It may be compared to a race demanding from the runners their last ounce of energy, with a medal awaiting all the participants at the finishing line.

Against this God-centred, eschatological and existential religion preached and practised by Jesus stands Christo-centric Christianity, which emphasizes the supernatural achievements of a God incarnate. Christianity does not primarily insist on the effort of humans to obey the teaching and follow the example of Jesus. It is characterized by belief in the redeeming power of the suffering, death and resurrection of Christ, a deified human being. This is a new religion, constructed not on the simple and down-to-earth gospel of the prophet from Nazareth, but on the mystical vision of the author of the Fourth Gospel and of St Paul, which has been developed into fully-fledged Christianity by the various Churches over the centuries up to the present day.

Sources: The Gospels. Josephus, *Ant.* 18:63–4.

JESUS SON OF ANANIAS

Jesus son of Ananias was a rural holy man who got himself into trouble with the authorities during the Feast of Tabernacles in 62 CE. *Josephus records that this Jesus, walking up and down the streets of the city day after day, proclaimed woe to Jerusalem and the sanctuary with a loud voice: 'A voice from the east, a voice from the west, a voice from the four winds; a voice against Jerusalem and the sanctuary, a voice against the bridegroom and the bride, a voice against the people!' These ill-omened prophetic words, reminiscent of Jeremiah, chapter 7, created disturbances. So the Jewish magistrates arrested Jesus and gave him a severe beating to bring him to his senses. It made no difference; Jesus persisted with his cries. Fearing that he might be inspired by God – Josephus believed that he was – instead of taking more drastic steps to silence him themselves, the magistrates passed the case to the Roman governor *Albinus. Albinus ordered another scourging, worse than the previous one, before examining the accused. But when Jesus son of Ananias refused to answer his questions, he concluded that the man was a lunatic and released him. Jesus continued with his daily laments until the outbreak of the first war against Rome in 66 CE. For seven years and five months he persisted with his wailing. He stopped only when a stone catapulted by a Roman war machine killed him in 69 CE.

The story of Jesus son of Ananias recalls that of *Jesus of Nazareth. The Gospels contain no hint that *Caiaphas and his colleagues imagined that Jesus was divinely inspired, but it is conceivable that a mixture of superstitious fear and an innate unwillingness actually to order the execution of a Jew played a subconscious part in their decision to deliver Jesus to Pontius *Pilate.

Source: Josephus, War 6:300–309.

JESUS SON OF DAMNAEUS

Jesus son of Damnaeus was appointed high priest by King *Agrippa II after the three-month pontificate of *Ananus son of Ananus. He was in office in 62/3 CE. Nothing is recorded about his tenure of the pontificate. His deposition and replacement by *Jesus son of Gamaliel may have been due to Agrippa's displeasure with the people's criticism of his generosity in foreign lands. In the years leading to the first Jewish war and during the war itself the sacred office of the high priesthood degenerated. *Josephus notes that Jesus son of Damnaeus was unwilling to relinquish his post and the rowdy partisans of the two Jesuses pelted one another with stones in the streets of Jerusalem.

Sources: Josephus, War 6:114; Ant. 20:203, 213.

JESUS SON OF GAMALIEL

Jesus son of Gamaliel or Joshua ben Gamla was chosen as high priest by King *Agrippa II in 63 CE in replacement of *Jesus son of Damnaeus. He came, according to the Mishnah, from the priestly family of Boethus through marriage, his wife being Martha daughter of Boethus. As Jesus son of Damnaeus was not prepared to be replaced, the supporters of the rival pontiffs resorted to street fighting in Jerusalem. According to the Talmud, Jesus son of Gamaliel introduced primary education for boys from the age of six or seven. He was deposed by Agrippa II in 64 CE in favour of *Matthias son of Theophilus, but he continued to remain at the centre of politics after the outbreak of the war. Although Jesus was a close friend of *Josephus, he is accused together with another former high priest, *Ananus son of Ananus, of trying to limit the power of Josephus in Galilee. He also criticized the Zealots for their choice of the last high priest, Phannias son of Samuel, in 67 CE. Later, Jesus son of Gamaliel vainly tried to pacify the Idumaean allies of the Zealots: he finally fell victim to them together with Ananus son of Ananus.

Matthias son of Theophilus was the last high priest created by Agrippa II in 64/5 CE. He was the son of Theophilus son of Ananus and the grandson of *Ananus (or Annas) son of Sethi, whose five sons preceded him on the pontifical throne. Nothing is known about him.

Sources: Jesus: Josephus, *War* 4:160, 238, 360; *Ant.* 20:213, 222; *Life* 193, 204. mYeb: 6:4; mYom. 3:9; bBB 21a. Matthias: Josephus, *War* 6:114; *Ant.* 20:223.

JESUS SON OF PHIABI

Jesus son of Phiabi was high priest under *Herod the Great. He belonged to a leading high-priestly family, which provided two further pontiffs, Ismael son of Phiabi (15–16 CE) and a second high priest with the same name (59–61 CE). Of Jesus son of Phiabi nothing is known apart from *Josephus' note that he was replaced by *Simon son of Boethus. The latter owed his promotion to the beauty of his daughter, whom Herod was to marry. The Boethus family supplied several further holders of the pontifical office in addition to Simon.

Source: Josephus, *Ant.* 15:322.

JESUS SON OF SEE

See under **Joazar son of Boethus**.

JOAZAR SON OF BOETHUS

Joazar son of Boethus was the last high priest appointed by *Herod (4 BCE). He was the king's brother-in-law, *Mariamme II's brother, and replaced *Matthias son of Theophilus, whom Herod dismissed on account of his involvement with a disturbance resulting in the removal of a golden eagle from the Temple. Joazar had a rather stormy career. Accused of supporting the revolt which followed the death of Herod, he was deposed in 4 BCE by the ethnarch *Archelaus, Herod's son, and replaced by his brother, Eleazar son of Boethus. Eleazar stayed in office for only a short period and Jesus son of See, about whom we know nothing, was appointed to replace him. For reasons equally unknown, Joazar was recalled by Archelaus, and as high priest he persuaded many of his compatriots to accept the census organized by *Quirinius, Roman governor of Syria, after the removal from office of Archaelaus in 6 CE. Joazar did not remain in favour with Quirinius for long. Influenced by the people, Joazar toed a nationalist line and Quirinius, no longer finding him useful, installed in 6 CE a new and powerful high priest, *Ananus or Annas son of Sethi, the head of another leading pontifical dynasty, who according to the Gospel of *John was later to interrogate *Jesus after his arrest before handing him over to his son-in-law, the high priest Joseph *Caiaphas.

Sources: Joazar: Josephus, *Ant.* 17:164. Eleazar: Josephus, *Ant.* 17:339.

JOHN OF GISCHALA

John of Gischala, from the Upper Galilean town of Gush Halab (hence the Hellenized Gischala), was one of the principal leaders of the rebellion against Rome, first in Galilee and then from 67 CE onwards in Jerusalem. As we owe his portrait to *Josephus, with whom he was on far from friendly terms, it is no surprise that he is portrayed as a most unsympathetic character: unscrupulous, crafty and malicious, a liar and a knave. Naturally Josephus needs to be taken here with a pinch of salt.

Surrounded by a small private army of 400 'brigands', the impecunious John, animated by a typically Galilean fighting spirit, was plundering the northern district, of which Josephus was the commander-in-chief at the start of the rebellion. While rebuilding the walls of his town of Gischala and practising a kind of monopoly in exporting the olive oil of the region, he enriched himself considerably. Josephus mischievously reports that John was a crook. He bought four amphorae of oil for four Attic drachms, but resold half an amphora for the same price!

John instigated a revolt against Josephus in the city of Tarichaeae by the Lake of Galilee and almost managed to get rid of him. Jewish resistance in Galilee did not last long and *Titus, commissioned by his father *Vespasian to complete the conquest of the province, easily occupied Gischala and forced John and his Zealots to flee to Jerusalem in early November 67 CE. In the capital John became one of the two main revolutionary leaders until the spring of 69 CE, a tyrant according to Josephus, responsible for the internecine fighting among Jewish factions. He commanded a force of twenty officers and 6,000 men. For a short while *Eleazar son of Simon, a renegade of John's party, became the captain of a third group, but at Passover in 70 CE John's partisans conquered the sector held by Eleazar, and the defence of the capital was once more directed by the duumvirate of John of Gischala and *Simon son of Giora, the former defending the Antonia fortress and the latter the upper city. The senseless bloody resistance continued until August 70 CE. At the end, fleeing the Romans, John of Gischala took refuge in the underground tunnels, but starvation forced him to surrender. Together with Simon son of Giora he was compelled to march in front of Titus at the victory parade in Rome in 71 CE. Luckier than Simon, who was ceremonially executed at the end of the triumph, John was given a life sentence for his part in the rebellion against the almighty empire of Rome.

Sources: Josephus, *War* 2, 4–7; *Life.*

JOHN THE APOSTLE

John son of Zebedee, the brother of *James, was one of the leading apostles of *Jesus and considered by Christian tradition as the author of the Fourth Gospel. He and James, both fishermen, were called by Jesus immediately after *Peter, and the three of them formed the inner circle of the apostles. They alone witnessed the raising of the daughter of Jairus and the Transfiguration. They questioned Jesus about the future destruction of the Temple and they were asked to stay close to him in the Garden of Gethsemane, but fell asleep.

John and his brother are portrayed as typical Galileans with a fiery temperament; hence the Aramaic nickname 'sons of thunder' (*Boanerges*) given them by Jesus (Mk 3:17). John's hot-headedness is signalled by his firm intervention against the exorcist who used the name of Jesus in expelling demons without being a member of Jesus' company. Together with his brother he threatened an unfriendly Samaritan village with fire from heaven, and adding ambition to impetuosity, John and James claimed for themselves the best seats at the Messianic banquet table.

In the Fourth Gospel neither James nor John is mentioned by name, though there is a single allusion to the sons of Zebedee, and Christian tradition considers John to be the person referred to as 'the disciple whom Jesus loved', who sat next to Jesus at the Last Supper, accompanied him to the cross, was entrusted with the care of Jesus' mother and outran Peter in checking the report about the empty tomb. It is odd that this important person remains anonymous, but the Fourth Gospel does not mention the name of Jesus' mother either.

In the Synoptic Gospels John disappears, together with the other apostles, after the arrest of Jesus and makes his re-entry into New Testament history in the Acts of the Apostles (3:1-4, 11; 4:13, 19; 8:14). In the Acts, he is listed among the disciples of Jesus and is the constant single associate of Peter. They went together to the Temple to pray; John witnessed the healing of a lame man by Peter; Peter and John were the apostles' spokesmen before the Sanhedrin and were qualified as 'uneducated, common men' by the authorities. Later John was sent with Peter to finalize the evangelization of the Samaritans. This leading role of John in the early Christian community is confirmed by Paul, who names him, together with James the brother of the Lord and Cephas, among the 'pillars' of the Church (Gal. 2:9). With this mention John vanishes from the New Testament, if we discard the author of the Book of Revelation, also called John, whose identity with the son of Zebedee is most unlikely. Nor can the three letters attributed to 'John' be credited to the apostle with any degree of certainty.

Irenaeus, bishop of Lyons, asserted around 180 CE, and Eusebius repeated, that John had settled in Ephesus and lived there to a great age. No earlier tradition supports this statement. In fact it is implicitly contradicted by Ignatius, bishop of Antioch, who, in a letter written to the Ephesians c. 110 CE, describes them as the people of *Paul without alluding to John's presence in their midst just a few years earlier.

As for John's authorship of the Fourth Gospel, the evidence is rather tenuous. Papias is silent on the subject and the earliest witness is Irenaeus, who reported that John had composed his Gospel in Ephesus. The Gospel itself does not disclose the identity of its author. A passage in the last chapter, which is patently a later gloss, implies that 'the disciple whom Jesus loved' wrote 'these things' (Jn 21:24). The Glossator also knew that the writer of the Gospel had already died (Jn 21:23). Whereas John is portrayed as active in the apostolic community from the start of the ministry of Jesus, no one is referred to as the beloved disciple before the Last Supper. So there is no specific reason to identify the two: the beloved disciple could be any one of the apostles apart from Peter and *Judas. On the other hand, the only friend who is explicitly said to have been loved by Jesus is Lazarus, but he was not an apostle, nor does any tradition designate him as an evangelist.

The contents of the Fourth Gospel are not helpful either. If, on the basis of the highly developed doctrinal message, culminating in the philosophical-mystical Prologue, we conclude that the Gospel of 'John' is more recent than the Synoptics – it is thought by many to date to 100–110 CE – it will become highly unlikely that its author was a contemporary of Jesus. The Fourth Gospel differs fundamentally from *Mark, *Matthew and *Luke in both its narrative structure and its doctrinal substance. With the exception of some parts of the account of the Passion (its dating to the day before the Jewish Passover and its omission of a religious trial before the Sanhedrin) and a small number of more or less or less similar anecdotes recorded in the other Gospels, the story-telling in 'John' stands on its own to such an extent that if 'John' is right, the Synoptics are wrong, and vice versa. In the Fourth Gospel Jesus' public life is extended to two to three years against the Synoptics' six months to one year. There is no conceivable reason for the earlier witnesses to abridge the story so much. Against the historical reliability of the Fourth Gospel speaks the absence of all the accounts of exorcism and of all the parables so typical of the first three Gospels. Another characteristic departure of 'John' from the Synoptics is his portrayal of the Jews as the mortal enemies of Jesus from the start of his activity. This all-pervading hostility, combined with the evangelist's familiarity with Hellenistic philosophy and mysticism, raise the question of whether 'John' was Jewish or not. No other New Testament writer goes so far as to depict the Jews as the bloodthirsty children of their murderous father, the Devil (Jn 8:44). The problem remains unresolved, the arguments for and against being roughly of equal strength. However, it is obvious that the audience addressed by 'John' was non-Jewish as the simplest Hebrew terms, such as Messiah or Rabbi, had to be accompanied by their equivalent in Greek.

The Gospel of 'John' relates not the story of a charismatic Galilean prophet, but that of a Stranger from Heaven, the eternal creative Word (*Logos*) of God who for a short time took on the flesh to redeem humanity, before returning from his earthly exile to rejoin his Father in his celestial home.

Sources: Gospel of John. Irenaeus in Eusebius, *Eccl. Hist.* 3:23.

JOHN THE BAPTIST

John the Baptist was the Jewish ascetic preacher who provided the springboard for the public career of *Jesus of Nazareth. *Josephus joins the four evangelists in representing John as a significant personality in Jewish religious life in the first century CE. He is the starting point of the main Gospel account. He first came into the limelight, *Luke tells us, in the fifteenth year of the emperor *Tiberius (29 CE) during the governorship of Pontius *Pilate (26–36 CE). The Synoptic evangelists introduce him as an independent religious leader with a special mission, but in the later Gospel of John his ministry is seen from the outset as secondary and preparatory to that of Jesus. Luke's legendary infancy narrative includes also an account of the birth of the Baptist and asserts that there was a family connection between him and Jesus: John's father, the priest Zechariah, was married to Elisabeth, a relative of Jesus' mother, who miraculously conceived in her old age. The New Testament story can be supplemented by Josephus' sketch of the mission of John and his independent account of the Baptist's death.

*Mark, *Matthew and Luke introduce John as an ascetic and a prophet whose God-given task was to preach repentance and make ready his Palestinian Jewish contemporaries for the impending arrival of the Kingdom of God. He was believed to fulfil Second Isaiah's prediction of a voice that would prepare in the wilderness the way of God (Isa. 40:3; Mk 1:3; Mt 3:3; Lk 3:4). Repentance and conversion are common prophetic themes in the religion of eschatological Judaism. Unlike the already liturgically regulated annual entry into the covenant through the spiritually cleansing baptism of the Dead Sea sectaries, the immersion preached and practised by John was a special one-off event. His summary proclamation voiced urgency: 'Repent, for the Kingdom of God is at hand!' (Mt 3:2), a proclamation which Jesus subsequently borrowed from John (Mt 4:17; Mk 1:15). The quintessence of John's exhortation, recalling the words of the prophets, lay in a sincere conversion. Awareness of being descendants of Abraham was not enough; they had to share their possessions with the poor; tax collectors and soldiers were to perform their duties correctly and humanely (Mt 3:7–10; Lk 3:7–14). In the messianic age in which he lived, John was bound to be asked whether he was the awaited Messiah. He firmly denied it, but assured his listeners that the Messiah was close by.

At their first meeting on the shore of the River Jordan nothing suggests that John and Jesus had known each other, let alone that they were relatives. The Gospels disagree on the question of whether John recognized Jesus as the Messiah. According to Mark and Luke, Jesus, like all the other repentant Jews, was simply baptized by John, and in the course of the ceremony had a vision and heard a heavenly voice declaring him to be God's beloved son (Mk 1:9–11; Lk 3:21–2). John the Baptist did not notice anything out of the ordinary. Even later, when in prison he learned about the growing fame of Jesus, he was still in two minds about the latter's status (Mt 11:3; Lk 7:19).

In contrast to Mark and Luke, Matthew and *John indicate straightaway that the Baptist knew who Jesus was. According to Matthew it was John, not Jesus, who saw the dove descending from heaven and heard the voice, 'This is my beloved son' (Mt 3:17). The same is true of the parallel account of the Fourth Gospel.

After Herod *Antipas had imprisoned John, Jesus set out to preach in Galilee his Master's message about repentance and the approach of the Kingdom of God (Mk 1:14–15; Mt 4:12–17; Lk 4:14–25). The Fourth Gospel alludes at this early stage to feelings of jealousy and rivalry between the disciples of the Baptist and those of Jesus (Jn 3:25–30). A careful reading of the Gospels can help to clear up the confusion. Jesus never seems to have made any derogatory remark about John. On the contrary, he always spoke of him in the highest terms. For him, John was the reappearing prophet Elijah, the greatest of all men in whom the Law and the Prophets culminated (Mt 11:11; Lk 16:16). Some even wondered whether Jesus was a reincarnation of the Baptist (Mk 6:14; Mt 14:2; 16:14; Lk 9:7).

According to the evangelists, Herod Antipas took umbrage at the Baptist's condemnation of his new marriage and, bullied by his wife *Herodias, imprisoned John but stopped short of putting him to death because of his renown and popularity. While in gaol, he learned about the growing fame of Jesus but remained in two minds about his status (Mt 11:3; Lk 7:19). The wily Herodias, the second wife of Antipas, wishing to take revenge on John, managed to get her own way. She told her daughter *Salome, to whom Antipas had promised anything she could dream of as a reward for her splendid dance on the king's birthday, to request the head of John the Baptist on a platter. She did so, and John was decapitated.

The historicity, importance and circumstances of the death of John are fully confirmed by Josephus, who gives him the 'surname' of the Baptist, just as he speaks also of Jesus 'surnamed' the Christ (*Ant.* 20:200). John is characterized in *Jewish Antiquities* as a 'good man' who encouraged his compatriots to undergo baptism and show justice to one another and piety to God. His eloquence attracted large crowds who were ready to do whatever John told them. This popular success led to his downfall in the revolutionary age in which he lived. The anxious Antipas, afraid of a potential uprising, decided to arrest John, imprison him in the fortress of Machaerus in Transjordan and put him to death. Josephus twice remarks that the Jewish people were shocked by the murder and saw in Antipas' defeat by the Nabataeans a few years later a divine punishment for the crime he had committed against the Baptist. Both the Gospel account and Josephus' report concerning the execution of John are plausible separately but can also be combined. Nevertheless, if one is forced to choose, Josephus seems to be the more reliable source.

The extent of the impact of John on his compatriots is hard to assess. We learn from the Acts of the Apostles that during Paul's ministry in Asia Minor his helpers and he himself came across Jewish people who had been baptized by John. The best known of them is the eloquent Alexandrian Jew Apollos, whom Paul encountered in Ephesus, but others are also mentioned in the same place. It is unlikely, however, that the fellowship of the Baptist survived for long after John's death in the grandiose Herodian hilltop stronghold of Machaerus, in 29 or 30 CE.

Sources: New Testament. Josephus, *Ant.* 18:116–19.

The Fortress of Machaerus where John the Baptist was beheaded

JOHN THE ELDER

John the Elder or the Presbyter was a disciple of Jesus according to Papias, bishop of Hierapolis in Asia Minor, who lived between *c.* 60 and 130 CE. Papias, quoted by the Church historian Eusebius of Caesarea, distinguishes this John the Elder from *John the Apostle. While both Johns lived in the Roman province of Asia and were buried in Ephesus, Papias had direct contact only with the disciples of the apostle, whereas he actually listened to the preaching of the Elder. The existence of John the Elder is of importance in the debate concerning the authorship of the Fourth Gospel and the Johannine literature. In particular, one should bear in mind that the writer of the second and third letters traditionally attributed to John simply identifies himself as 'the Elder', with no personal name mentioned in the title of either epistle.

Sources: 2 and 3 John. Eusebius, *Eccl. Hist.* 3:39.

JOHN THE ESSENE

John the Essene was a Jewish general during the first rebellion against Rome (66–70 CE). Unlike the other three Essenes named by *Josephus (Judas, *Menahem and *Simon), John is not portrayed as a charismatic prophet, but as one of the military leaders of the war who was entrusted with the command of the southern Judaean region of Thamna together with the cities of Lydda, Ioppa and Emmaus. In the company of two other outstandingly courageous and able generals, Niger of Peraea and Silas of Babylon, John attacked the Hellenistic city of Ascalon. However, the Jewish forces were defeated by the Romans and John, together with Silas and 10,000 of their men, fell on the battlefield. An Essene presence in the Jewish high command implies that some members of the sect, contrary to the ideas of pacifism, which they are generally thought to have professed, took part in the national uprising. The survival of a Qumran manuscript, the Angelic Liturgy, in the Zealot fortress of Masada may also indicate that some sectaries continued the fight until the last stand of *Eleazar son of Jairus and his company in that desert stronghold. This would imply that extreme religious piety and revolutionary zeal could go hand in hand, as may have also been the case among some of the followers of Jesus who shared the aspirations of the Jewish nationalists.

Source: Josephus, *War* 2:566–8; 3:9–21.

JONATHAN SON OF ANANUS

Jonathan was the second son of *Ananus (or Annas) son of Sethi to be appointed high priest. The first was Eleazar(16–17 CE), chosen by the Roman prefect of Judaea *Valerius Gratus. Jonathan owed his promotion to the legate of Syria, *Vitellius, and held the office from 36 to 37 CE. Vitellius sacked Jonathan in favour of his brother Theophilus son of Ananus, about whom no record has survived. He may have kept his position until the appointment of *Simon Kantheras son of Boethus by King *Agrippa I in 41 CE.

Jonathan nevertheless remained influential even after losing the high priesthood. He was one of the leaders of the Jewish delegation who met the Roman governor of Syria, Ummidius Quadratus, to complain against the Samaritans for murdering Galilean Jewish travellers and against the Roman procurator of Judaea, *Cumanus, for abstaining from intervention. The emperor *Claudius condemned the Samaritan ringleaders to death, sent Cumanus into exile and replaced him, on Jonathan's request, with Antonius *Felix in 52 CE. The government of the new procurator was intolerable and Jonathan was a constant critic of his administration. To silence him, Felix connived with the Jewish revolutionaries called Sicarii who assassinated Jonathan. They slipped into Jerusalem pretending to be pilgrims but concealing daggers under their cloaks. The high priest Jonathan was the first of their many victims.

Jonathan son of Ananus is no doubt the John mentioned after Annas and *Caiaphas in the story of the interrogation of the apostles *Peter and *John by the Jewish high court (Acts 4:5–6).

Sources: Jonathan: Josephus, *War* 2:240–43, 256; *Ant.* 18:95, 123; 19:313; 20:163. Theophilus: Josephus, *Ant.* 18:123.

JOSEPH

Joseph was the husband of *Mary and the father or, according to Christian tradition, the putative father of *Jesus of Nazareth. The iconography of Christmas represents St Joseph as a man of considerable age, accompanied by a heavily pregnant young woman riding a donkey from Nazareth to Bethlehem. These picturesque details do not figure in the books of the genuine New Testament and originate in the legendary accretions of the later apocryphal Gospels.

The four canonical Gospels tell us little about Joseph. The so-called Infancy narratives relating to the birth and childhood of Jesus constitute the principal source of information. Only two of the four Gospels, *Matthew and *Luke, open with a birth story. The fact that *Mark, the earliest of the Gospels, contains nothing of the sort suggests that the Infancy narratives are secondary creations prefixed by Matthew and Luke to the main account of the life of Jesus. Their purpose is to demonstrate the belief of the Church in the messianic character of Jesus, legitimate descendant of King David, and the doctrine of his supernatural conception and birth. Joseph plays the leading role in the argument of the Davidic genealogy of Jesus, but in the finally formulated Gospel tradition he is denied real paternity. The conception of Jesus was the work of the Holy Spirit and in consequence he was the 'Son of God'.

In Jewish religious tradition the King-Messiah must be a descendant of King David and this descent must be proved from father to son on the male line. For this reason Matthew and Luke insert into their Gospels a detailed genealogy of Jesus. Matthew (1:1–17) lists the ancestors of Jesus from Abraham through David to Joseph, while Luke (3:23–34) gives an even longer version in the reverse order from Joseph through David and Abraham up to Adam. The names of the early forefathers are borrowed from various biblical genealogical tables, but those which follow the Babylonian exile (after 540 BCE) are not only unknown, but are completely different in the two lists of Matthew and Luke down to the father of Joseph, Jacob in Matthew (1:16) and Heli in Luke (3:23). Neither genealogical tree is reliable.

Matthew calls Joseph the 'husband' (anêr) (Mt 1:16) to whom

Mary was betrothed (Mt 1:18). The latter detail implies that she was legally a minor since Jewish law permitted betrothal only for girls who were minors. Majority was reached at the age of twelve years or at the onset of puberty, whichever came first. Matthew dates the birth of Jesus to the reign of *Herod the Great, but makes no reference to Nazareth as the place of residence of Joseph and Mary at that time. He mentions no journey before the childbearing, which implies that Joseph and Mary lived in Bethlehem, in 'a house' (Mt 2:11). According to Matthew as we now have it, the miraculously conceived Jesus was not Joseph's child (Mt 1:20–21). He is said to have refrained from 'knowing' his wife, i.e. from having intercourse with her. What happened after the birth of Jesus is not specified, but the text does not imply that the temporary self-restraint – 'until she had borne a son' (Mt 1:25) – was converted into permanent sexual abstention. In Matthew's Infancy narrative the protagonist is Joseph. He is warned by an angel in a dream and organizes the flight of the family to Egypt to escape from Herod's murder plot (Mt 2:13–14). He is the one who is instructed by an angel in several dreams after the death of Herod (4 BCE) not to return to Judaea, which was ruled by a son of Herod (*Archelaus), and to settle in Nazareth in Galilee (Mt 2:19–23). That Galilee too was administered by another son of Herod (*Antipas) is ignored.

In Luke Joseph is never called the husband of Mary; he is only her fiancé or the *supposed* father of Jesus (Lk 3:23). Both are regular residents of Nazareth (Lk 1:26–7) and Joseph's journey to Bethlehem is necessitated by an imperial decree of tax registration, issued in Rome by *Augustus and implemented in Palestine by *Quirinius, governor of Syria. The census recounted by Luke is unhistorical (see the article on Quirinius). The journey to Bethlehem ensures that Jesus, the future Messiah, is born in the city of David in conformity with prophetic tradition. Luke knows nothing about the murder of the infants ordered by Herod, about the visit of the wise men (Magi) or about the escape of Joseph, Mary and Jesus to Egypt. On the contrary, the whole family is portrayed as quietly and strictly observing in Bethlehem and Jerusalem the Jewish religious rules associated with the birth of a son (Lev. 12:1–8): the circumcision on the eighth day after his birth (Lk 2:21) and a purification offering made in the Temple of Jerusalem on the fortieth day (Lk 2:22–4). In short, in Luke's narration Joseph and his family remain undisturbed in Judaea until it is time for them to return home to Nazareth and live there in obscurity for the next three decades (Lk 2:39). The father of Jesus again figures in the Lukan account of the family pilgrimage to Jerusalem for Passover when Jesus was twelve years old. When the parents had lost the youth in the crowded Jerusalem, they searched anxiously for him until they finally discovered him among the teachers in the Temple (Lk 2:41–50). Mary, reprimanding Jesus, refers to Joseph as 'your father'.

In the finally edited version of their genealogies, both Matthew and Luke insinuate that despite all the appearances to the contrary, Joseph was not really the father of Mary's son. The wording of the traditional text of Matthew (1:16) tries to evade the problem: 'Jacob begot Joseph, the husband of Mary, *of whom Jesus was born* [or: *begotten*], who is called the Christ'. Nevertheless, several textual witnesses, some Greek manuscripts and the Sinaitic Syriac translation positively state that Joseph was the father of Jesus: 'Joseph, to whom was betrothed the virgin Mary, *begot* Jesus who was called the Christ'. The fifth-century Greek 'Dialogue of Timothy and Aquila', representing an argument between a Jew and a Christian, succinctly asserts that 'Joseph *begot* Jesus who was called the Christ'. Luke attests no textual variations in his genealogical list but inserts a saving clause: 'Jesus, when he began his ministry, was about thirty years of age, being the son – *as was supposed* – of Joseph' (Lk 3:23). The attempt by some early editors of Matthew's genealogy to weaken or remove any plain reference to the paternity of Joseph reveals special efforts to correct the impression that Joseph might have been the father of Jesus. The substitute statements, 'Jesus was born of the virgin Mary' or 'the virgin Mary gave birth to Jesus', were inserted at the cost of spoiling the proof of the Davidic descent of Jesus. Incidentally, the view that Joseph was the normal father of Jesus was professed by the ancient Jewish-Christian community of the Ebionites.

In the main Gospel dealing with the public life of Jesus, he is simply the son of Joseph or the son of the carpenter (Mt 13:55; Lk 4:22; Jn 6:42; cf. also Mk 6:3). Indeed, it is inferred too that Joseph and Mary were also the parents of the four younger brothers of Jesus, *James,

Joses, Simon and Judas or *Jude, and of his several sisters (Mk 6:3; Mt 13:55). The same conclusion can be reached from the tradition of the Jewish-Christian Ebionites, reported by the Church Father Irenaeus at the end of the second century, and – if authentic – from the contents of the ossuary inscription of 'James, son of Joseph, brother of Jesus' (see the article on James brother of the Lord).

The Church's doctrine regarding the perpetual virginity of Mary, progressively developing from the second century onwards, naturally influenced the Christian representation of Joseph. The earliest and most influential source is the legendary apocryphal Gospel, the Protoevangelium of James, the Greek original of which may go back to the last decades of the second century. It is the source of most of the traditional stories regarding Mary's association with Joseph.

The Protoevangelium, of Gentile-Christian origin, recounts the unlikely story that at the approach of the puberty of Mary, who spent her childhood in the Temple of Jerusalem, entrusted to the priests, the high priest decided to choose a widower to be her guardian, by casting lots. The lot fell on Joseph, who had four sons and two daughters from his first marriage, the stepbrothers and sisters of Jesus. Joseph's advanced age in the Protoevangelium helps to account for the couple's sexless 'marriage' and Mary's perpetual virginity.

The later years of Joseph's life and his death are unknown, though some fictional details may be found in the 'History of Joseph the Carpenter', a legend written in Coptic not before the fourth century CE. According to this account, Joseph was forty years old when he first married. That marriage produced four sons and two daughters. A further forty-nine years passed before Mary was entrusted to Joseph, by then aged eighty-nine, and he lived with her for twenty-two years. He was 111 years old at his death and was buried by the twenty-year-old Jesus.

Sources: The Gospels. 'Protoevangelium of James', in M. R. James, *The Apocryphal New Testament*, 38–49; 'The History of Joseph the Carpenter', ibid., 84–6.

JOSEPH KABI SON OF SIMON KANTHERAS

See under **Ismael son of Phiabi II**.

JOSEPH SON OF ELLEM

See under **Matthias son of Theophilus I**.

JOSEPH SON OF KAMEI

King *Herod of Chalcis (44–48 CE), having been granted by the emperor *Claudius the right of supervision of the Temple of Jerusalem, appointed two high priests. He first removed *Elionaeus son of Kantheras in 44 CE and replaced him with Joseph son of Kamei or Kamydus (possibly of the same family as *Simon son of Kamithus who was high priest in 17–18 CE). Joseph remained in charge for three years, but nothing is recorded about his activities.

His successor was Ananias son of Nedebaeus who remained active for the unusually long time of twelve years (47–59 CE). He was involved in the troubles between the Jews and the Samaritans and was one of the Jewish leaders arrested by the governor of Syria, Ummidius Quadratus. He was sent to Rome to appear before the emperor Claudius together with the disgraced procurator of Judaea, *Cumanus. All this happened just before Passover in the year 52 CE. The high priest Ananias and his colleagues were released after King *Agrippa II had intervened on their behalf and they were allowed to return to Judaea where Ananias continued in office for a further seven years. The Talmud reproaches him for gluttony. At the outburst of the revolt in 66 CE Ananias, his brother Ezechias and other leaders took refuge in Herod's palace in the upper city of Jerusalem, but they were caught and murdered by the rebels led by the Zealot *Menahem, a descendant of *Judas the Galilean.

According to the Acts of the Apostles (23:2; 24:1), Ananias as high priest presided over the investigation of the case of St *Paul at the request of the Roman tribune who had arrested the apostle. With the typical hostility attributed by the author of the Acts to the Jewish authorities dealing with Paul, Ananias is presented as a judge illegally ordering the beating of the accused. When the council meeting became disorderly, Paul having succeeded in gaining the sympathy of the Pharisee members of the Sanhedrin and turning them against the Sadducees, the Roman military spirited him away from the tumult and dispatched him to Caesarea to be judged by the procurator of Judaea, *Felix. The high priest Ananias led a deputation to Caesarea and employed an advocate called Tertullus to prosecute Paul. The request of the Jewish authorities to have the case returned to their jurisdiction was pre-empted by Paul's appeal to be judged by the emperor himself.

Sources: Joseph: Josephus, *Ant.* 20:16, 103. Ananias: Josephus, *War* 2:243; *Ant.* 20:103, 131.

JOSEPHUS

Josephus, or Flavius Josephus as he was known after adopting the surname of his imperial patron, *Titus Flavius Sabinus Vespasianus, was the most important Jewish historian in antiquity. Joseph son of Matthias was born of an illustrious priestly family in Jerusalem in the first year of the emperor *Caligula (37/8 CE). His family tree is traced to the time of the Hasmonaean high priest John *Hyrcanus I, and one of his ancestors married the daughter of the king-high priest Alexander Jannaeus (103–75 BCE). Josephus was educated in Jerusalem and boasted a precocious expertise in the Law. He studied the teaching of the Pharisees, Sadducees and Essenes at the age of sixteen and spent three further years with an ascetic, the hermit *Bannus. At nineteen he opted for the party of the Pharisees. He doubtless learned Greek as a child or a youth, but at the beginning of his writing activity his expertise in the Greek language was not sufficient, so that he composed the *Jewish War* in Aramaic and afterwards relied on assistants when he prepared the Greek edition of the work. In 64 CE Josephus sailed to Rome where he became a favourite of Poppaea, wife of the emperor *Nero.

At the outbreak of the uprising against Rome in 66 CE, the twenty-nine-year-old Josephus, like many upper-class Jews, opposed the war. He soon changed his mind and was appointed commander-in-chief of the rebel forces in Galilee. His inglorious leadership ended in 67 CE with the fall of his fortress at Jotapata and his capture by the Romans. Taken before *Vespasian, he foretold the commander of the Roman army his elevation to the imperial throne, and when his prophecy came true two years later in 69 CE, the grateful Vespasian set his prisoner free. Josephus accompanied him as far as Alexandria on the newly proclaimed emperor's journey to Rome. From Alexandria he returned to Jerusalem and assisted *Titus, Vespasian's son, who was left in charge of the operations in Jerusalem until the end of all resistance in 70 CE. Josephus' particular task was to parley with the defenders of the city and persuade them to surrender. He claims to have obtained freedom for many Jewish prisoners, including his brother, and even to have rescued three acquaintances already crucified, of whom one actually survived after medical treatment. Josephus then followed Titus to Rome after the victory; he was granted Roman citizenship and financial security by the emperor Vespasian, which enabled him to devote the rest of his life to literary pursuits. He also enjoyed the patronage of the sons of Vespasian, the emperors Titus (79–81 CE), and *Domitian (81–96 CE), and remained in Rome until his death in around 100 CE.

The marital history of Josephus was characteristic of an upper-class Jew in the troubled days of the first revolution. His first wife was in Jerusalem during the siege, but while Josephus was prisoner of war, he was ordered by Vespasian to marry a captive Jewish woman from Caesarea. She left him when he travelled to Alexandria with the future emperor. In Egypt Josephus promptly remarried and had three children by his third wife. This marriage ended in divorce, and in Rome Josephus acquired a fourth wife in the person of a Cretan Jewess who came from an illustrious family and bore him two more sons. Three of his boys, Hyrcanus of the third marriage and Justus and Simonides of the fourth, born respectively in 73, 76 and 78 CE, were alive when Josephus was writing his autobiography.

Most of the works of Josephus have survived. Written in Greek, they were transmitted by Christian copyists. He was primarily address-ing educated Graeco-Roman readers with the avowed intention of glorifying the Jewish people. No doubt this emphatic apologetical intent was meant to counteract the bad impression created among some of his compatriots by Josephus's turncoat behaviour during the war.

His first major work, the *Jewish War* in seven books, was completed in the late seventies, the latter part of the reign of Vespasian, to whom his volumes were dedicated. They contain a full account of the hostilities, preceded by a summary version of Jewish history from the persecution of the Jews by Antiochus Epiphanes (175–164 BCE) to the start of the rebellion against Rome in 66 CE. Josephus proudly reports that he was in possession of written approval by the emperor Titus and the Jewish king *Agrippa II of the reliability of his *History* (*Life* 363–6). Agrippa declares: 'You seem to me to have written with much greater care and accuracy than any who have dealt with the subject' (*Life* 365).

Josephus' largest work, the *Jewish Antiquities* in twenty books, is a tour de force describing biblical and Jewish history from the creation of the world to the outbreak of the rebellion against Rome in 66 CE. It was completed in 93/4 CE when Josephus was in his mid-fifties. The first ten books, ending with the Babylonian captivity of the Jews in the sixth century BCE, follow the Greek Septuagint account of the Bible and frequently embroider on it with the help of non-biblical books and popular Jewish interpretative traditions. The second half of the *Antiquities*, from Cyrus and Alexander the Great to the war, relies on a medley of sources: partly Greek (Polybius, Strabo, *Nicolaus of Damascus, *Herod the Great's teacher and adviser; official documents from the age of Julius *Caesar and *Augustus), partly Jewish (Letter of Aristeas, 1 Maccabees, and a document deal-ing with the Jewish high priests). *Jewish Antiquities* offers a unique insight into Jewish history of the Roman period (63 BCE–66 CE). Thanks to Josephus, the age of Herod the Great and of his heirs, that is to say, the age of Jesus in the broad sense, is better known than any other period in ancient Jewish history.

Josephus' *Life* followed his *Jewish Antiquities*. It is not a real autobiography, but an account of his office as commander of the revolutionary forces in Galilee from 66 to 67 CE, and offers an obviously biased apologia of his handling of the affairs against the political machinations of his opponent *John of Gischala and charges expressed by *Justus of Tiberias in his rival account of the Jewish war. The substance of the *Life* is sandwiched between biographical details about Josephus' family and his domestic history, including mention of his fall from his horse, which resulted in a broken wrist. The *Life* was written sometime after 93/4 CE.

The last surviving work of Josephus is a defence of the Jewish religion and the Jewish people in two books, entitled *Against Apion or On the Antiquity of the Jews*. Apion was an Egyptian grammarian who led the anti-Jewish delegation of Alexandrian Greeks to the emperor *Caligula, with *Philo of Alexandria heading the Jewish counter-embassy. Apion was only one of several opponents of the Jews taken to task by Josephus, who skilfully rebutted the ridiculous distortions by Apion and his colleagues of the history of the Jews in Egypt and of their religion, such as the alleged worship of the head of an ass. *Against Apion* contains a first systematic short synopsis of the Law of Moses (2:164–219).

A number of other works by Josephus have been lost. His important project entitled *On Customs and Causes*, in which he intended to discuss 'the opinions that we Jews hold concerning God and his essence as well as concerning the laws' (*Ant.* 20:268), seems never to have matured.

Opinions relating to the reliability of Josephus as a historian have varied greatly. He is clearly not wholly trustworthy in matters where he himself is the subject of controversy. Also, in both the *War* and the *Antiquities* we find long speeches on the lips of historical personalities which are plainly apocryphal. Josephus gives Greek philosophical colouring to the Jewish schools of thought, comparing the Pharisees to the Stoics and the Essenes to the followers of Pythagoras. He seeks to put all the responsibility for the war on a revolutionary minority and for political reasons he plays down messianism, which would have been regarded with suspicion by the Romans. However, on the whole he is judged favourably by present-day scholarship. One of the leading Roman historians, Fergus Millar, has called the *Antiquities* of

Josephus arguably 'the most significant single work written in the Roman empire' (JJS 38, 1987, 147).

Josephus' role in illuminating New Testament history is unique. He provides a solid and structured background to the story of *Jesus and of the early Palestinian Church. Without him we would possess only fragmentary bits and pieces. To crown his contribution, Josephus supplied three references to Gospel personalities: *John the Baptist, *James the brother of the Lord, and Jesus himself. The first two are generally accepted as genuine. John the Baptist is described as a 'good man', who exhorted the Jews 'to lead a righteous life', and was beheaded by Herod *Antipas on the grounds of being a potential revolutionary (Ant. 18:117–18). As for James 'the brother of Jesus surnamed the Christ', Josephus reports that he was stoned to death in 62 CE by order of the high priest *Ananus son of Ananus. The act met with the disapproval of the most fair-minded and strictly observant Jews of Jerusalem. They complained to Agrippa II and obtained the dismissal of the high priest (Ant. 20:200). The third reference, the famous Testimonium Flavianum or the Jesus notice of Josephus, is more problematic as it certainly contains elements which cannot be authentic (for example, 'if indeed one might call him a man'; 'he was the Messiah', and a reference to the resurrection). On the other hand, the description of Jesus as a 'wise man', the performer of 'paradoxical deeds', sounds genuine and typical of the style of Josephus. He also mentions the crucifixion of Jesus by Pontius *Pilate. Taken together, the three Josephus passages furnish the most important external information to the study of New Testament history. It is therefore no surprise that Josephus was almost regarded as a fifth evangelist in Christian circles. According to the Church historian Eusebius (Eccl. Hist. 3:9), a statue was erected in his honour in the city of Rome, almost certainly by Christians.

Sources: Josephus (Loeb edition) and Tessa Rajak, Josephus: The Historian and his Society (2002).

JUDAS ISCARIOT

Judas Iscariot is presented in the New Testament as the villain among the apostles of *Jesus who betrayed him to the Jewish priestly authorities. The etymology of Iscariot is uncertain. The commonest interpretation is that it stands for his place of origin, 'the man from Qeriot or Qariot', but since Qiryah means 'town', it is of little help. A derivation from *Sicarius*, daggerman, the title of an anti-Roman terrorist, has also been suggested, though nothing in the Gospel accounts of Judas points in that direction. According to *John (12:6), Judas was the bursar of the apostolic community, which would suggest that he was a leading member of the group. But he is depicted as a thief and a man who sold his leader for thirty silver coins.

The tragic end of Judas is sketched in two different ways in the New Testament. In the Gospel of *Matthew (27:5) Judas repents and returns the thirty pieces of silver, but being blood money they were declared unfit by the high priest for the Temple treasury and could only be used for the purchase of a burial ground for strangers. Judas then commits suicide by hanging himself. In the Acts of the Apostles (1:18–19) there is no question of repentance. Judas buys a field with his ill-gotten gain and dies there in an accidental fall that causes his belly to burst. It would seem that both stories serve to explain the Aramaic name of a field in Jerusalem known as Akeldama (*haqal dema*) or 'Field of Blood'.

How Judas, if he was an embezzler, could have maintained his position among the twelve until the end of the life of Jesus is left unexplained in the Gospels. The many speculations about the honourable motivation of Judas, such as his wish to compel Jesus to reveal his Messiahship, or to force him into open rebellion and thus precipitate the arrival of God's Kingdom, are entirely without evidential basis.

Source: New Testament.

JUDAS SON OF SAPPHORAEUS

Judas son of Sapphoraeus and Matthias son of Margalothus were two learned teachers, probably Pharisees, who stood behind a religious uprising in Jerusalem in 4 BCE. The cause of the trouble was the setting-up of the Roman symbol of a golden eagle on one of the gates of the newly reconstructed Temple by King *Herod the Great. When it became public knowledge that Herod was terminally ill, Judas and Matthias, who headed a school of enthusiastic young people, concluded that it was time to perform a brave act in defence of the ancestral Law, even at the risk of their lives. So when the false rumour reached them that the king had died, they exhorted their pupils to act and the youngsters climbed on to the roof of the Temple, pulled down the eagle and hacked it to pieces in full view of the bystanders. The two teachers and forty of the rioters were arrested and taken to Jericho where the moribund Herod, lying on a couch as he was no longer able to sit, tried them and condemned the two teachers and the pupils who actually pulled down the eagle to be burned alive and the rest of the prisoners to be executed. They were all keen to suffer martyrdom for their belief in the sanctity of the Law of Moses. The episode demonstrates that in the age of *Jesus rebellion against the civil authority often contained an amalgam of religious and political motivation.

Sources: Josephus, *War* 1:648–50, 655; *Ant.* 17:149–57, 167, 206, 214.

JUDAS THE GALILEAN

Judas the Galilean, or Judas of Gamala, a town in the Golan, was the co-founder of the revolutionary party of the Zealots–Sicarii. He is no doubt identical with the Judas son of *Ezechias who was already involved in revolutionary activities after the death of *Herod the Great. His father Ezechias should be identified with the robber captain executed by Herod in 47 BCE. In 4 BCE Judas the Galilean recruited a small army and captured the arsenal of Sepphoris in Galilee. Well equipped with the stolen weapons, his men were terrorizing the region. Rumour had it at this stage that Judas had royal aspirations. The arrival of *Varus, the Roman governor of Syria, forced the revolutionaries to go underground and wait for another favourable opportunity. This chance arose in 6 CE when, after the deposition of the ethnarch *Archelaus, Herod's son, the governor of Syria, *Quirinius, set about implementing the imperial census of the Jews necessary for regulating taxation in the new Roman province of Judaea. The high priest *Joazar son of Boethus endeavoured to calm down the outraged population, but much disgruntlement remained and was exploited by Judas. Assisted by a Pharisee by the name of Zadok, he founded a revolutionary party with the aim of pursuing a religiously and politically motivated rebellion.

While 'Zealotism' was more than an extreme form of nationalism and possessed intellectual and doctrinal elements, *Josephus, though wholly opposed to it politically, rather flatters the followers of Judas by depicting them as representatives of a philosophical school. This school, Josephus states, mostly agrees with the teaching of the Pharisees, but claims that, God being the only master of Israel, Jews should serve him alone and have no earthly lords. Judas thus launched a movement of extreme chauvinism powered by religious fanaticism, which was continuously active during the first six decades of the first century CE and culminated in the war, which put an end to institutional Jewish life in Palestine for nineteen centuries.

Judas the Galilean was not a solitary rebel, but the founder of a dynasty of revolutionaries. In fact, being the son of the Ezechias who was killed by Herod, he himself followed in the footsteps of his father. His sons Jacob and Simon were crucified as anti-Roman rebels by Tiberius Julius *Alexander, the Romanized nephew of *Philo of Alexandria, who was procurator of Judaea from 46 to 48 CE. Another of his sons, or possibly a grandson, *Menahem, was among the principal nationalist leaders in Jerusalem at the outbreak of the war against Rome in 66 CE. Finally the last prominent descendant of Judas the Galilean was *Eleazar son of Jairus, the captain of Masada, the fortress where Jewish resistance to the Romans continued until as late as 73/4 CE.

Judas the Galilean figures in the New Testament. *Gamaliel the

Elder mentions him in his speech when the apostles of *Jesus were investigated by the Sanhedrin (Acts 5:34–9). Judas is introduced to illustrate the principle that if a movement is not willed by God, it is bound to fail. Gamaliel asserts that Judas perished after the uprising inspired by him, a fact unattested by Josephus. Anachronistically, the author of the Acts of the Apostles places Judas the Galilean after *Theudas, another revolutionary leader. In fact, Judas rose at the time of the census in 6 CE, while Theudas came some forty years later. The error is due to Luke rather than to Gamaliel.

Sources: Josephus, *War* 2:118, 443; *Ant.* 18:4–10, 23–5.

JUDE

Jude (a variant form of Judas) was one of the four brothers of *Jesus of Nazareth of whom *James is the most famous and the other two, Joseph (or Joses) and Simon, are completely unknown (Mk 6:3; Mt 13:55). Jude is nowhere else mentioned in the Gospels. If we include him among the relatives of Jesus, he would share the blame with the others for opposing Jesus (Mk 3:21) and the same cool reception that Jesus gave to his mother and his brothers (Mk 3:32–4; Mt 12:46–50; Lk 8:20–21). Without being mentioned by name, Jude must be included among the brothers of Jesus who, together with Mary, joined the primitive community after the first Easter (Acts 1:14).

According to the questionable traditions handed down by the Church historian Eusebius in the name of the second-century authority Hegesippus, the grandsons of Jude, that is, the great-nephews of Jesus, were still considered sufficiently important at the end of the first century to appear on the political blacklist of the emperor *Domitian (81–96 CE) among the impoverished members of the royal House of David. Since the Davidic descent of Jesus is more theological than historical – in order to be proclaimed the Messiah he had to be a son of David – the story is probably legendary.

The attribution of the short letter of Jude (twenty-four verses) in the New Testament to this brother of Jesus is equally dubious. The indirect testimony in the writing itself describes the author as 'a servant of Jesus Christ and the brother of James' (verse 1). The Greek of the letter is far too good to have derived from an uneducated Galilean. Because of its concern with Christian heretical movements and its similarity to the second epistle of Peter, the letter of Jude is often dated to the early second century CE. The author was surely a Jew specially interested in non-canonical Hebrew and Aramaic literature, as is apparent from his allusion to the apocryphal work the *Assumption of Moses* and his explicit reference to the first *Book of Enoch*.

Sources: New Testament. Eusebius, *Eccl. Hist.* 3:20–21.

JUSTUS OF TIBERIAS

Justus of Tiberias was a first-century CE Jewish politician, historian and writer. He is particularly unlucky in that all that we know about him comes from his arch-rival and bitter enemy, Flavius *Josephus. A substantial portion of Josephus' *Life* is devoted to polemics against Justus and more precisely to the demonstration that Josephus's *Jewish War* is a better-informed and more reliable source of history than the lost work of Justus on the same subject.

Justus and his father Pistus were leading citizens of Tiberias. Justus had received a thorough Hellenistic education. Even Josephus admits that he was not 'unversed in Greek culture' and possessed rhetorical gifts (*Life* 40). This special emphasis on Hellenistic education shows that it was not common among Jews, but was the privilege of upper-class citizens. The idea widely held nowadays in certain scholarly circles that the Galileans were thoroughly Hellenized and bilingual, speaking Aramaic and Greek, is without real foundation.

Josephus and Justus hold each other guilty for inciting the inhabitants of Tiberias to rebel against Rome. Justus is even accused of leading the Tiberians' attack against localities in Transjordan, which belonged to the cities of Hippos and Gadara in the Decapolis. In reality, however, Justus, like Josephus, was a moderate politician who joined the revolutionary party only out of necessity. In fact, his family suffered at the hands of the Galilean and Gaulanite rebels, who murdered Justus' brother-in-law and cut off his brother's hand as punishment for forging a letter (*Life* 177). Before the Romans had completed the conquest of Galilee, Justus left for Berytus (Beirut) and joined King *Agrippa II whose sister *Bernice interceded on his behalf with *Vespasian, as a result of which his death sentence was cancelled. Thereafter Justus prospered in the royal court of Agrippa II, and after the war he was even appointed secretary to the king. But Josephus did not miss the opportunity to report later the sacking of his opponent for incompetence. Justus kept his *History* unpublished for twenty years and released it only after the death of the protagonists of the events, Vespasian, *Titus and Agrippa II. Josephus implies that Justus's version of the account would have displeased the authorities, and boasts that in a letter Agrippa II wholeheartedly endorsed his own version of the war: 'King Agrippa to dearest Josephus ... You seem to me to have written with much greater care and accuracy than any who have dealt with the subject. Send me the remaining volumes' (*Life* 365).

Justus must have lived until the beginning of the second century since his book apparently mentioned the death of Agrippa. According to the testimony of the Church historians Eusebius, Jerome, the Byzantine Suda and Photius, Justus of Tiberias was the author of three (now lost) works: *History of the Jewish War, Chronicle of the Jewish Kings* (from Moses to Agrippa II) and, if Jerome is to be believed, *Commentaries on the Scriptures*.

Sources: Josephus, *Life*, 175–8; 336–67. Eusebius, *Eccl. Hist.* 3:10, 8. Jerome, *De viribus illustris* 14. The Suda, under 'Justus of Tiberias'. Photius, *Bibliotheca* 33.

L

LUCILIUS BASSUS

See under **Silva**.

LUKE

Luke was the author of the Third Gospel and tradition also attributes the Acts of the Apostles to him. He is thought to be identical with the Luke three times mentioned in the corpus of St *Paul's letters: once with no specification in 2 Timothy 4:11; the second time as Paul's 'fellow worker' in Philemon 24; and the third time as 'the beloved physician' in Colossians 4:14. As he is not listed as one of the 'men of circumcision' among Paul's Colossian associates, Luke appears to have been a Gentile, a native of Antioch according to Eusebius, possibly the only non-Jewish New Testament writer. No reference to the Gospel of Luke is quoted by Eusebius from Papias, who had written about *Matthew and *Mark. The earliest testimonies relating to his authorship of the Third Gospel and the Acts come from the Muratorian canon and Irenaeus, bishop of Lyons, of *c.* 180 CE. The same view is confirmed by Eusebius in his *Ecclesiastical History*. Eusebius further asserts without supporting evidence that Luke translated into Greek Paul's letter to the Hebrews, the original of which was in Hebrew or Aramaic. The main reasons for questioning the attribution of the Third Gospel and the Acts to Luke, the companion of Paul, arise from the many contradictions between the autobiographical statements in Paul's letters and Luke's relevant comments on Paul's biography in the Acts and the absence of Pauline theology in works attributed to Luke, although the presentation of the institution of the Eucharist in the Third Gospel and in 1 Corinthians points in the opposite direction.

As far as the start and the finish of Luke's Gospel are concerned, they are more developed than the corresponding narratives in Matthew. The genealogy of the Infancy Gospel traces *Jesus back to Adam, and the names of the ancestors, which are not directly borrowed from the Bible, totally differ from those in Matthew. Luke alone links, erroneously, the birth of Jesus with a census ordered by the emperor *Augustus and implemented by *Quirinius, governor of Syria (see the article on Quirinius), and, contrary to Matthew, outlines a journey of *Joseph and *Mary from Nazareth to Bethlehem, and their return to Nazareth via Jerusalem, but without a detour to Egypt. Luke further adds an account of the birth of John the Baptist and the anecdote of the twelve-year-old Jesus revealing his precocious knowledge to the teachers of the Law in the Temple. His special doctrinal material includes many otherwise unrecorded sayings of Jesus and some fourteen parables, including those of the Good Samaritan and the Pharisee and the Publican, unknown in Mark and Matthew. His narration of the resurrection appearances is considerably enriched compared to Matthew's account.

Luke, himself a Gentile and addressing an almost exclusively non-Jewish readership, deliberately omitted any reference to the restriction of the mission of Jesus and his original disciples to the house of Israel alone. He also deleted the chauvinistic comments of Jesus concerning non-Jews being 'dogs' or 'swine'. A universalistic outlook opens and closes his Gospel. The elderly Simeon, after meeting the infant Jesus in the Temple, speaks of the salvation prepared by God for 'all the nations', and the order to preach repentance and forgiveness to the whole universe figures at the end of the Third Gospel. In reverse, the Acts of the Apostles overemphasizes Jewish hostility towards the apostles and the nascent Church. The most striking exaggeration appears in the assertion that a second ambush with a view to murdering Paul was plotted by 'the chief priests and the principal men of the Jews' (Acts 25:2). The inner logic of the whole account is that the Sanhedrin intended to try Paul on a capital charge, not to assassinate him.

There is furthermore a tendency in the Gospel of Luke to water down the eschatological urgency of the message of Jesus. His opening appeal to repentance because of the proximity of the Kingdom of God is omitted by Luke. Eschatological sayings tend to be softened and apocalyptic images are again and again left out. Luke gently opens the gate towards a Church with a long-lasting future.

Sources: New Testament. Eusebius, *Eccl. Hist.* 2:22; 3:4.

M

MARCELLUS

See under **Fadus**.

MARCUS AMBIVALUS

See under **Coponius**.

MARIAMME I

Mariamme I, to be distinguished from Mariamme II, daughter of the high priest *Simon son of Boethus and third wife of *Herod the Great, was a Jewish princess engaged to Herod in 42 BCE and married to him during the siege of Jerusalem by her husband and *Sosius, the Roman governor of Syria, in 37 BCE. This union between a representative of Hasmonaean royalty and a man of common Idumaean stock promised to be glorious, but ultimately it turned into an unmitigated disaster. While Herod adored her, Mariamme felt no respect for her husband and, aided and abetted by her mother *Alexandra, the daughter of *Hyrcanus II, engaged in the royal court in wily intrigues with the leading female members of her husband's family, Cyprus the mother and *Salome the sister of Herod. The king's jealous possessiveness caused the marriage to collapse. On two occasions, when Herod had to depart on politically dangerous journeys to visit his patron *Mark Antony and later Octavian, the future emperor *Augustus, he left secret instructions with his uncle Joseph in the first case and with his friend Soemus in the second, to kill Mariamme in the event of his not returning, so as to ensure that she would not marry another man. In both cases the secret was divulged to Mariamme and she did not hide her anger and resentment from her husband. On both occasions, Salome, the mischief-making sister of Herod, made matters worse by fabricating a false charge of adultery against her sister-in-law. The first scheme failed, and Mariamme escaped, but the second succeeded, and in 29 BCE the insanely jealous Herod ordered the execution of his adored wife. Mariamme died a true princess. Beautiful, proud and calm, she met her fate without any change in colour, revealing her 'nobility of descent' (*Josephus). Her unreasonableness and quarrelsome nature were contributory factors to her tragedy. Mariamme's death drove Herod out of his mind. During the days following her execution his desire for her grew stronger and he kept calling for the woman whom he had so foolishly destroyed.

Mariamme bore Herod three sons and two daughters. The youngest son died in Rome, where he was educated, and the two older ones, Alexander and Aristobulus, shared their mother's fate: like Mariamme, they were murdered by the brutal Herod.

Sources: Josephus, *War* 1; *Ant.* 15.

MARK

Mark, or John Mark, was the son of a Jewish woman from Jerusalem called Mary who was an associate of *Peter. Mark, a cousin of *Barnabas (Col. 4:10), joined him and *Paul on their first missionary journey to Cyprus. However, when the trio set out to continue their preaching in Asia Minor, Mark abandoned them, thereby angering Paul. On the occasion of their second expedition Barnabas insisted on taking Mark with them and the violent argument which ensued between Paul and Barnabas irremediably spoiled their friendship. Nevertheless Mark later renewed his association with Paul and remained with him even after the imprisonment of the apostle in Rome (Philem. 24). The pseudonymous author of the first letter of Peter alludes to a companion of his as 'my son Mark' (1 Pet. 5:13). This reference is the basis of the tradition which presents Mark as the author of the gospel preached by Peter. Papias, the second-century bishop of Hierapolis, cited by Eusebius, declares that Mark was the 'interpreter of Peter', who 'wrote down carefully, but not in order, all that he had remembered of the Lord's sayings and doings'. Papias explicitly states that Mark did not hear or follow

*Jesus, and consequently was not an eyewitness of the Gospel events. According to Eusebius, Mark became the first bishop of Alexandria and as such was responsible for the monastic ascetics whom we know as the Therapeutae from *Philo's book, *The Contemplative Life*.

Mark's is considered to be the oldest of the canonical Gospels, written possibly during the Jewish rebellion against Rome (66–70 CE), but probably shortly after it. Mark already contains the idea of the Second Coming of Christ, the imminence of which is forecast by the destruction of the Temple at the end of a terrible war (Mk 13). The Gospel of Mark is independent from the works of the other three evangelists; in fact, literary comparison shows that *Matthew and *Luke rely on Mark's narrative structure. Mark is the shortest of the Synoptic Gospels for two reasons. It contains less doctrinal material; Matthew and Luke have been enlarged by adding to Mark extracts from a now lost collection of the sayings or *logia* of Jesus. Also Mark's chronological framework is narrower than that of Matthew and Luke as it begins without the preamble of an Infancy Gospel and lacks the happy ending of the apparitions of the risen Jesus. In fact Mark stops with the disconcerting picture of three terrified and dumbfounded women fleeing from an empty tomb. The longer ending (Mk 16:9–20) is absent from all the older Gospel manuscripts.

As would befit the oldest of the sources, Mark shows far fewer signs of doctrinal revision than Matthew and Luke. Passages alluding to emotions, ignorance or imperfections in Jesus are not touched. For example, before healing a leper, Mark's Jesus is moved by *pity* towards the sick man, or according to a manuscript variant by *anger* (Mk 1:41). Neither Matthew nor Luke refers to Jesus' state of mind. Again, in Mark Jesus looks at his critics with *anger* (3:5). Luke omits 'with anger' (Lk 6:10) and Matthew deletes the whole sentence (cf. Mt 12:12–13). The comment by Jesus' relatives that *he is out of his mind* recorded in Mark (Mk 3:21) is ignored altogether by Matthew and Luke. In Mark Jesus groans before replying to the Pharisees' request for a sign from heaven (Mk 8:12); Luke implies that Jesus did not answer at all (Lk 11:16), and Matthew overlooks the undignified sigh (Mt 16:2). Mark's Jesus frequently displays ignorance: he asks for information, for instance for the name of a demon (5:9). Instead of curing 'many' sick persons in Mark (1:34; 3:10), Jesus cures them 'all' in Matthew (8:16) and Luke (4:40). In Mark Jesus was unable to perform 'mighty works' in Nazareth apart from a 'few' cures (Mk 6:5); in Matthew 'he did not do *many* mighty works there' (13:58); Luke is silent on the matter.

A particular feature of Mark, his liking for the quotation of Aramaic words in the sayings of Jesus, deserves emphasis. Only he reports that Jesus nicknamed the hot-headed apostles James and John *Boanerges*, 'sons of thunder' (3:17), or uses the word *Ephphatha*, 'Be opened' when healing a deaf-mute (7:34). He calls a sacrificial gift *Corban*, for which the Greek paraphrase 'given to God' is provided (7:11). The blind men of Jericho bears the Aramaic name *Bartimaeus*, correctly explained as 'the son of Timaeus' (10:46), and Bartimaeus calls Jesus *Rabbuni*, which is left untranslated as everyone was expected to know that it signified 'My Master' (10:51). Matthew and Luke shied away from the use of these words. *Talitha cum* is Jesus' command to the daughter of Jairus, 'Little girl [literally, little lamb], I say to you, arise' (Mk 5:41). These words are ignored in Matthew (9:25) and appear in Luke only in Greek as 'Child, arise' (Lk 8:54). In Mark Jesus addresses God in Aramaic as *Abba* (14:36). Matthew substitutes 'My Father' (Mt 26:39) and Luke 'Father' (Lk 22:42), both in Greek. Finally, Mark reproduces fully in Aramaic the cry of Jesus on the cross, '*Eloi, Eloi lama sabachthani?*' ('My God, my God, why hast thou forsaken me?') (Mk 15:34). Matthew substitutes the Hebrew *Eli, Eli* for the Aramaic *Eloi, Eloi* (Mt 27:46).

Mark's Gospel brings us nearer to the Jesus of history than any other New Testament writing. Moreover, Mark is the only evangelist who enables the reader to hear an occasional echo of what may have been Jesus' own words in his own language.

Finally, a frequently repeated misconception about the Gospel of Mark should be disposed of once and for all. Late nineteenth- and early twentieth-century New Testament scholarship created the notion of 'messianic secrecy' in connection with the repeated instruction given by Mark's Jesus to his disciples or to the persons cured by him not to reveal that he was the Messiah. A better explanation for this prohibition is that Jesus considered the traditional political concept of the royal Messiah ill suited and misleading as a definition of his mission and for this reason discouraged its use.

Sources: New Testament. Eusebius, *Eccl. Hist.* 2:16–17; 3:39; 6:14.

MARK ANTONY

Marcus Antonius (*c.* 83–30 BCE) was a Roman general and statesman. He was a triumvir with Octavian (the future *Augustus) and Lepidus, and husband of the Egyptian queen *Cleopatra VII. He was the ruler of the Roman East while he himself was dominated by Cleopatra. His involvement with Jewish history consisted of appointing *Herod and his brother *Phasael as tetrarchs of the Jewish territory, and later in 40 BCE he made Herod king. He further interfered with the integrity

Mark Antony

of Judaea when he donated the balsam plantations of Jericho to Cleopatra. Bribed by Herod, he also gave the order for the decapitation of the last Hasmonaean priest-king *Antigonus in Antioch. Under Cleopatra's influence he forced Herod to appoint the young Hasmonaean prince *Aristobulus III as high priest and after the young man had become the victim of an arranged swimming-pool accident, on receiving another large financial enticement he let Herod escape the consequences of his crime. Mark Antony was defeated by Octavian first in the battle of Actium in 31 BCE and finally at Alexandria in the following year. Soon afterwards both Antony and Cleopatra committed suicide.

Sources: Josephus, *War* 1; *Ant.* 14–15.

MARULLUS

See under **Fadus**.

MARY

Mary, the mother of *Jesus and the wife of *Joseph, lived in the town of Nazareth in Galilee during the time of the public career of her son Jesus. The scant evidence about her in the New Testament may be divided into three categories: *Mark, *Matthew and *Luke dealing with Jesus in Galilee; *John describing Jesus in Galilee and at the scene of the crucifixion; and Matthew and Luke presenting the birth and childhood of Jesus. The portrait of Mary varies greatly according to the sources.

Leaving aside the Infancy narratives of Matthew and Luke, Mary is first referred to in the Synoptic Gospels by acquaintances and neighbours in her home town of Nazareth (Mk 6:3; Mt 13:55). They identify Mary as the mother of Jesus and the wife of Joseph the carpenter (see also Jn 1:45; 6:42). Four more sons (*James, Joses or Joseph, Judas or *Jude and Simon) and several unnamed daughters are also mentioned by them. Nothing in the text would suggest that

Mary was not the mother of five sons, of whom Jesus was the eldest, and of two or more daughters. The next reference to the mother of Jesus, his brothers and, according to manuscript variants, his sisters appears in the passage where they turn up unannounced and demand that Jesus should interrupt his teaching and come to see them. From Jesus' less than obliging reaction – 'Who are my mother and my brothers?' – and his description of his pupils as 'my mother and my brothers' it is obvious that the family were not welcome. They represented the attitude of the relatives who were determined to prevent him from pursuing his charismatic mission (Mk 3:21). Several further sayings of Jesus with disparaging remarks about parents ('He who loves father and mother more than me' or 'any one [who] does not hate his own father and mother' is unworthy to be my disciple) clearly point to a serious disagreement between him and his nearest and dearest. In fact, neither his mother nor any other member of the family is mentioned again in the Synoptic Gospels. Several named Galilean women watched Jesus die on the cross, but Mary was not among them.

John gives a somewhat different picture. He intimates in the story of the wedding at Cana that there was warmth and understanding between mother and son despite Jesus' apparent unwillingness to use his charismatic powers to supply additional wine for the improvident organizers of the feast. Mary knew that, the brusque reply of Jesus notwithstanding ('What have you to do with me?', no doubt meaning, 'Why don't you leave me alone?'), her son would fulfil her request. During the remainder of Jesus' ministry Mary disappears from John's account, only to reappear with *Mary Magdalene and two other Galilean women under the cross, where the dying Jesus entrusts her to the care of his beloved disciple (Jn 19:25–7). Finally, the mother (and the brothers) of Jesus suddenly surface in the Acts of the Apostles in the company of the disciples of Jesus before the first Pentecost (Acts 1:14). At this point Mary vanishes for good from the New Testament. The only indirect allusion to her in *Paul is that Christ was born of a nameless Jewish mother ('born of woman, born under the Law', Gal. 4:4).

The birth stories of Matthew and Luke include a different kind of evidence regarding Mary, which introduces a virgin mother who miraculously, with the help of the Holy Spirit, produces a son without a human father. In Jewish and non-Jewish religious tradition the birth of heroes is often surrounded by signs and wonders. Noah's arrival into the world was marked by shining light; and the patriarchs Isaac, Jacob and Joseph as well as the prophet Samuel were conceived through divine intervention by previously sterile, aged mothers. Jesus, the son of a virgin mother, is depicted as surpassing them all.

The word 'virgin' figures only once in connection with Mary in each of the two Infancy Gospels. In Luke the virginal conception of Jesus is announced in a vision by an angel who explains to the baffled young girl that she will bear the son of God (Lk 1:26–35). The matter is never raised again in Luke. Matthew handles the issue in a more roundabout fashion by citing the prophet Isaiah (7:14): 'A virgin [parthenos] shall conceive and bear a son and his name shall be Emmanuel [God is with us]' and applies the prediction to Mary in the form of a fulfilment interpretation (Mt 1:22–3). Disregarding the inexact rendering in Matthew of Isaiah's Hebrew almah ('a young woman') by the Greek 'virgin', the notion of Mary as virgin mother seems to be forgotten in the rest of the Gospel of Matthew. For readers of the Hebrew Bible the Isaiah passage meant that the name Emmanuel (God is with us) given to the son of a young woman in an age of threatening war symbolized divine protection promised to beleaguered Israel. It was only in the cultural atmosphere of Hellenistic Gentile Christianity that the birth of a miraculously conceived 'God with us' became theologically significant.

The virgin birth story in Matthew and Luke constitutes the springboard of the Christian religious speculation about Mary. The apocryphal Gospels produced by the early Church further developed this speculation, emphasizing the holiness and perpetual virginity of the mother of Jesus. The earliest and most influential source is the legendary Protoevangelium falsely attributed to *James the brother of the Lord. Its Greek original is not earlier than the last decades of the second century CE. It is the source of most of the traditional ideas regarding the birth and childhood of Mary and her association with Joseph.

The Protoevangelium, the work of a non-Jewish writer, recounts that the three-year-old Mary was handed over by her elderly parents, Joachim and Anne, to the priests of Jerusalem in order to be brought up in the holy atmosphere of the Jerusalem sanctuary. The story is baseless since the presence of young girls in the Temple is a mere figment of the Gentile author's imagination. Later, when Mary approached the age of twelve years and with it puberty, the priests had to remove her from the sacred precincts to avoid the ritual pollution of the Temple. The high priest therefore decided to look for a widower, to be chosen by casting lots, who would take care of her. This widower was Joseph, the father of four sons and two daughters from his first marriage, later to be known as the brothers and sisters of Jesus. The Protoevangelium depicts Joseph as an elderly man, an idea that conveniently accounted for the sexless marriage and the permanent virginity of Mary. The apocryphal evangelist also solved the problem of the messianic descent of Jesus from King David, even though Joseph was not his genuine father. In the Protoevangelium not only Joseph but Mary, too, is of Davidic origin. The writer did not know that for the inheritance of the messianic title Jewish law demanded proof of descent on the paternal line.

The theological and religious process which by the fourth century evolved into the doctrine of the perpetual virginity of Mary culminated in the definition by the Council of Ephesus (431 CE) of the doctrine of Mary being the 'Mother of God' (*theotokos*). By the sixth century belief in her bodily assumption to heaven also became part of the Christian belief. It was even proclaimed dogma in the Roman Catholic Church in 1950. The doctrine of the Immaculate Conception, that is to say, that Mary was born without original sin, still a matter of debate in the Middle Ages, was officially defined by Pope Pius IX in 1854 – a far cry from the scant information preserved in the New Testament.

Sources: New Testament. Protoevangelium of James.

MARY MAGDALENE

Mary Magdalene, a native of the fishing town of Magdala by the Sea of Galilee, was a close companion of *Jesus. No family connection, such as the name of her father or husband, is supplied by the evangelists. The Gospel of Luke (8:2) describes her before the account of the crucifixion and resurrection as one of the women who looked after Jesus and his disciples during their itinerant ministry. This implies that Mary Magdalene was a person of means who devoted herself to Jesus who had healed and exorcized her. The remark that she had been freed of seven demons is no doubt responsible for the otherwise unfounded association in some layers of Christian tradition of Mary Magdalene with a repentant prostitute, 'the woman of the city who was a sinner' (Lk 7:37). Her identification with another Mary, sister of Martha and of Lazarus, is equally far-fetched.

In the Gospel account of the crucifixion of Jesus, *Mark and *Matthew list Mary Magdalene in the first place among the Galilean women who watched the cross from a distance (Mk 15:40–41; Mt 27:55–6). In *John, Mary Magdalene is the last in the group consisting also of *Mary, mother of Jesus, and Mary, wife of Clopas.

Mary Magdalene is also the chief witness of the resurrection of Jesus. She is named first by Mark and Matthew as one of the women who went to the tomb to complete the funeral rites. According to Matthew and *Luke, she and her female companions report the news of the resurrection to the disciples of Jesus. In John, too, Mary Magdalene is the chief witness of the resurrection. She alone visits the empty tomb and carries the news to the apostles. She is also the first to be granted a vision of the unrecognizable risen Jesus whom she mistakes for the gardener in charge of the graves.

The Gospel tradition implies, without providing an explanation, a very close bond between Jesus and Mary Magdalene. Christian tradition further elaborates the story. The Eastern Church brings her to Ephesus with the mother of Jesus and St John, while in Western Christianity Mary, together with her sister Martha and her brother Lazarus, are believed to have landed in Marseilles and founded the Christian Church in Gaul.

Source: Gospels.

MATTHEW

Matthew was one of the twelve apostles of *Jesus and tradition attributes to him the authorship of the First Gospel. The New Testament supplies only the scantiest of information about him. His name is Matthew in the lists of the apostles (Mk 3:18; Mt 10:3; Lk 6:15; Acts 1:13) and in one of the accounts of his call by Jesus (Mt 9:9), but in the parallel story in the other Synoptics he is known as Levi son of Alphaeus (Mk 2:14; Lk 5:27, 29). By profession Matthew was a tax collector employed by Herod *Antipas and he was sitting in the tax office when Jesus invited him to become his disciple. The Synoptic evangelists report that Matthew gave a party for Jesus, attended by many tax collectors, and that the Pharisees or scribes objected to Jesus' eating with such people. This and other similar episodes illustrating Jesus' sympathy for social outcasts earned for him the disparaging title of 'friend of tax collector and sinners' (Mt 11:19; Lk 7:34). Nothing else about Matthew survives in the New Testament; his link with the Gospel of Matthew is due to early Church tradition, but it is questioned by a large number of modern scholars.

The earliest mention of Matthew as an evangelist derives from a lost work of Papias, bishop of Hierapolis (died *c.* 130 CE), quoted by the Church historian Eusebius: 'Matthew arranged in an orderly manner the sayings in the Hebrew [i.e. Aramaic] dialect and everyone interpreted (or translated) them as he could' (*Eccl. Hist.* 3:39). Whether these Aramaic sayings refer only to doctrinal, as opposed to narrative, passages of Matthew is debatable, but by the latter part of the second century (around 180 CE) Irenaeus, bishop of Lyons, definitely speaks of a written Gospel recorded in script during the apostolic ministry of *Peter and *Paul in Rome. The majority of contemporary experts attribute the work in its final form to a Judaeo-Christian or Gentile-Christian writer of the last decades of the first century (80–100 CE). Perhaps the best compromise is to see him as a Greek-speaking Jewish Christian.

The author of the Gospel of Matthew was the first to add a highly theological Infancy Gospel to the main story of Jesus borrowed from *Mark. It consists of a genealogy of Jesus demonstrating his descent from King David through *Joseph and an account of his birth, the flight to Egypt to escape Herod's murderous soldiers and the return of the family to Nazareth in Galilee. The quotation of Isaiah 7:14 about the birth of Emmanuel from a virgin (*parthenos*), based on the Greek Bible, is meant to announce already at the beginning of the Gospel the late first-century CE concept of Jesus as a miraculously conceived Messiah, Son of God (Mt 1–2). Moreover, Matthew's Gospel is the first to provide a rudimentary description of a vision of Jesus by the women who had found the empty tomb, followed by a single apparition of the risen Christ to the eleven apostles on a Galilean mountain in which some of them believed while others doubted it (Mt 28:9–10, 16–17).

In regard to Jesus' attitude to Jews and Gentiles, Matthew's evidence is self-contradictory. On the one hand, he displays more Jewish elements in his Gospel than do any of the other evangelists. He has the largest number of prophetic proof texts applied to Jesus and devotes a great deal of space to discussions relating to Jewish laws and customs. He emphatically restricts the mission of Jesus and of his apostles and disciples to 'the lost sheep of the house of Israel', excluding Gentiles and Samaritans (Mt 10:6; 15:24).

Side by side with Jewish exclusivism, the Gospel of Matthew exhibits strongly, even violently, anti-Jewish ideas. The same Jesus who declared himself concerned only with Jews declares later that non-Jews will sit at the messianic banquet while the Jews will be cast into the outer darkness (Mt 8:11–12). His final command to the eleven apostles is to make disciples of all the nations (Mt 28:19). Matthew's occasional anti-Jewish venom is astonishing. When trying Jesus, the Jewish authorities sought *false* testimony against him (Mt 26:59) and Matthew makes *all the people* shout, 'His blood be on us and on our children' (Mt 27:25)! To account for these contradictions in the same Gospel it is best to assume that after a highly optimistic beginning, the Christian mission among Jews in both Palestine and the Diaspora ran into increasing difficulties and ended with the idea that Jesus himself chose the non-Jews and proclaimed the rejection of Israel.

Christian tradition has nothing to report on Matthew beyond the time of the New Testament. According to Eusebius, the Alexandrian scholar Pataenus claims to have found during his visit to India the Gospel of Matthew written in Aramaic characters and taken there by the apostle *Bartholomew when he evangelized that country.

Sources: Gospel of Matthew. Irenaeus, *Against the Heretics* 3:1, 1 cited in Eusebius, *Eccl. Hist.* 5:8, 2.

MATTHIAS

See under **James son of Alphaeus**.

MATTHIAS SON OF ANANUS

See under **Simon Kantheras son of Boethus**.

MATTHIAS SON OF MARGALOTH

See under **Judas son of Sapphoraeus**.

MATTHIAS SON OF THEOPHILUS I

Matthias son of Theophilus succeeded *Simon son of Boethus as high priest at the end of the reign of *Herod the Great (5/4 BCE). We know nothing about him apart from the episode, recorded by *Josephus and the Talmud, which states that because of the ritual uncleanness caused by a wet dream the night before he was to celebrate a fast, Matthias was deposed by Herod and replaced for one day as high priest by a relative of his, the otherwise unknown *Joseph son of Ellem or son of the Mute. Matthias was dismissed by Herod for being partly responsible for the removal of a golden eagle decorating the reconstructed Temple.

Sources: Matthias: Josephus, *Ant.* 17:78, 164–6. Joseph: Josephus, *Ant.* 17:166.

MATTHIAS SON OF THEOPHILUS II

See under **Jesus son of Gamaliel**.

MENAHEM

Menahem, the son or grandson of *Judas the Galilean, was one of the leaders of the rebellion against Rome in 66 CE. Before joining in the fight in Jerusalem, he and his associates had broken into the arsenal established by *Herod the Great at Masada and armed themselves and their allies. Surrounded by such a powerful bodyguard, Menahem entered Jerusalem and, behaving like a king, took over the leadership of the revolution and attacked the palace of Herod. The Jewish garrison was allowed to leave the besieged fortress while the Romans withdrew to the royal towers. Menahem's troops massacred some Romans as well as the former high priest Ananias son of Nedebaeus (47–59 CE) and his brother Ezechias. Success went to Menahem's head and turned him into a tyrant. Another rebel leader, *Eleazar son of Simon, attacked him in the Temple, where Menahem paraded wearing royal garments, pretending to be the King-Messiah. After a short resistance Menahem and his companions ran away. Some, among them a relative of Menahem, *Eleazar son of Jairus, the future captain of the last Jewish centre of resistance to the Romans, managed to reach safety at Masada. Menahem took shelter on the Ophel in Jerusalem, but was discovered and killed, after prolonged torture, together with one of his lieutenants, Absalom. He was the penultimate rebel leader who descended from Judas son of Ezechias, the last being Eleazar son of Jairus.

Like Judas the Galilean, Menahem is called by *Josephus a sophist, a false teacher of whom the historian disapproved. It is conceivable that the memory of Menahem and his messianic dreams is preserved in the rabbinic tradition according to which the name of the Messiah will be Menahem son of Ezechias (bSanh. 98b). In a theory floated in the early days of Dead Sea Scrolls research, but now discarded, Menahem was seen as the Teacher of Righteousness, and his deputy

Absalom was linked to the House of Absalom, mentioned in the Commentary on Habakkuk from Cave 1.

Source: Josephus, *War* 2:433–48.

MENAHEM THE ESSENE

Menahem was a member of the Essene sect in the mid-first-century BCE whom *Josephus celebrated as a man endowed with the gift of prophecy. One of his predecessors, Judas the Essene, foretold at the end of the second century BCE the death of Antigonus, the brother of the high-priest-king Aristobulus I. He is presented by Josephus as a master surrounded by a large group of pupils engaged in the study of how to predict the future (*Ant.* 13:311–13; *War* 1:78–81). Menahem proved his prophetic ability when he greeted the young boy *Herod as the future 'king of the Jews'. Herod, uncertain whether Menahem was mistaking him for someone else or was just joking, told him that he was an ordinary citizen, only to be smacked gently on the buttocks by Menahem and reassured of his future elevation to the kingship of Judaea. He was advised to love justice and piety and practise gentleness towards his subjects, but was also warned that he would fall short of these requirements and at the end of his life would be punished by God. At first Herod took no notice of Menahem's prediction, but when it came true, he inquired about the length of his future reign. Menahem first remained silent, but when pressed, he forecast that Herod might sit on the throne for twenty or thirty years. Herod treated him with kindness and also showed sympathy to all the other Essenes, while he treated his Pharisee critics harshly. Josephus attributed the supernatural knowledge of Menahem and the other Essenes to their virtuous life.

Source: Josephus, *Ant.* 15:373–9.

N

NERO

Claudius Caesar Germanicus Nero, the fifth Roman emperor of the Julio-Claudian dynasty (54–68 CE), was born Lucius Domitius Ahenobarbus. He was the son of Agrippina, *Augustus' great-granddaughter and wife of *Claudius. Claudius adopted Nero as his son and heir. Under the influence of Nero's wife, Poppaea Sabina, who was a sympathizer of Judaism (*Ant.* 20:195; *Life* 16), Jews enjoyed imperial favour during the earlier part of Nero's reign. His final years, however, coincided with the ever-worsening political turmoil in Palestine and ended with the outbreak in 66 CE of the first Jewish rebellion against Rome.

Nero's rule also marks the beginning of hostilities between the Roman empire and nascent Christianity. Christianity was regarded by Rome as a Jewish movement. The Christians came into the limelight after the great fire in the capital, which destroyed much of Rome in 64 CE. Popular suspicion put the blame on the emperor for starting the conflagration, and we learn from Tacitus that to escape the charge, Nero decided to use the unpopular new sect of the Christians as a scapegoat.

Nero substituted as culprits, and punished with the utmost refinement of cruelty a class of men, loathed for their vices, whom the crowd styled Chrestians. Christ, the founder of the sect, had undergone the death penalty in the reign of Tiberius, by sentence of the procurator Pontius Pilate, and the pernicious superstition was checked for a moment, only to break out once more, not merely in Judaea, the home of the disease, but in the capital itself, where all things horrible or shameful in the world collect and find vogue.

Many of the Christians were crucified and burned alive 'to serve as lamps at night'. Christian tradition, recorded by the fourth-century historian Eusebius, connects the martyrdom of the apostles *Peter and *Paul with the persecution launched by Nero against Christians: 'In

The Emperor Nero

his reign Paul was beheaded in Rome itself, and Peter likewise crucified, and the record is confirmed by the fact that the cemeteries there
are still called by the names of Peter and Paul' (Eusebius).

In 68 CE, while the first Jewish war was raging, the Roman armies
of Spain and Gaul turned against Nero and the ill-fated emperor
committed suicide.

Sources: Josephus, *War* 2–4; *Ant.* 20. Tacitus, *Annals* 15:44, 2–4.
Eusebius, *Eccl. Hist.* 2:25, 1.

NICOLAUS OF DAMASCUS

Nicolaus of Damascus, historian, philosopher and statesman, born *c.* 64 BCE, came from a leading non-Jewish family in Damascus. His father, Antipater, had a distinguished public career. Nicolaus received a thorough Greek education and became a follower of the philosophy of Aristotle.

He is said to have tutored the children of *Mark Antony and *Cleopatra before becoming a courtier of *Herod the Great sometime prior to 14 BCE. He acted as Herod's teacher in philosophy and rhetoric, his political adviser and occasionally his ambassador. In 14 BCE he negotiated on behalf of the Jews of Asia Minor with Marcus Agrippa, the representative of *Augustus, and in 8 BCE with Augustus himself in Rome after Herod had fallen into disgrace with the emperor as a result of his conflict with the Nabataeans. Nicolaus was the king's chief adviser in his troubles with his sons, Alexander, Aristobulus and Antipater, who were all executed by Herod. After Herod's death in 4 BCE Nicolaus accompanied Herod's son *Archelaus to Rome and persuaded Augustus to confirm the king's last will, which made Archelaus his successor although without obtaining for him the title of king.

Nicolaus' best-known work is his *Universal History* in 144 books in which he deals at length with Jewish history in the age of Herod. The relevant sections of this *History* constitute the principal source of the very detailed account of Herod's reign in Josephus' *Jewish War* and *Jewish Antiquities*, books 15–17.

Sources: Josephus, passim; B. Z. Wacholder, *Nicolaus of Damascus* (1962).

P

PAUL

Paul, or Saul of Tarsus, to use his original Jewish name, is the most influential and best-known New Testament character next to *Jesus of Nazareth. He wrote at least eight authentic letters (Romans, 1 and 2 Corinthians, Galatians, Philippians, Philemon, 1 and 2 Thessalonians) and his pupils and imitators produced six other epistles (1 and 2 Timothy, Titus, Ephesians, Colossians, Hebrews). The authentic letters include autobiographical passages in which Paul describes his past life. In addition, half of the Acts of the Apostles, attributed to his companion, *Luke, contains an account of Paul's career and missionary activities. The two sets of evidence mostly supplement and complete, but occasionally also contradict, each other. Regrettably, his contemporary *Josephus never refers to Paul.

Paul was born in Tarsus, a city in Cilicia (Southern Turkey). The Acts assert that he was a Roman citizen by birth and that he was a young man when he witnessed the stoning of the deacon *Stephen, probably in the mid-30s CE. Paul tells us that his family belonged to the tribe of Benjamin and that he joined the Pharisee movement. He studied in Jerusalem at the feet of the famous *Gamaliel the Elder (Acts 22:3). His Pharisee training is revealed by his expert handling of biblical arguments in his letters, and by his belief in bodily resurrection, which serves as the foundation stone of his teaching about the crucified and risen Christ. However, Paul's later ease in freeing himself and his Jewish brethren from the scriptural dietary obligations in the company of non-Jewish Christians would suggest that his Pharisee convictions were not as deep-seated as those of *James the brother of the Lord and his 'circumcision party'.

Paul was a native Greek speaker; he dictated his letters in Greek, but sometimes added autograph greetings to them. According to the Acts he was also able to deliver an impromptu speech in Aramaic. He suffered from an undefined illness, and he admitted that his physical presence was not impressive and his rhetorical gifts were limited. He failed to impress philosophers, but his influence on simple, uncultured listeners was remarkable.

Paul's letters and the Acts of the Apostles testify to his initial violent hostility to the Jesus movement. Apparently he acted against its members on behalf of the priestly authorities in charge of maintaining communal peace. Once he is depicted as the special envoy of the high priest, dispatched to cleanse the Jewish community of Damascus of Christian heretics. If this is true, he could have acted only in an advisory capacity since outside Judaea the high priest had no executive power, especially not in Damascus, which was under the control of the Nabataean king.

On the way to Damascus Paul had a vision which completely transformed his life: the ferocious enemy of the Christians was on the spot metamorphosed into a disciple of *Jesus and asked to be baptized. According to the Acts of the Apostles the new convert immediately infuriated the Damascene Jews with his preaching of Jesus, to such an extent that Paul had to run for his life. He fled to Jerusalem where he was introduced to the apostles by *Barnabas, his later missionary companion. Having immediately turned his fire on the Greek-speaking Jews of the city, Paul once more had to escape, this time to his home town, Tarsus. Paul's own account of these events is quite different and no doubt more reliable. His sudden flight from Damascus was necessitated not by Jewish hostility but by the governor of the Nabataean king who saw in Paul an unwelcome troublemaker in the local Jewish community. Also, he did not go straight away to Jerusalem but to the Arabian desert of Transjordan, where he enjoyed further mystical experiences. He then returned to Damascus and three years later journeyed to Jerusalem to introduce himself to *Peter and *James the brother of the Lord, but not to the other apostles. This story, emphasizing Paul's independence, is more plausible than that of the author of the Acts, whose aim is always to reconcile differences between Church leaders.

Referring to his relationship with the original disciples of Jesus, Paul was always keen to insist on his equal apostolic status. He regularly met with opposition. In the eyes of the early members of the Jesus movement Paul was an upstart and was not entitled to call himself an apostle. Unable to argue against them on their ground,

Paul based his claim of equality with Peter and James on his direct vision of Jesus, the effective source of his apostolic mission to the Gentiles. The incident at Antioch, described in chapter 2 of the letter to the Galatians and implicitly alluded to in Acts 15:1, proves that the last commissioned apostle was not afraid to stand up to, and even reprimand, the leader of the Church. In fact, his evangelizing policy dispensing prospective Gentile converts from prior circumcision and the observance of the entire Jewish law was vindicated by the council of the apostles held in Jerusalem in 49 CE and presided over by James the brother of the Lord.

Paul was often at the centre of conflicts. The Corinthian community was split into three parties, those of Cephas, Apollos and Paul. In fact the believers who were sick of the discord between them claimed to belong to the fourth party of Christ (1 Cor. 1:12). As Paul normally began his preaching in the local synagogue, he often clashed with the Jewish communal leaders as well. They used against him their legal powers of imprisonment, corporal punishment (thirty-nine lashes on five occasions) and, no doubt extra-legally, one attempted but unsuccessful stoning (2 Cor. 11:23–5). According to the Acts (16:19–39), Paul was also chastised and imprisoned by Greek magistrates in Philippi, but was released with apologies when they learned about his Roman citizenship.

Paul devoted his life to the propagation of the gospel in the course of three missionary journeys taking him to Cyprus, to various regions of Asia Minor and to mainland Greece where he established churches in Thessalonica, Philippi and Corinth. His activity in Corinth can be dated thanks to a reference to his appearance before *Gallio (Acts 18:12–16), who was proconsul of Achaia between 51 and 53 CE. Paul also preached in Athens, but without much success. He planned to travel to Rome and even to Spain, the western extremity of the Mediterranean world. He reached Rome not of his own free will, but as a prisoner awaiting trial before the law court of the emperor *Nero.

In 58 CE, at the end of his third missionary trip, Paul travelled to Jerusalem with several of his followers (see Acts 21–6). While in the city, he was accused by Diaspora Jews of having preached abroad against the Law and of having introduced a non-Jew, the Ephesian

Trophimus, into the area of the Temple which Gentiles had to avoid on pain of death. The charge was apparently without foundation, but sufficed to create a tumult resulting in the intervention of the Roman military forces which were keeping an eye on the Temple. Paul was arrested under the misapprehension that he was the notorious revolutionary nicknamed 'the *Egyptian'. The Roman tribune intended to extract the truth from the suspect by flogging him, but quickly thought better of it when he discovered that Paul was a Roman citizen.

The following day a confrontation between Paul and the high priest *Ananias son of Nedebaeus and his council ended in chaos – if the account of the Acts can be accepted as historically true. (The author of the Acts loves to portray Jews, even the highest Jewish authorities, when opposed to (Jewish) Christians, as a bloodthirsty mob.) Paul apparently cleverly set the Pharisee members of the Sanhedrin against the Sadducees by declaring that he stood before the court because of his belief in the resurrection of the dead. Immediately the Pharisees took his side against the Sadducees, who rejected the doctrine of the resurrection. As the members of the Sanhedrin – once more according to the author of the Acts – were on the point of exchanging blows, the Roman commander spirited Paul away to safety behind the walls of the fortress of the Jerusalem garrison.

Having learned from Paul's nephew that a gang of Jewish fanatics were plotting an ambush to murder his uncle on the way to the tribunal, Claudius Lysias, the Roman tribune, arranged for Paul's transfer to Caesarea under strong military escort to bring him before the procurator of Judaea, Antonius *Felix (52–60 CE). Felix invited the Jewish authorities to present their charges against Paul and apparently the high priest Ananias himself, with several elders and a lawyer by the Latin name of Tertullus, took the trouble to journey from Jerusalem to Caesarea to accuse Paul of being the ringleader of a heretical sect who attempted to profane the Temple. The authorities asked for Paul's extradition to their own religious jurisdiction with a view to passing the death sentence on him. Ultimately the governor did not accept the plea of Tertullus, but did not release Paul either. He was kept under house arrest. On one occasion Felix and his Jewish wife *Drusilla listened to Paul expounding his faith in Jesus Christ. The lecture did not move Felix; nevertheless he frequently met Paul,

*Caesarea with the Praetorium in the forefront where Paul was imprisoned
from 58 CE to 60 CE*

hoping, according to Acts, to obtain a suitable bribe, a not unusual attitude among Roman provincial governors.

The legal dilemma of which court should try Paul and where lingered on for over two years. Porcius *Festus, who in 60 CE replaced Felix as governor of Judaea, inherited the unresolved case of Paul. The Jewish chief priests and leaders, apparently having nothing more important to do, at once petitioned the procurator to hand over Paul to them. The author of the Acts asserts that the authorities themselves were plotting to murder Paul on the way – as though after a first attempt easily frustrated by the Romans a second would have had any chance to succeed! Festus flatly refused the request and ordered them to come to Caesarea if they still wanted to pursue the case against Paul. A delegation sent from Jerusalem duly appeared and renewed their threefold charge, which, reconstructed from Paul's reply, related to crimes against the Law, the Temple and the emperor. Festus, no doubt wishing to settle the matter once and for all, suggested to Paul that he should agree to a trial in Jerusalem by the Sanhedrin. In order to ensure fairness in the proceedings, Festus promised to attend the hearing himself. Paul, unwilling even in the presence of Festus to face a Jewish court, successfully appealed to the supreme tribunal of Caesar in Rome. When the Jewish king *Agrippa II and his sister *Bernice came to visit the new procurator in Caesarea, they were given an opportunity to hear Paul. Festus counted on Agrippa, with his deeper understanding of Jewish matters, to help him with the preparation of a brief for the emperor *Nero about the case against Paul. Paul recounted his life story before them. Festus concluded that Paul was mad, and Agrippa, politely and no doubt ironically, remarked before terminating the audience that if Paul went on a little longer he might even convert him to Christianity!

On the way to Italy in the autumn of 60 CE the ship carrying Paul and other prisoners ran into a heavy storm alongside Crete (see Acts 27–8). The sailors tried their best to save the situation – the Acts contains perhaps the most detailed description we have of the ancient technology of navigating a disabled ship – but the vessel and its occupants remained entirely in the hands of the elements. Having been tossed about by the raging seas for over two weeks, miraculously, so Paul believed, the ship ran aground in Malta. Paul and his travel companions were saved, and Paul even escaped a viper which wound itself around his arm after he had landed on the island.

Paul finally reached Rome where he was allowed to stay in a rented room, guarded by a soldier. He was free to receive visitors and preach the gospel. The account of the Acts abruptly ends two years after Paul's arrival in Rome while he was still awaiting his trial by the emperor. Whether the trial ever took place is not recorded, nor does the New Testament relate how Paul died. According to Church tradition, transmitted by the historian Eusebius, he was decapitated in Rome about the end of the reign of the emperor Nero, sometime before 68 CE.

This unfinished story of Paul's life needs to be complemented by a synopsis of his teaching and an outline of his contribution to the establishment of the Christian Church. What were the sources of Paul's gospel to the Gentiles? Not having met the living Jesus, Paul admits that some of his information is secondhand, such as the teachings relative to the death, burial and resurrection of Jesus, the expectation of his impending return, the prohibition of divorce followed by remarriage (which Paul revised in favour of a Christian whose pagan spouse refused to continue the marital union) and the right of the preacher to be maintained by the community (though Paul himself preferred to earn his own living as a tentmaker). The institution of the Eucharist is often named among the doctrines which Paul had inherited from tradition, but it seems more likely that when he declared that he had received it from the Lord, he meant from the Lord by means of a personal revelation.

Paul was not interested in the historical Jesus. He never mentions Galilee, *Herod and his sons, any of the high priests or even Pontius *Pilate. The parents of Jesus and *John the Baptist are ignored, but *James the brother of the Lord is referred to twice. Among the apostles we encounter only *Cephas, *James and *John. By contrast, Paul names many of his own pupils and helpers: *Barnabas, *Timothy, *Titus, *Luke the physician, *Silvanus, Sosthenes, Apollos from Alexandria, Aquila and Priscilla, refugees from Rome, Mark, Aristarchus, Demas and others. This would suggest that his silence over the contemporaries of Jesus was deliberate.

Paul was not concerned with the activity and teaching of the living

Jesus, but with the accomplishment of the dying and rising Christ for believers. For him Jesus was not God, but a highly elevated true human being who was 'designated Son of God in power' after his resurrection from the dead (Rom. 1:3). Paul's central mystery drama is played by two leading actors, the first Adam and Jesus, the last Adam. The first Adam brought sin into the world; the last Adam, the innocent Christ, by offering himself in sacrifice atoned for all sins and potentially revivified mankind through his death and resurrection. Paul's basic message was that mystical union with the dying and rising Christ through the symbolic act of baptism purifies the new Christian from sin and allows him to share the supernatural life of the risen Lord.

In the new existence of the baptized all the differences between rich and penniless, freeman and slave, man and woman, Jew and Gentile disappear. The proclamation of such universal equality in Christ was greatly welcomed and gladly listened to by the poor and the oppressed classes of the Graeco-Roman world, which formed Paul's primary clientele.

The Parousia or Second Coming was the focus of Paul's religious vision and determined the framework of his apostolic activity and moral outlook. The shortness of the future fired his dynamism: as the apostle of the Gentiles he had to bring the gospel of Jesus to Spain, the westernmost limit of the inhabited universe. The same short-term future also determined his moral outlook. Stay as you are was his rule of thumb: if you are circumcised, do not try to hide it; if uncircumcised, keep your foreskin. If you are a freeman, consider yourself the slave of Christ; if you are a slave, Christ will grant you freedom. The conditions of the world will soon change. The Churches were frenzied. Paul even had to pour cold water on the enthusiasm of some of his believers in Thessalonica who spread the rumour that Christ had already returned.

The burning expectation of the new age when the dead would rise and together with the living would meet the descending Christ and his angels in mid-air threatened the Pauline Churches with universal chaos. Far-sighted and wise, Paul took precautionary measures by appointing local bishops, presbyters and deacons to look after the flock, keep excesses under control and provide spiritual nourishment for all. The early Christians in the Greek cities were a mixed bag: charismatic enthusiasts speaking with tongues and prophecy (1 Cor. 14) stood side by side with brethren guilty of immorality and greed, idolaters, revilers, drunkards, or robbers (1 Cor. 5:11). Paul did not hesitate to excommunicate a Christian who shared the bed of his stepmother and to 'deliver [him] to Satan for the destruction of the flesh' (1 Cor. 5:1–5). The strong social organization set up for the spiritual safety of the religiously and morally untrained Gentile Christian communities turned out to be a blessing when the imminence of the return of Christ was no longer felt and the steadying protective influence of the Church became a necessity.

Paul's total dedication to the cause of the evangelization of the Gentiles and his struggle with Judaizing Christians did not make him anti-Jewish. He tried to please all men in everything (1 Cor. 10:33). He envisaged his successful mission to the non-Jewish world as part of a divine ploy to bring Israel to Christ. He was convinced that the ancient chosen people of God would not watch passively the takeover by the Gentiles of their religious heritage. Competition would excite their jealousy and prompt them to advance fast so that by the time the totality of the Gentiles is gathered in all the Jews will also be saved (Rom. 11:25–6).

Paul never reached Spain; the Second Coming is not yet here and Jews and Christians are still divided. But the Church continues thanks to the powerful theological vision and the organizational skill and wisdom of the Jew from Tarsus, the real founder of the world religion which bears the name of Christianity.

Sources: New Testament. Eusebius, *Eccl. Hist.* 2:25.

PETER

Simon son of Jonah or John, surnamed Peter (the Rock, in Aramaic *Kefa*, Cephas), is always listed as the first of the twelve apostles chosen by *Jesus of Nazareth. Simon Peter was a native of Bethsaida by the Lake of Galilee. He was the head of a team of fishermen and the proprietor of a boat. At the time of his association with Jesus he resided together with his brother *Andrew in the small lakeside town of Capernaum where he owned a house. Peter was married, and his mother-in-law, who lived with them, was healed by Jesus (Mk 1:29–30). According to *Paul, Peter was accompanied by his wife on his missionary journeys (1 Cor. 9:5). No children are mentioned.

Peter was the head of the inner circle of Jesus' company and was regularly addressed by Jesus when in fact the question was aimed at all the apostles. Conversely, Peter was the spokesman of the group vis-à-vis Jesus. In the Gospel of *Matthew, Peter declared on behalf of all his colleagues that Jesus was not the risen *John the Baptist, the returned Elijah or some other prophet, but the Messiah. He was wholeheartedly devoted to Jesus and according to the Fourth Gospel he was ready to protect him with the sword. Yet this devotion did not stop him from behaving in a cowardly manner in Jesus' hour of need. When challenged in the high priest's courtyard, Peter denied that he was a follower of Jesus and swore that he did not even know 'that man'. Afterwards he vanished, like all his pusillanimous fellow apostles. Only some Galilean women showed enough courage to stay with Jesus until the end, according to the testimony of the Synoptic Gospels.

The resurrection appearances recounted in the Gospels enhance Peter's role among the apostles. According to *John, he hurried to check the report about the empty tomb and corrected the initial disparaging judgement of the apostles about the women's 'idle talk' (Lk 24:11). Also both *Luke (24:34) and *Paul (1 Cor. 15:5) state that Peter was the first to be granted a private vision of the risen Jesus before he was seen by the other apostles.

Peter's primacy over his colleagues is also manifest in the early chapters of the Acts of the Apostles where the beginnings of the Christian movement are sketched. It was on his proposal that the vacancy caused by the betrayal of Judas was filled. Again it was Peter who addressed the assembled Jewish crowd about Jesus on the first Pentecost and later in the court of the Temple. He spoke on behalf of the apostles when they stood before the Sanhedrin. In short, Peter behaved as the head of the new Jesus movement with regard to both the outside world and internal affairs, such as the collecting of private property by the Church leaders when the Jerusalem community lived

An ancient fishing boat discovered in the Lake of Galilee in 1985

from a common purse, as did the members of the Essene sect. In the eyes of the chief priests and their Sadducee allies Peter's standing was not high; for them he was an uneducated common man (Acts 4:13).

From the start Peter was the person in charge of preaching the gospel to the Jews alone. Jewish exclusiveness denying Gentiles access to the Jesus movement was taken for granted in the early years of the Palestinian Church. It was only challenged after the success of the mission of Paul and *Barnabas among non-Jews, and was prepared, if Peter's part in the account is true, by the episode of the acceptance of the Roman centurion *Cornelius and his household into the Christian fellowship. These Gentiles were dispensed from the requirement of first becoming Jewish proselytes on account of the charismatic gifts they had received. The innovation did not go down well with the traditional Jewish majority of the primitive community. Peter, with John, also initiated the evangelization of the Samaritans, against the express command of Jesus, and it was Peter who condemned *Simon the Magician's attempt to buy charismatic power with money. During the reign of *Agrippa I (41–44 CE) Peter was apparently gaoled, but according to the Acts of the Apostles (12:3–17) an angel helped him escape from prison.

The great turning point of Peter's career was marked by St Paul's entry into the primitive Church. The former enemy of the Christian 'heresy' and persecutor of the followers of Jesus was introduced to the leaders by Barnabas, and Paul explicitly records that on his first visit to Jerusalem after his 'conversion' he paid his respects to Cephas and *James the brother of the Lord. The venue of the next personal encounter between Peter and Paul was Antioch in northern Syria, where Barnabas and Paul had created a mixed Church, consisting of Jews and non-Jews who were the first to be called Christians. When Peter came to inspect them, he was willing to sit at the common table of Jews and non-Jews and share their meals. But when members of the strictly observant 'circumcision party' of James arrived in Antioch from Jerusalem, Peter, not wishing to be seen eating with Gentiles, withdrew from their table and persuaded the Jewish Christians, including Barnabas, to do the same. He was publicly rebuked by Paul for his duplicity (Gal. 2:11). As usual, the author of Acts tries to pour oil on troubled waters and while recording a conflict, omits to mention the presence of Peter (Acts 15:1).

If Peter's participation in the council of the apostles in Jerusalem in 49 CE is accepted as historical, that was the last occasion mentioned in the New Testament when Peter and Paul met. The main item on the agenda of the council was to decide whether a male Gentile could be baptized without being converted to Judaism through circumcision as a preliminary to his becoming a Jewish Christian. Peter apparently spoke first at the meeting. Recalling the Cornelius episode, he pronounced against putting on the Gentiles the burden of the yoke of the Law of Moses which neither the apostles' fathers nor they themselves had been able to bear (Acts 15:7–11). In the light of the stand taken by Peter in Antioch, and since he continued his mission exclusively among the Jews – he was, in Paul's colourful terms, the 'apostle of the circumcision', as Paul was the 'apostle of the foreskin' (Gal. 2:7) – Peter's proposal, *preceding* that of Barnabas and Paul, is questionable. It is probably an attempt by the author of the Acts intended to paper over the breach between the two church leaders by presenting Peter as a champion of the non-Jews. In fact, when the apostles came to decide the conditions in which Gentiles could be admitted to the Church, the president of the council who issued the decree was not Peter, but James the brother of the Lord, the head of the Jerusalem community. By that time James was probably the most influential person in Palestinian Judaeo-Christianity. It is worth noting that when in this connection Paul listed the 'pillars' of the Church, Peter was no longer the obvious leader: James was the first, Cephas the second and *John the son of Zebedee the third (Gal. 2:9).

The nickname Peter, meaning the 'Rock', which Simon may have possessed long before his meeting with Jesus, does not quite match his character. He panicked on the Lake of Galilee when he began to sink, denied and abandoned Jesus after his arrest, and later on made his famous volte-face in Antioch for which the irate Paul called him a plain hypocrite. Foreseeing the problems arising from Peter's weakness, the evangelists and the author of the Acts sought to conceal his clay feet, and correspondingly tried to raise his status. The betrayal of his Teacher was predicted, so it had to happen. It filled Peter with remorse and made him cry bitterly. *Luke places a special prayer on the lips of Jesus with a view to protecting the faith of Peter and enabling him to strengthen his brethren (Lk 22:31). *Matthew, and Matthew alone, makes Jesus proclaim Peter the foundation stone of the Church (Mt 16:18–19), and in John Peter thrice confesses his great love for Jesus, who appoints him the shepherd of his flock. Also to disguise Peter's conflict with Paul, the pseudonymous author of the second letter of Peter refers to him as Peter's 'beloved brother Paul'. But he pronounces his praise with his tongue in his cheek when he adds that Paul's letters contain things 'hard to understand' and dangerous for 'the ignorant and the unstable' (2 Pet. 15–16). Positively, the chief fisher-of-men is depicted as a charismatic healer, a friend of non-Jews and a loving, devoted and enthusiastic personality.

After the conflict in Antioch and the council in Jerusalem Peter disappears from the New Testament records. The two letters which bear his name are quasi-unanimously held by critical scholarship to be apocryphal; 1 Peter is dated to about 100 CE and 2 Peter to 125 CE or later, long after the death of the apostle Simon Peter.

Christian tradition, chiefly recorded by the Church historian Eusebius, asserts that after leaving Jerusalem Peter became the first bishop of Antioch. From Antioch he went to Rome during the reign of *Claudius (41–54 CE) in hot pursuit of his adversary from Samaritan days, Simon the Magician. In Rome he destroyed both the man and his influence. In the imperial capital Peter preached the Christian message and his Roman converts prevailed on Mark, Peter's companion, to write down Peter's teaching in what is known as the Gospel of Mark. Eusebius further relates that Peter also met *Philo of Alexandria in Rome and that both Peter and Paul were executed in Rome about the end of the reign of *Nero (54–68 CE): Paul, the Roman citizen, was beheaded, and the Jew Peter, like Jesus, died on the cross.

Sources: New Testament. Eusebius, *Eccl. Hist.* 2:14, 17; 3:36.

PETRONIUS

Publius Petronius, governor of Syria (39–41/2 CE), was a wise and decent Roman high official who found himself in the unenviable position of being the middleman between the insane emperor *Caligula and the infuriated Jews. The upheaval began in the coastal town of Jamnia (Yavneh) where the Jewish majority destroyed the altar set up by the Gentile inhabitants in honour of the emperor. Caligula was quick to take revenge by ordering his statue to be installed in the Temple of Jerusalem. To ensure the implementation of the order, Caligula instructed Petronius to hasten to Judaea in the winter of 39/40 CE and take with him half of the legions stationed in Syria. Petronius the diplomat tried to negotiate with the Jewish representatives, but they would not consider any compromise. Mass protests followed in Ptolemais, the headquarters of Petronius, and the governor, moved by the plea of the Jews, sought to delay matters. Further negotiations followed which resulted in Petronius begging the emperor to cancel his edict. This petition was supported by the Jewish king *Agrippa I, who was visiting his friend Caligula in Rome. The intervention brought temporary relief, but Caligula soon changed his mind, and ordered a new statue of himself to be made in Rome and shipped to Judaea. Also in a letter addressed to Petronius the emperor directed him to commit suicide. Bad weather delayed the delivery of the letter, which Petronius received twenty-seven days after the news of the murder of Caligula had reached him. So the decent and kindly Roman escaped with his life and no longer felt obliged to erect the statue in the Temple. Petronius' fairness towards the Jews was also manifest in his reassertion of their religious freedom in the Hellenistic city of Dora, north of Caesarea, though his cautious attitude towards Mesopotamian Jewry was based more on strategic considerations than on a sentiment of friendship.

Sources: Philo, Legatio 576–84. Josephus, Ant. 18:261–309; 19:299–311.

PHANNIAS

Phannias son of Samuel, known also as Phanni (Pinhas), was the last high priest in Jewish history. The Zealots, after occupying the Temple in 67 CE, selected him by lots. He was a laughable character. Not only did he not descend from high priests, he was also a mere simple-minded stonemason, who did not have the first idea what the high priesthood was about. His masters regarded him as a joke and dictated to him what he was supposed to do.

The tragic end of the Temple and the pontificate thus became a comedy.

Sources: Josephus, *War* 4:155; *Ant.* 20:227.

PHASAEL

Phasael, a Judaean statesman, was the elder son of *Antipater and the brother of *Herod the Great. Appointed governor of Jerusalem by his father, he earned the sympathy of the ordinary people of the city, but the civic leaders were jealous of the success of Phasael and Antipater and complained about them to *Hyrcanus II. The mild Hyrcanus was unwilling to act against them although he ordered Herod to appear before the tribunal of the Sanhedrin when he was accused of putting the Galilean rebel leader *Ezechias and his men to death without a trial. Phasael and Antipater dissuaded the furious Herod from taking revenge and attacking Jerusalem. In 41/40 BCE *Mark Antony elevated both Phasael and Herod to the rank of tetrarch under Hyrcanus who still possessed the higher dignity of ethnarch.

During the Parthian invasion of Judaea Herod escaped to the Nabataeans, but Phasael and Hyrcanus II were captured and handed over to the last Hasmonaean priest-king *Antigonus. Antigonus mutilated his uncle Hyrcanus by biting off one or both of his ears and condemned Phasael to death. The courageous Phasael took matters into his own hands and killed himself by smashing his head against a rock. In remembrance of his brother, Herod named one of the towers of

Jerusalem Phasael. He also built the town of Phasaelis, ten miles north of Jericho, and donated it before his death to his sister *Salome.

Sources: Josephus, *War* 1:181–275; *Ant.* 14–17.

PHILEMON

Philemon was the addressee of a short and very special letter of *Paul on behalf of a fugitive slave by the name of Onesimus who belonged to Philemon. Since Onesimus is described as a Colossian (Col. 4:9), Philemon must have been a Colossian too. He was a wealthy member of the Christian community and his house served as a venue for Church meetings. He is described as Paul's 'fellow worker' and the note sent to him was written by Paul's own hand.

Onesimus appears to have stolen something from his master and successfully escaped to Rome where he met up with Paul. He was converted and became Paul's servant. Paul would have loved to keep him, but not without Philemon's consent. So he returned Onesimus to his master with the plea that he should be received as a 'beloved brother', that is to say, implicitly asking Philemon to make Onesimus a freedman. If Philemon suffered any financial damage as a result, Paul was willing to compensate him. Whether Onesimus bishop of Ephesus in the 110s CE, mentioned by Ignatius of Antioch and Eusebius, was the same person as the ex-slave is rather doubtful, but chronologically not impossible.

Sources: Letters to Philemon and Colossians. Ignatius of Antioch: Eusebius, *Eccl. Hist.* 3:36.

PHILIP THE APOSTLE

The apostle Philip is just a name on a list in the Synoptic Gospels and in the Acts of the Apostles without playing any part in the story of *Jesus of Nazareth (Mk 3:16–19; Mt 10:2–4; Lk 6:14–16; Acts 1:12–14). Philip grows in importance in *John. A native of Bethsaida, the fishing town of birth of *Peter and *Andrew, he brought Nathanael to Jesus and acted as a guide for some pilgrims from the Greek Diaspora who wanted to meet Jesus. He was also used as a kind of not very clever partner in conversation when Jesus intended to emphasize an idea (Jn 14:8–11).

Later Christian tradition, contained in a late second-century CE letter of Polycrates bishop of Ephesus to Pope Victor, quoted by the Church historian Eusebius (fourth century), places the apostle Philip in the Roman province of Asia. He is said to lie buried in Hierapolis together with his two unmarried daughters, while his two other daughters rest in Ephesus. It would seem that Eusebius confused the apostle Philip with *Philip the Deacon, whose four prophesying daughters are mentioned in the Acts of the Apostles (Acts 21:8–9).

Source: Eusebius, *Eccl. Hist.* 3:31.

PHILIP THE DEACON

Philip was one of the seven Greek-speaking members of the Jerusalem Church who were appointed deacons or ministers by the apostles in order to take care of the poor and the widows among the 'Hellenists', that is to say, the Jewish Christians who originated in the Diaspora. The other six, all with good Greek names, were *Stephen, Prochorus, Nicanor, Timon, Parmenas and the proselyte from Antioch, Nicolaus (Acts 6:1–5).

Philip went to preach the gospel to the Samaritans. (By that time the original prohibition of Jesus on addressing Gentiles and Samaritans was forgotten.) His evangelization, accompanied by charismatic exorcism and healing, was very effective and converted even *Simon the Magician, who became Philip's constant companion. *Peter and *John arrived from Jerusalem to convey the Holy Spirit to the Samaritans in a visible manner through the laying on of hands. Simon offered money to Peter to buy some of this power, but was firmly rebuked.

The second recorded episode in Philip's evangelizing career concerns his meeting on the road from Jerusalem to Gaza with an Ethiopian convert to Judaism. This treasurer of the Queen of Ethiopia was returning from his pilgrimage to the Temple. The official was reading

Isaiah 53, the passage about the suffering servant of the Lord, and, unable to understand it, asked Philip for an explanation. Philip told the Ethiopian that the words came true in Jesus and promptly baptized him at the next pool of water they came to.

Philip is last encountered in 58 CE when Paul paid him his respects on landing in Caesarea, while heading to Jerusalem for the last time. Paul stayed in Philip's house and met his four daughters who were charismatic prophets.

Sources: Acts 8:5–6, 12–13, 26–40; 21:8.

PHILIP THE TETRARCH

Philip, *Herod's son by Cleopatra of Jerusalem, inherited the regions lying north-east and east of Galilee, Batanaea, Gaulanitis, Auranitis, Trachonitis and Panaias, as well as Ituraea, according to Luke 3:1. He ruled over the mostly Gentile (Greek and Syrian) population from 4 BCE to 33/4 CE. He is the only son of Herod about whom *Josephus' report is wholly positive. The only accomplishments attached to his name concern building projects. He reconstructed the old city of Panaias at the source of the Jordan, and renamed it Caesarea in honour of *Augustus. In the New Testament it is known as Caesarea Philippi. Philip also renovated Bethsaida, the town of the apostles *Peter, *Andrew and *Philip, situated on the north side of the Lake of Galilee, and dedicated the refurbished fishing village to Julia, daughter of Augustus, calling it Julias. He married *Salome, daughter of the wife of Herod *Antipas, *Herodias. According to the Gospels, mother and daughter were instrumental in obtaining the decapitation of *John the Baptist. Philip is praised for his gentleness and love of justice. He was very approachable and his servants always carried a judgement seat wherever he went so that he could hear cases and pronounce sentence wherever he was requested to do so. Being in charge of a largely non-Jewish population, he struck coins with the effigies of Augustus and *Tiberius on them, and his own image figures on one of them. As he died childless in the twentieth year of Tiberius (33/4 CE), his territory was attached to the Roman province of Syria, but

Philip the Tetrarch, son of Herod the Great

was later, in 37 CE, restored by the emperor *Caligula to Philip's nephew, the Jewish king *Agrippa I, son of *Aristobulus and grandson of *Mariamme, both murdered by Herod the Great.

Sources: Josephus, *War* 2:167–8, 181; *Ant.* 18:27–8, 106–8, 237.

PHILO

Philo of Alexandria was the greatest philosopher of Hellenistic Judaism. He was also a theologian and a statesman. He was born around 20 BCE to a leading Jewish family in Alexandria, his brother being Alexander the Alabarch, the Roman customs superintendent, and his nephew the procurator of Judaea, Tiberius Julius *Alexander

(46–8 CE). In 39/40 CE he led the delegation of the Alexandrian Jews to Gaius *Caligula. A Roman citizen and a great admirer of the emperor *Augustus, Philo was deeply involved in the conflict between Greeks and Jews in Alexandria, exacerbated by the anti-Jewish leanings of the Roman governor Flaccus before his fall from grace, banishment and subsequent execution by order of Caligula in 38 CE. Neither the Jewish nor the Greek ambassadors succeeded in winning the emperor over to their cause, for Caligula was more interested in 'being acknowledged as a god' (*Legatio* 372).

Philo was an extremely productive writer and the bulk of his works has survived. Most of them are devoted to an allegorical interpretation of the Pentateuch, especially of Genesis, and to a systematic exposition, tinged with philosophy and allegory, of the Law of Moses, in particular in his four books on the *Special Laws*. In *Every Just Man Must Be Free* and *The Contemplative Life* he has left important descriptions of the Jewish sects of the Essenes and of the Therapeutae or Healer-Worshippers, the former mostly located in Palestine and the latter in the neighbourhood of Alexandria. Eusebius has preserved many fragments of Philo's defence of the Jewish religion under the title *Hypothetica or an Apology for the Jews*.

Philo's works testify to a happy marriage between Hellenistic thought and Jewish religion. His thorough familiarity with Greek philosophy, most of all with Plato, went hand in hand with fidelity to the Bible, which he used in the Septuagint translation, his knowledge of Hebrew being revealed as somewhat limited by his etymologies of biblical names. As the child of two worlds, he could propose to Jews that Moses had taught them the essentials of Greek philosophy and to the Greeks that their most cherished ideas had been known to, and borrowed from, Moses. His influence on rabbinic Judaism is negligible. By contrast, it has left a deep mark on the beginnings of Christianity, from the letter to the Hebrews and the prologue of the Fourth Gospel to the early Church fathers, especially Clement of Alexandria, Origen, Ambrose and Jerome.

Philo's popularity in Christian circles inevitably led to legends associating him with the primitive Church. The Church historian Eusebius of Caesarea reports that Philo met and had discussions with St *Peter in Rome, and the Therapeutae of his *Contemplative Life* were Judaeo-Christian ascetics from Egypt (*Eccl. Hist.* 2:17). Later Church tradition was not satisfied with making Philo a Christian sympathizer, but turned him into a fully-fledged Christian who was baptized by the apostle *John and wrote the Greek Book of the Wisdom of Solomon among the Apocrypha.

Sources: Philo (Loeb edition). HJP III, 2, 809–89.

PILATE

Pontius Pilate is the best known of all the Roman governors of Judaea. He held his office from 26 to 36 CE. A Latin inscription, discovered in 1961 in Caesarea, discloses that officially he bore the title 'prefect' (*praefectus*) and not that of 'procurator', as subsequent sources, including the Roman historian Tacitus, tell us. Pilate's Judaean performance is assessed in some detail by *Josephus and *Philo, but his lasting notoriety is unquestionably due to the New Testament, that is, to the part he played in the condemnation to death and crucifixion of *Jesus. His name even entered the Christian Creed. There exist two very different portraits of Pilate, one drawn by the first-century CE Jewish writers Philo and Josephus, and the other by the evangelists and the early Church. The two have manifestly little in common.

The Pilate of Josephus is a harsh, insensitive and cruel official who fully earned his dismissal from office by his regional superior *Vitellius, the Roman governor of Syria in 36/7 CE. Apparently, soon after his arrival in Judaea, Pilate broke with the custom of his predecessors, who respected the religious sensitivities of the Jews, and commanded his soldiers to march into Jerusalem carrying Roman standards bearing the image of the emperor, thus unnecessarily causing provocation and offence. Next, he gave rise to a popular upheaval when he unlawfully appropriated the money called *Corban* (offering) from the Temple treasury and used it for the construction of an aqueduct bringing water to Jerusalem. Crowds of Jews protested. Though unarmed, many were slaughtered by the legionaries on Pilate's order, while others were trodden to death in the ensuing tumult. The so-called *Testimonium Flavianum*, *Josephus' notice on Jesus, is inserted in this context of calamities. It refers to the crucifixion of Jesus as one of the outrages brought about by Pilate. A further criminal act, which finally led to Pilate's dismissal, was a murderous attack on a group of Samaritans. On the complaints lodged by Jewish notables, Vitellius relieved Pilate of his office and ordered him to appear before the emperor in Rome to account for his misdeeds. A further act of cruelty, unrecorded in Josephus but attested in the Gospel of Luke (13:1), relates to the massacre of Galilean Jewish pilgrims travelling to Jerusalem with their sacrificial offerings.

Philo, a contemporary of Pilate, has no personal testimony to offer, but quotes at length a letter of the Jewish king *Agrippa I (37–41 CE) to the emperor *Caligula, in which Pilate is described as a stubborn, irascible and vindictive man. He is said to have been naturally inflexible, a blend of self-will and obduracy. As a governor he was guilty of insults, robberies, outrages and wanton injuries, in addition to accepting bribes; he was also responsible for numerous executions without trial as well as for numerous acts of grievous cruelty. It would be hard to paint a darker picture.

In contrast, the Pilate of the New Testament is a totally different person. He appears as a fair-minded weakling, who found Jesus innocent of the charges levelled against him by the Jewish leaders. He sought to avoid the need to pass judgement by attempting to hand Jesus over to Herod *Antipas, tetrarch of Galilee, who happened to be in Jerusalem for the Passover festival. Only after Antipas had declined to get involved in the case and had returned Jesus to Pilate did the governor half-heartedly consent, against the advice of his wife, who had a nightmare about Jesus, to sentence him to crucifixion, not without further protesting his innocence by washing his hands of a righteous man's blood.

As far as the respective characterizations go, the Pilate of Josephus and Philo is irreconcilable with the Pilate of the evangelists. In support of the Gospel portrayal one may cite the usual reluctance of the Roman authorities to get involved in strictly Jewish matters (for instance, whether being the Christ-Messiah amounted to political rebellion). The Gospel of *John brings this aspect of the affair to the fore with Pilate declaring that Jesus had broken no Roman law and suggesting that his accusers should judge him by their own rules and regulations.

Latin inscription found in Caesarea, referring to the dedication of a building to Tiberius by Pontius Pilate, Prefect of Judeae. The surviving text reads: ... TIBERIEVM ... [PON]TIVS PILATVS ... [PRAEF]ECTVS IVDA[EA]E

Only their objection of questionable validity – namely, that Jewish courts had no right to execute Jewish criminals – provides ground in the Fourth Gospel for Pilate continuing the case against Jesus.

Another detail in the Gospel account which is intended to show Pilate's sympathetic attitude towards Jesus is the anecdote of the so-called paschal privilege (*privilegium paschale*) connected with the Barabbas episode. On the eve of the Feast of Passover it was the governor's custom to liberate (or the Jews' custom to ask for the release of) a prisoner. Pilate was holding a notorious criminal by the name of Barabbas, who had been involved in murder in the course of an uprising. He offered the Jewish crowd the choice between the wicked Barabbas and the innocent Jesus. The crowd opted for the villain. However, the historicity of the story is debatable. No ancient document, narrative or legal, Jewish or Roman, attests a Passover amnesty.

It is often thought that the New Testament image of a kindly, hesitant and indecisive Pilate stems from the desire of the evangelists not to place full blame for the death of Jesus on the representative of Rome. However, the most convincing evidence for Pilate's disregard for the law is the fact that it was on account of his cruelty that he was demoted from his office by the emperor and sent into exile.

Later Christian tradition developed two different pictures of Pilate. According to the negative version he was either executed by *Tiberius or *Nero, or he committed suicide and his body, accompanied by demons, was transported to Vienne in Gaul. As the River Rhône spat out his corpse, it was finally transported to Switzerland and buried in a well on a mountain close to Lake Lucerne known as Mount Pilate or Pilatusberg. But there is also a favourable Christian portrait of Pilate. Eusebius is credited with a legendary report that Pilate informed Tiberius about the resurrection of Jesus and about the belief of Christians that he was God. The emperor referred the matter to the senate, which rejected the idea. The Latin Church father Tertullian believed that Pilate was a crypto-Christian at the time of the trial of Jesus, and the fourth-century legendary Acts of Pilate describes his dealings with Jesus in a favourable light. But the posthumous fame of Pilate reached its climax when the Egyptian Coptic Church decided to canonize the former prefect of Judaea and venerate him as a saint.

Sources: New Testament: Mk 15:2–15; Mt 27:11–26; Lk 23:2–25; Jn 18:28–19:22. Josephus, *War* 2:169–77; *Ant.* 18:35–89. Philo, *Legatio* 299–305. Tertullian, *Apologeticum* 21:24. Eusebius, *Eccl. Hist.* 2:2. 'Acts of Pilate' in M. R. James, *The Apocryphal New Testament*, 94–146.

POMPEY

Cnaeus Pompeius Magnus, or the Great Pompey (106–48 BCE), a Roman general and statesman, was one of the members of the first triumvirate governing Rome, together with Julius *Caesar and Crassus. Pompey's name casts a dark shadow on Jewish history. He was the Roman conqueror of the Near East who in 63 BCE put an end to the national independence enjoyed by the Jewish people for nearly a century under the Maccabaean–Hasmonaean rulers (152–63 BC). With the exception of the seven years of self-government during the two uprisings against Rome (66–70 and 132–5 CE), Jews had to wait for renewed political autonomy until the creation of the State of Israel in 1948.

Pompey conquered Pontus in Asia Minor and defeated Tigranes, King of Armenia, who also ruled Syria. By 65 BCE Pompey's general, Marcus Aemilius *Scaurus, entered Damascus, the capital of Syria. His next target was Judaea, where civil war raged between *Aristobulus II and *Hyrcanus II, the two sons of the high-priest-king Alexander Jannaeus. The Romans first favoured Aristobulus, who offered Pompey a golden grape-vine as a gift, but this did not prevent the Roman general from switching his patronage to Hyrcanus. (The details of this political game are dealt with in the articles on Aristobulus II and Hyrcanus II.) The meeting in Damascus between Pompey, the representatives of the two competing high priests and a deputation of the Jewish people, who sought the removal of the Hasmonaean rule and the restoration of the previous high-priestly dynasty supplanted by the Maccabees, was inconclusive, and in 63 BCE Pompey captured Jerusalem and upset the Jews by entering the Temple. He celebrated his triumph in Rome in 61 BCE, where the Hasmonaean ruler

Pompey the Great

Aristobulus II, along with his family and many Jews captured during the campaign, had to march in front of Pompey's chariot.

Pompey was involved again in Jewish history when during the civil war against Julius Caesar he received support from the high priest Hyrcanus II and from *Antipater, the Idumaean administrator who was the father of the future *Herod the Great. However, Hyrcanus and Antipater soon realized that they were backing the wrong horse and promptly transferred their allegiance to Caesar after his victory over Pompey in the battle of Pharsalus in Greece. Pompey's defeat was followed not long afterwards by his assassination in Egypt on 28 September 48 BCE.

Jews who later mourned the murder of Caesar had no tears to shed for Pompey. They blamed on him the loss of both their political independence and the Hellenistic cities situated on the Mediterranean coast, which Pompey removed from the national territory. The first-century BCE Jewish poet who wrote the Psalms of Solomon (2:29–31) metaphorically describes Pompey as a 'dragon', rejected by God and slain on the mountains of Egypt. His body lay there unburied, which was regarded as the ultimate dishonour in the ancient world.

Sources: Josephus, *War* 1:127–58; *Ant.* 14:34–79. Psalms of Solomon 2; 17.

Q

QUIETUS

Lusius Quietus, a Spanish prince, was the Roman governor of Judaea in 117 CE. He earned his post for his part in the suppression of a Jewish revolt in Mesopotamia at the end of the reign of *Trajan. The Church father Eusebius reports that Lusius Quietus treated the Jews with barbaric ferocity, slaughtering a large number of them. Since rabbinic writings also refer to a 'war of Quietus' (mSot. 9:14; Seder

Olam Rabbah), it is possible that there were disturbances in Palestine as well during Quietus' governorship. His initial luck ran out when it was suspected that he wished to replace *Hadrian and become emperor. As a result, Quietus was dismissed from the army and subsequently put to death.

Sources: Eusebius, *Eccl. Hist.* 4:2. Dio 68:32, 15.

QUIRINIUS

Publius Sulpicius Quirinius was Roman governor of Syria under the emperor *Augustus in 6 CE. In the New Testament he is associated with a universal census in the Roman empire which he implemented in Syria and in Judaea. This census, according to *Luke (2:1–6), necessitated the journey of *Joseph and *Mary from Nazareth to Bethlehem immediately before the birth of *Jesus. Historically, Luke's account is highly questionable. He appears to antedate Quirinius' tax registration, which according to *Josephus occurred in 6/7 CE, to the end of the rule of *Herod the Great, who died in 4 BCE and under whose reign Jesus was born (see Lk 1:5; Mt 2:1).

The census of 6/7 CE being unquestionable, we have to ask whether, as Luke asserts, there was also a Roman property registration in the kingdom of Herod some ten to twelve years earlier, a census also organized by Quirinius. Five substantial arguments can be marshalled against Luke's claim. 1) No Roman historical source mentions a worldwide census under Augustus. 2) Herod having been recognized by Rome as a *client* king (*rex socius*), no imperial interference with the government of his territory in the form of a census (*apographê*) would have been allowed under Roman law. 3) The presumed duty of Joseph to travel to Bethlehem, the city of his forefather David, in order to declare his land and property would also have been contrary to Roman practice which stipulated that the financial declaration be made either in Joseph's home town (Nazareth) or in the main town of his taxation district (Sepphoris) rather than in the town of his presumed tribal ancestor. 4) Joseph was not required to be accompanied by his wife as the declaration was to be made by the head of the household on behalf of the whole family. 5) Indirectly the silence of the historian Flavius Josephus about a census under Herod seriously undermines the reliability of the account of Luke, since Josephus was especially well informed about all matters pertaining to the final years of Herod's reign.

The historicity of the census ordered by Quirinius in 6/7 CE is firmly established. It is reported by Josephus and had a clear purpose. When Judaea's government was taken away from *Archelaus, the son of Herod, and transferred to an administrator directly answerable to Rome, fresh assessment of property for taxation purposes became necessary *ipso facto*.

Finally, the hypothesis of two consecutive censuses – one under Herod and a second after Archelaus – runs into further insurmountable difficulties. Quirinius' census in 6/7 CE, that is to say in the thirty-seventh year after *Caesar's defeat of Antony at Actium (2 September 31 BCE), is presented by Josephus as unprecedented. It was indeed such a shocking innovation for the Jews that it led to a major rebellion by *Judas the Galilean, known also as Judas of Gamala. Furthermore, a tax registration enacted by the order of Quirinius under Herod is rendered impossible by the fact that there is no mention of his governorship of Syria prior to 6 CE; nor is there any vacant period in the series of governors during the relevant years. The names and dates of the Syrian imperial legates at the turn of the era are known: Caius Sentius Saturninus (10/9–7/6 BCE), Publius Quinctilius *Varus (7/6–4 BCE), Lucius Calpurnius Piso (4–1 BCE), Caius Julius Caesar, grandson of *Augustus (1 BCE–4 CE), and Lucius Volusius Saturninus (4–5 CE). Hence Quirinius could not have held office before 6 CE.

Quirinius made yet another mark on New Testament history when, after deposing in 6 CE the uncooperative Jewish high priest *Joazar, he appointed as his successor *Ananus son of Sethi, who held the office until 15 CE. This Ananus is identical with the former high priest Annas, who is said to have played a leading role in the trial of Jesus (Jn 18:13, 24) and at a later date in that of *Peter and the other apostles before the Jerusalem Sanhedrin (Acts 4:6).

Sources: Lk 2:1. Josephus, *Ant.* 18:1–2, 26.

S

SALOME I

Salome I, to be distinguished from *Salome II, daughter of *Herodias and associated with the story of *John the Baptist, was the sister of *Herod the Great, king of Judaea from 37 to 4 CE. She was a clever, cruel and scheming woman, responsible for the death of many of her close relations. She and her mother Cyprus, suffering from an Idumaean inferiority complex, plotted constantly against the Hasmonaean royal side of Herod's family, first against *Mariamme I and her mother *Alexandra, daughter of the Jewish ethnarch and high priest *Hyrcanus II, and later against Mariamme's sons, Alexander and Aristobulus. Salome also engineered the downfall of two of her husbands. The first of these was Joseph, who was also her uncle. He was appointed guardian of Mariamme by Herod who, when summoned by his Roman patron *Mark Antony, undertook a risky trip to Egypt to account for the suspicious death of the high priest Aristobulus III, the son of Alexandra. On Herod's return in 34 BCE, Salome accused Joseph of having had an affair with Mariamme during Herod's absence, and the king put his uncle to death without further ado. The next victim was Mariamme herself. Salome, supported by her mother Cyprus, repeated the false charge of adultery, namely, that Mariamme had misbehaved with her second guardian, a certain Soemus, while Herod was visiting the emperor *Augustus in Rhodes. The jealous Herod executed both his wife, whom he loved passionately, and his close friend Soemus in 29 BCE. Shortly afterwards, Salome grew tired of her next husband, the Idumaean Costobar. Disregarding Jewish law, which denied a wife the right to initiate such proceedings, she sent Costobar a bill of divorce. But to ensure that she would have it her own way, she also charged her husband with disloyalty to Herod and promptly obtained his execution. Finally, together with Herod's eldest son *Antipater, she had a hand in turning the king against the two sons of Mariamme. Their plot succeeded when Herod sentenced Alexander and Aristobulus to death and they were strangled in 7 BCE.

Salome's third husband Alexas fared better than the first two. In fact, he and his repentant (?) wife saved the lives of a group of imprisoned Jewish notables whose execution was entrusted to them by the dying Herod, who in his final madness tried to make certain that his passing would be accompanied by widespread lamentation and mourning. But Salome and her husband refused to carry out this outrage and let the prisoners go home.

In his final will Herod left Salome the cities of Jamnia, Azotus and Phasaelis as well as 500,000 silver coins. She died c. 10 CE, a rich woman with horrible memories. Remembering the long-term friendship of her brother with the emperor of Rome, she bequeathed part of her estate, including the famous palm groves of Phasaelis, to the empress Livia, wife of Augustus.

Sources: Josephus, *War* 1–2; *Ant.* 14–17.

SALOME II

Salome II, to be distinguished from *Salome I, the sister of *Herod the Great, was the daughter of *Herodias and her first husband, Herod. Salome married *Philip the Tetrarch and after his death Aristobulus, son of King *Herod of Chalcis. The effigy of Salome has been preserved on a coin of Aristobulus.

In the New Testament Salome appears nameless, referred to simply as the daughter of Herodias, but her lasting notoriety derives from the part she played in the death of *John the Baptist. According to the account given in the Gospels, but unknown to *Josephus, in order to reward Salome for the dance performed at his birthday celebration, her stepfather Herod Antipas gave her a blank cheque, metaphorically speaking: he would grant her whatever she asked. Following the instruction of her mother Herodias, the girl stipulated the head of the Baptist on a plate.

Sources: Mk 6:21–8; Mt 14:6–11. Josephus, *Ant.* 18:136–7.

*Queen Salome, daughter of Herodias and wife of
King Aristobulus of Chalcis*

SAMAIAS AND POLLION (OR SHEMAIAH AND
ABTALION)

Samaias and Pollion, as they are called in *Josephus, were mid-first
century BCE Pharisee teachers, probably identical with Shemaiah and
Abtalion of the Mishnah. They came to prominence after the trial
and acquittal of the young *Herod the Great by the high priest
*Hyrcanus II and the Jewish Sanhedrin in 47 BCE when they foretold
that in due course Herod would take revenge on the judges. Indeed,
after Herod entered Jerusalem as king in 37 CE, of all the members of
the Sanhedrin he spared only Pollion and his pupil Samaias, who
found further favour with him by persuading the people of Jerusalem
to accept Herod and thus atone for their sins. Also, when in the
eighteenth year of his reign the Pharisees refused to swear an oath of

allegiance to Herod, he let all of them go scot-free on account of what Pollion had previously achieved.

Samaias and Pollion are usually identified with Shemaiah and Abtalion, the pair of Pharisee masters who in the Mishnah were the immediate successors of *Simeon ben Shetah, the brother of Queen Alexandra Salome. The main discrepancy is that in Josephus Pollion is senior to Samaias, whereas in the Mishnah Shemaiah is always named before Abtalion. The principal saying of each of them consists of a warning, advising prudence when dealing with the authorities. Rabbinic tradition venerates them as great sages and Bible interpreters and attributes to them the ruling, popularized by their pupil, *Hillel, that Passover has precedence over the Sabbath. Their doctrinal authority greatly enhanced the influence of the Pharisee teachers in the first century CE.

Sources: Josephus, *Ant.* 14:172–6; 15:3–4, 370. HJP II, 362–3.

SCAURUS

Marcus Aemilius Scaurus, a Roman administrator and general, was the first governor of Syria from 65 to 62 BCE. He was sent to Syria by *Pompey while he was still campaigning in Armenia. From Damascus Scaurus entered Judaea, where civil war raged between the two sons of the Hasmonaean high-priest-king Alexander Jannaeus, who were competing for the Jewish high priesthood. The elder, *Hyrcanus II, assisted by the Nabataeans, was besieging his brother *Aristobulus II in Jerusalem. Both rivals sought to buy Scaurus' support, but he opted for Aristobulus and his ultimatum to the Nabataeans relieved the siege of the capital. Scaurus, however, was unable to capture the Nabataean stronghold of Petra in Transjordan, and stopped molesting the Nabataeans on receiving a large sum of money successfully negotiated for him by his envoy, *Antipater, father of *Herod the Great. *Josephus makes no reference to any ill-treatment of the Jews by Scaurus, but a badly preserved historical calendar from Qumran Cave 4 among the Dead Sea Scrolls twice asserts that 'Aemilius killed . . .' (4Q333 1, 4 and 8). Since other historical names such as Hyrcanus and Shelamzion

(Alexandra Salome) point to the same period, and since no other Aemilius played any leading part in the Roman conquest of Judaea under Pompey, the person alluded to in the Qumran fragments is bound to be Marcus *Aemilius* Scaurus.

After his governorship of Syria, Scaurus returned to Italy where he occupied several high offices of state, but ended his life in exile having been found guilty of corruption.

Sources: Josephus, *War* 1:127–9, 132, 157, 159–60; *Ant.* 14:29, 33, 37, 79–81.

SEXTUS VETTULENUS CERIALIS

See under **Silva**.

SHAMMAI

Shammai and *Hillel form the most influential pair among the early Pharisees and chronologically straddle the eras. Each of them was known as the Elder, not Rabbi or Rabban. Shammai, himself a rigorous master, founded a rabbinic school to rival Hillel's and both the founder and the school were noted for severity in legal matters.

Of the biography of Shammai practically nothing is known. He was apparently a builder by profession, and had an irascible temperament. No doubt in order to counteract this weakness of character, he recommended in his favourite saying that one should always receive people with a friendly countenance.

In the anecdote of the Gentile who declared himself ready to become a proselyte if someone taught him the whole Torah while he was standing on one leg, the short-tempered Shammai sensibly threw him out, but the mild and obliging Hillel revealed to him the Golden Rule – 'What is hateful to you, do not do to your fellow' (bShab. 31a) – which was part of the teaching of *Jesus too. By contrast, in *Matthew's version of Jesus' doctrine on divorce, where the dissolution of a marriage in the case of the wife's 'unchastity' is allowed, the evangelist reflects the more stringent doctrine of Shammai. Shammai authorized divorce only in the case of a wife's sexual misbehaviour, as against Hillel's lax ruling in favour of anything causing displeasure to the husband.

Sources: HJP II, 363–7.

SILAS OR SILVANUS

Silas, also called Silvanus, a 'prophet', was a leading member of the Jewish Christian community at the time of the council of the apostles in Jerusalem in 49 CE. He and Judas Barsabbas were charged to carry a letter from the council to the Churches in Antioch and Cilicia and announce the apostolic decree excusing prospective Gentile Christians from the obligation to embrace Judaism before being baptized.

After *Paul's row with *Barnabas, Silas became Paul's chief companion on his second evangelizing expedition, with *Timothy as Paul's junior partner. Silas appeared with Paul before the magistrates in Philippi and shared his imprisonment. Silas and Timothy participated with Paul in founding the Church in Thessalonica, Beroea and Corinth, but did not follow Paul to Athens. After Corinth Silas is no longer mentioned in the Pauline context, but a Silvanus (not necessarily identical with Silas) is referred to as a 'faithful brother' in the first letter of Peter.

Sources: Acts 15–18; 2 Cor. 1:9; 1 Thess. 1:1; 2 Thess. 1:1; 1 Pet. 5:12.

SILVA

Lucius Flavius Silva was the Roman governor of Judaea from 73/4 to 81 CE. Of his two predecessors in charge of Palestinian Jewish matters very little is known. Sextus Vettulenus Cerialis was the officer in command of the fifth legion during the siege of Jerusalem and as governor took over the command of the tenth (Fretensis) legion. His successor, Lucilius Bassus, continued the subjugation of the Jews and occupied the mountain-top fortresses of Herodium in the Judaean desert and Machaerus in Transjordan, where *John the Baptist had been beheaded.

Silva's fame in Judaea is linked to the conquest of the apparently impregnable rock fortress of Masada, the last stronghold of the Jewish rebels led by *Eleazar son of Jairus, a descendant of *Judas the Galilean. The ingenuity of Silva's military engineers overcame the difficulties first by erecting a wall to prevent escape from the fortress and then by building a ramp, which still stands today, to allow the battle engines and the troops to reach and breach the fortified walls of the stronghold. The second wooden wall, hastily improvised by the defenders, was destroyed by the fire lit with the help of burning torches propelled towards it by the Roman soldiers. When the Romans finally entered, they met no resistance as the defenders were all dead, having made a pact to kill their families and one another or commit suicide rather than be taken alive by the enemy. According to *Josephus the Romans counted 960 bodies. Only seven Jews escaped, two women and five children found alive hiding in underground aqueducts. Israeli archaeologists who excavated Masada between 1963 and 1965 claim to have found some twenty-five skeletons of the last Jewish Zealots. Among the manuscript remains discovered is an incomplete Hebrew scroll of the Book of Ecclesiasticus or Wisdom of Jesus ben Sira, a sectarian liturgical writing known from the Qumran find of the Dead Sea Scrolls and, amazingly, a mutilated fragment of a Latin papyrus, the oldest of its kind, containing a line of Virgil's *Aeneid*.

Sources: Josephus, *War* 7:252, 275–9, 304–15. Y. Yadin, *Masada* (1966).

SIMEON BAR KOSIBA

Simeon bar (or ben) Kosiba, also known as Bar Kokhba, was the leader of the second revolt of the Jews against Rome under the emperor *Hadrian between 132 and 135 CE. The most likely causes of the rebellion were either the prohibition of circumcision imposed by Hadrian, as is reported by the Roman historian Spartianus in the *Historia Augusta*, or the emperor's decision to erect a Roman city,

Aelia, on the ruins of Jerusalem (as stated by Cassius Dio). Bearing in mind the general historical context, the second explanation appears to be the more likely. Cassius Dio relates that the construction of the city of Colonia Aelia Capitolina – Aelia for short – started during Hadrian's stay in Egypt, Judaea and Syria around 130 CE. It is conceivable that hostile Jewish reactions provoked by the building of the new city combined with the outrage felt by Jews in face of the legislation outlawing circumcision. It is quite possible, however, that the prohibition of circumcision was imposed on the Jews as a measure of punishment after the end of the war. If so, it was the penalty for, and not the cause of, the rebellion.

The uprising, inspired and led by Simeon bar Kosiba, broke out in 132 CE. Until the discovery of documents relating to the second revolt in caves in the Judaean desert in the 1950s and 1960s not even his name was known with certainty. The Church fathers Justin and Eusebius call him Kochebas or Barchochebas and the rabbinic writings use Ben or Bar Kokhba, signifying Son of the Star. Surviving correspondence between leaders of the rebellion and their chief and among themselves shows that his name was Bar Kosba or Kosiba and his first name, attested also on some of the coins of the rebellion, was Simeon. His official title was Prince (Nasi) of Israel according to both the coins and the new texts. Numismatic evidence indicates that in the first and second years of the revolt Simeon shared the leadership with Eleazar the Priest. This Eleazar may have been Eleazar of Modiim, whom rabbinic sources designate as Simeon's uncle. According to the same sources, Eleazar was sentenced to death by his nephew who erroneously suspected him of treason. Apart from these not altogether reliable data no information has survived about the family background and life of Bar Kosiba.

Little documentary evidence has been preserved concerning the course of the rebellion. It started as guerrilla warfare in the various regions but some of the coins and a document testify that Jerusalem was liberated by the rebels. Soon the whole country was under their control and Cassius Dio implies that the uprising spread beyond the frontiers of Palestine.

Military governors appointed by Simeon ruled the districts and the localities had their own leaders or parnasin who liaised with the district commanders. They were in charge of leasing the land which all belonged to the head of state and they also collected the rent.

As one might expect from a revolutionary leader, Simeon reveals himself in his letters as a harsh and authoritarian commander. He threatened one of his lieutenants, by the name of Joshua son of Galgula, with putting his legs in irons should he disobey orders. The district commanders of Engedi also faced severe punishment if they failed to carry out orders. The same officers were instructed to arrest, disarm and send to Simeon a certain Joshua of Palmyra. Lack of enthusiasm for fighting in Engedi and Tekoa among the brothers, as the rebels called themselves, was met with stern rebuke.

Strict obedience to the leader went parallel with full observance of the Jewish religion. Bar Kosiba made arrangements for the dispatch of four kinds of tree branch (palm, citron, myrtle and willow) required for the Feast of Tabernacles. The civic leader of Kiriat Arabaya was to ensure that the branches had been tithed.

Simeon's letters are in Hebrew and Aramaic, but one was written in Greek because there was no Hebrew/Aramaic scribe on hand. It contained urgent orders relating to the feast of Tabernacles. At least one of the letters is signed by '[Si]meon s[on of] . . .' If the missing word is Kosiba, we have here an autograph document from the chief of the second revolt.

The military success of the uprising forced Hadrian to mobilize substantial forces. *Tinneius Rufus, Roman governor of Judaea at the outbreak of the war, the Tyrannos Rufus of the rabbis, remained in charge for a while, but was later replaced by Quinctilius Certus Publicius Marcellus, and at the end by Sextus Julius Severus, Hadrian's outstanding general, who had to be summoned from one end of the empire to the other, from Britain to Judaea. He could not engage Bar Kosiba's guerrillas in open battle and had to search for them in caves and underground hiding places such as those found in the Judaean desert by an Israeli archaeological team directed by Yigael Yadin. Jerusalem was reconquered by the Romans and the remains of the Jewish city were demolished to make place for Hadrian's new Aelia.

Simeon's final refuge was the mountain fortress of Bether, some 10 kilometres south of Jerusalem, which was surrounded and taken in 135 CE. The rabbinic legend speaks of a bloodbath, and the reality was probably the same. The leader of the rebellion fell there together with his last remaining brethren.

In some Jewish circles Simeon bar Kosiba enjoyed a messianic reputation and became Bar Kokhba, the Son of the Star. On coins struck by the rebels a symbol appears above the representation of the Temple, which some experts identify as a star, though other numismatists prefer to describe it as a rosette. Moreover, no less an authority than Rabbi Akiba saw in Simeon the fulfilment of the biblical prophecy, 'A star shall come forth out of Jacob' (Num. 24:17), and proclaimed him the King-Messiah. But other rabbis disagreed and changed his honorific title, Son of the Star (Bar Kokhba), to the sarcastic sobriquet of Liar, literally Son of the Lie (Bar Koziba).

Simeon did not have a good press in Christian circles either. According to Justin Martyr, Palestinian Christians felt unable to join the revolt led by a false Messiah without denying their true Christ. Jerome accuses Simeon of performing magic tricks and pretending that they were miracles, and Eusebius and Justin attribute to Bar Kokhba a severe persecution of the Church.

Sources: Bar Kokhba letters and coins: HJP I, 547. Dio 69:12–14. Justin, 1 *Apologia* 31:6. Eusebius, *Eccl. Hist.* 4:5–6.

SIMEON BEN SHETAH

Simeon ben Shetah was a rabbinic teacher and Jewish statesman from the first century BCE. *Josephus knows nothing about him and all the information relating to Simeon is borrowed from the writings of the rabbis and as such is of uncertain historical value. He is presented as a figure of great significance from both the political and the doctrinal points of view. His activity falls in the first half of the first century BCE and coincides with the rule of the Hasmonaean high-priest-king Alexander Jannaeus (103–76 BCE) and of his widow and successor, Alexandra Salome (76–67 BCE). These were the last years of the century-old Jewish independence under the Maccabaean-Hasmonaean dynasty, which came to an end in 63 BCE with the conquest of Jerusalem by the Roman legions of *Pompey.

Rabbinic tradition presents Simeon ben Shetah as the leading Pharisee teacher of his age; he is one of the famous *zuggot* or 'pairs', listed in the *Sayings of the Fathers* (1:8–9), who were thought to have been the leading authorities in the Jewish high court, or Sanhedrin. But in addition to the weight of his scholarship, Simeon's influence depended also on his family connection with the Hasmonaean royal house. According to rabbinic tradition he was the brother-in-law of Alexander Jannaeus, being the brother of Queen Shelamzion or Alexandra Salome (Genesis Rabbah 91:3), and as such he wielded considerable power over the king and queen.

The reigns of Jannaeus and of Alexandra who, despite being a woman, inherited and exercised the government of the Jewish people, witnessed major changes in the position of the religious parties, the Sadducees and the Pharisees, as is reported by Josephus and the rabbinic historical calendar known as the Scroll of Fasting (Megillat Taanit). The Sadducee ascendancy which prevailed under Jannaeus progressively gave way to Pharisee domination, finally achieved under Alexandra Salome, who gave the Pharisees her undivided support. We learn from Josephus that the Pharisees stirred up the population against Jannaeus and provoked a war, which also involved the participation of the Seleucid king Demetrius III (*Ant.* 13:372–415; *War* 1:88–112). After some initial reverses Jannaeus triumphed and took cruel vengeance on his opponents. Eight hundred of them were crucified in Jerusalem and their wives and children were murdered before their eyes. Confirmation of Josephus' gruesome account is found in one of the Dead Sea Scrolls, the commentary on Nahum from Cave 4 (4Q169, frg. 3–4, col. 1, 6–8), which alludes to the 'Furious Young Lion', the nickname of Jannaeus, as the ruler who 'hanged men alive on the tree', a phrase explained by most interpreters as meaning crucifixion. While Josephus does not explicitly identify the opponents of Jannaeus as Pharisees, or Jews led by Pharisees, the identity of the king's former foes is revealed in advice given on his deathbed to his wife Alexandra Salome, whom he urged to make peace with the Pharisees. Indeed, during the nine years of the queen's rule the Pharisees held the reins of government or, as Josephus puts it, 'If she ruled the nation, the Pharisees ruled her' (*War* 1:112), and, 'While she had the title of sovereign, the Pharisees had the supremacy' (*Ant.* 13:409).

By implication, therefore, it must be said that if the Pharisees were the ruling party under Salome, her brother, Simeon ben Shetah, the leader of the Pharisees, was the power behind the throne in the Hasmonaean state.

The doctrinal impact of Simeon appears to have matched his political influence. The number of decisions attached to the name of this early representative of Pharisaism is remarkably high. In particular, the introduction of various rules of judicial procedure is credited to him. To Simeon is imputed also, though more questionably, the obligation to produce a written marriage contract and the creation of an elementary school system. However, the launching of primary education in Palestinian Jewry probably happened more than a century later, in 63–5 CE under the high priest *Jesus son of Gamaliel.

The Mishnah (mSanh. 6:4) reports that Simeon ben Shetah was responsible for hanging (or crucifying) eighty women (witches) in Ashkelon. This would have been contrary to later rabbinic legislation, which ruled against the judging and subsequent execution on the same day of more than one person charged with a capital offence. In fact, the whole gruesome story seems to have been made up, because in the time of Simeon the Hellenistic city of Ascalon was not part of the Jewish territory over which he possessed jurisdiction.

The renown of Simeon ben Shetah ranked very high among the rabbis and his age, according to the Talmud, had the reputation of a golden age: 'In the days of Simeon ben Shetah rain fell every Wednesday and Sabbath night, so that the grains of wheat were like kidneys, the grains of barley like olives, and the lentils like golden denarii' (bTaan. 23a).

Sources: Enc. Jud. 14:1563–5. HJP II, 362.

SIMEON SON OF GAMALIEL

Simeon son of *Gamaliel the Elder was an important leader of the Pharisees in the second half of the first century CE. Although his ancestors *Hillel and Gamaliel the Elder remain unmentioned, Simeon is several times alluded to in the writings of *Josephus. Apart from the disabused saying attributed to him in the tractate *Sayings of the Fathers* in the Mishnah regarding words excessively multiplied by the sages – 'I have found nothing better than silence,' he apparently remarked – little is known about his teaching. Most of the passages ascribed to Simeon son of Gamaliel in rabbinic literature are thought to belong to his grandson Simeon son of *Gamaliel II. Our best source of information is Josephus. He portrays Simeon as one of the two main Jewish leaders in Jerusalem at the time of the first war against Rome (66–70 CE), the other being the former high priest *Ananus son of Ananus. Together with Gorion son of Joseph and the former high priest *Jesus son of Gamaliel, they were the chief opponents of the Zealots in the city. Simeon was a friend of *John of Gischala, the Galilean revolutionary leader who sought to unseat Josephus from his post as military commander of the province. Yet despite his hostile attitude towards him Josephus praised Simeon in the highest terms: 'This Simon was a native of Jerusalem, of a very illustrious family, and of the sect of the Pharisees, who have the reputation of being unrivalled experts in their country's laws. A man highly gifted with intelligence and judgement, he could by sheer genius retrieve an unfortunate situation in affairs of state.'

Sources: Josephus, *War* 4:159; *Life* 38–9, 44, 60, 191–2. mAb. 1:17–18.

SIMON KANTHERAS SON OF BOETHUS

King *Agrippa I (41–4 CE) was responsible for the appointment of three high priests of whom scarcely anything is known beyond their names.

The first, Simon son of Boethus, surnamed Kantheras (the 'Scarab'?), was chosen to replace *Theophilus son of Ananus in 41 CE.

Agrippa soon changed his mind and proposed to reinstate Jonathan, another son of the high priest Ananus, who had been in office in 36/7 CE. Jonathan, displaying a rare example of humility among members of the pontifical families, declined the offer and recommended to the king his brother Matthias son of Ananus as a worthier candidate than himself. Agrippa, deeply impressed, followed Jonathan's advice and as a result another son of *Ananus son of Sethi was able to wear the high-priestly vestments.

The third incumbent of the high-priestly post was Elionaeus son of Kantheras. If he is the same as the Mishnah's Elihoenai ha-Qoph or ha-Qayyaph (son of Caiaphas?), he was one of the rare high priests, the others being Hanamel (or *Anael) the Egyptian and *Ismael son of Phiabi, who had the opportunity of performing the burning of the red heifer, the ceremony prescribed in Numbers 19 in connection with a ceremony of ritual purification.

Sources: Simon: Josephus, *Ant.* 19:297, 313. Matthias: Josephus, *Ant.* 19:316. Elionaeus: Josephus, *Ant.* 19:342. mPar. 3:5.

SIMON OF PERAEA

Simon, a giant Peraean slave of *Herod the Great, proclaimed himself king on his master's death in 4 BCE and, wearing a crown, led a band of insurgents to plunder and set on fire the royal palaces and property at Jericho and elsewhere. Gratus, the commander of Herod's infantry, pursued them and his soldiers massacred many Peraeans. Gratus himself caught up with the fleeing Simon and beheaded him, thus putting an end to his ephemeral reign.

Sources: Josephus, *War* 2:57–9; *Ant.* 273–7.

SIMON SON OF BOETHUS

Simon son of Boethus was a member of an Egyptian priestly family living in Jerusalem, who was appointed high priest by *Herod the Great in 25/4 BCE. His promotion to the pontificate was due not to his religious qualities or his leadership but to the beauty of his daughter Mariamme, who beguiled Herod. To increase the standing of the future bride's father, the king removed the high priest in office, *Jesus son of Phiabi, in favour of Simon.

The new wife, *Mariamme II, after bearing Herod Philip, was

charged with complicity in a plot fomented against Herod by his eldest son *Antipater and was divorced. As Simon's elevation to the pontifical post was motivated by Herod's wish to marry his daughter, Mariamme II's disgrace resulted in Simon's demotion and replacement by *Matthias son of Theophilus shortly before the king's death in 4 BCE.

Four further high priests came from the Boethus family.

Sources: Josephus, *Ant.* 15:320–22; 17:78, 164–6.

SIMON SON OF GIORA

Simon son of Giora – the Aramaic *Giora*, like the Hebrew *Ger*, means proselyte – was one of the leading revolutionaries during the siege of Jerusalem. Born in Gerasa of a father who had converted to Judaism and a Jewish mother, Simon first joined the *Sicarii* of Masada. Thereafter he set out with his band of outlaws to plunder Judaea, where he occupied Hebron, and the whole of Idumaea. In the spring of 69 CE, Simon and his men entered Jerusalem on the invitation of the chief priest Matthias son of Boethus. It was mistakenly thought that they might put an end to the tyrannical rule of *John of Gischala. In fact, with his fifty officers and 10,000 men plus the 5,000 Idumaean auxiliaries commanded by ten chiefs, Simon became an even greater despot and threat to his co-citizens than John of Gischala was. He harassed the wealthy and murdered many of them, including his erstwhile patron the chief priest Matthias, together with three of his sons. The vileness of spirit prevailing in besieged Jerusalem is revealed by Simon's order to butcher the sons before the eyes of their father, who planned to desert, and then kill him in view of the Romans with the comment: 'Let him see whether his friends to whom he intended to desert will assist him' (Josephus, *War* 5:531). During the final stages of the siege Simon was in charge of the defence of the upper city of Jerusalem. He was the last rebel leader to be caught by the Romans when he emerged from his subterranean hideout. He was kept alive to appear as the principal rebel chief during the triumph of *Titus in Rome in 71 CE at the end of which, in conformity with ancient custom, he was ceremonially scourged and executed in the Mamertine prison at the north-east end of the Roman Forum.

Sources: Josephus, *War* 2–7; *Life* 191–2.

SIMON SON OF KAMITHUS

See under **Ananus (or Annas) son of Sethi.**

SIMON THE ESSENE

Simon the Essene was a charismatic dream-interpreter at the beginning of the first century CE. According to *Josephus he volunteered in 6 CE to interpret a dream of *Archelaus, the ethnarch of Judaea, which the other experts, soothsayers and Chaldaeans, were unable to explain. The dream was vaguely similar to that of Pharaoh in Genesis 41. In it the ethnarch saw ten thick ears of corn (nine according to *War* 2:112) being eaten by oxen. Simon, having obtained a guarantee of safety irrespective of the nature of his interpretation, explained the dream as foreshadowing a change at the end of ten (or nine) years. Josephus notes that five days later an envoy of *Augustus arrived to put an end to Archelaus' rule and took him to Rome for trial before the emperor, which resulted in his dismissal from office, the confiscation of all his possessions and his banishment to exile in Vienne in Gaul.

The Essene Simon is depicted as a professional dream-interpreter who knew how to ensure his survival when he had to proclaim a bad omen. Josephus, himself of priestly extraction and with some Essene training, also claimed to possess the gift of a dream-interpreter. He attempted to justify his surrender to the Romans by the knowledge gained from his dreams concerning the future sovereignty of Rome over the Jews (*War* 3:351–2).

Sources: Josephus, *War* 2:111–13; *Ant.* 17:342–4.

SIMON THE MAGICIAN

Simon was a famous professional magician among the Samaritans in the early years of Christianity. He was called the great divine power and became highly influential in Samaria until the arrival of *Philip the Deacon who converted the Samaritans to the gospel of *Jesus about the Kingdom of God. Simon himself is said to have believed and was baptized. His conversion was superficial because when the apostles *Peter and *John communicated the Holy Spirit to the Samaritans, Simon offered them money to acquire charismatic power. He was strongly rebuked but apparently repented (Acts 8:9–25).

Subsequent Christian tradition depicts him in wholly unfavourable colours. The Church historian Eusebius (fourth century CE) refused to accept that Simon was ever sincere in his repentance and conversion, and called him the founder of a 'disgusting sect'. Peter followed Simon to Rome and destroyed him and his power.

According to the second-century Church father Justin Martyr, a certain Simon of the Samaritan village of Gittha gained influence during the reign of the emperor *Claudius (41–54 CE) and was worshipped in Rome according to a Latin inscription dedicated to 'Simon the holy god' (*Simoni deo sancto*). Eusebius's identification of Simon Magus with Simon of Gittha is unfounded. His source, Justin, does not make the same mistake. His version of the Latin inscription on Simon's statue is also incorrect: it was dedicated not to Simon, but to a Sabine deity called Semo. Nevertheless, the New Testament figure is an important negative mirror image of the charismatic individual made popular by Jesus and his immediate followers in the Christian community. Simon's ill fame has been perpetuated by the word 'simony', meaning the attempt to purchase spiritual values or ecclesiastical offices with money.

Sources: Justin, 1 *Apologia* 1:26. Eusebius, *Eccl. Hist.* 2:13.

SIMON THE ZEALOT

See under **James son of Alphaeus**.

SOSIUS

Caius Sosius, governor of Syria from 38 to 37 BCE, played an important part in Jewish history when he lent a powerful hand to *Herod the Great and established him as King of the Jews and ruler of Jerusalem. The event took place in 37 BCE, three years after Herod's appointment as king by *Mark Antony. To achieve it, Sosius brought a large Roman contingent to Jerusalem and together with the army of Herod they stormed the city which was defended by the last Hasmonaean priest-king, *Antigonus, son of *Aristobulus II. Antigonus surrendered to Sosius and was taken by him in chains to Antioch in Syria where he was beheaded by order of Antony and in conformity with the wishes of Herod. Antigonus was the first defeated king executed by the Romans. With his death the century-long role of the Hasmonaean Jewish priestly dynasty came to an inglorious end. To celebrate his victory in Jerusalem, Sosius dedicated a golden crown to the God of the Jews in the Temple. For his success in Judaea he was rewarded with the title *imperator* and a ceremony of triumph in Rome in 34 BCE.

Sources: Josephus, *War* 1:345–57; *Ant.* 14:468–9, 481, 484–8; 15:1. Dio 49:23.

STEPHEN

Stephen was the first of the seven assistants or deacons chosen by the apostles in Jerusalem to take over the distribution of food to widows and poor members of the community after complaints from the 'Hellenists', that is, people of Greek Diaspora origin. The seven deacons all bear Greek names and were no doubt themselves Hellenists. The account in the Acts of the Apostles is politically biased, written from the viewpoint of Gentile Christianity.

Stephen, like most leaders of the primitive Church including *Peter and *Paul, is presented as a charismatic miracle-worker, accused before the Jerusalem Sanhedrin by Jews of the Greek dispersion of blasphemy against Moses and God and of speaking against the Law and the Temple. In self-defence Stephen delivered a long and rather irrelevant sermon on Jewish history from Abraham until David and Solomon, ending with the building of the Temple. Then, quoting prophetic words critical of a man-made house of God, he turned on his accusers: their fathers persecuted the prophets and they themselves murdered Jesus.

The charge infuriated the audience. The situation was further aggravated by Stephen's claim of a mystical vision of Jesus seated on God's right hand. The audience went berserk; they rushed him out of the city and stoned him to death while a young man by the name of Saul, the future Paul, witnessed and fully approved the killing.

The account is intended to convey the message of the breach of Christianity with Judaism and the Temple. The historical reality behind the story of the Acts probably consisted of a provocative outburst by a leader of the Jesus movement which resulted in turning the easily excitable Jerusalem crowd into a lynch mob. Stephen is depicted as an imitator of Christ, offering his spirit to Jesus and begging God to forgive his murderers.

Source: Acts 7:8–8:1.

SYMEON SON OF CLOPAS

Symeon son of Clopas was the second bishop of Jerusalem, according to the Church historian Eusebius quoting the second-century author Hegesippus. Symeon's father Clopas was the uncle of *Jesus of Nazareth, consequently Symeon was his cousin. Symeon succeeded *James the brother of the Lord as head of the Jerusalem Church. So the leadership of the Mother Church was kept in the family of Jesus. Symeon died a martyr's death. Eusebius, following Hegesippus, reports that Christian heretics denounced Symeon to a Roman judge as both a descendant of David and a Christian and he was crucified under the emperor *Trajan in 106/7 CE, apparently at the age of 120 years.

If the testimony of Eusebius is acceptable, the two relatives of Jesus, James and Symeon, were followed on the episcopal throne of Jerusalem by thirteen more bishops 'of the circumcision', i.e. of Jewish descent, from 106/7 to 135 CE. Nothing is recorded about them apart from their names: Justus, Zacchaeus, Tobias, Benjamin, John, Matthias, Philip, Seneca, Justus, Levi, Ephres, Joseph and Judas. After 135 CE all Jews, including Jewish Christians, were banished from the pagan city of Aelia, built on the ruins of Jerusalem by *Hadrian.

Source: Eusebius, *Eccl. Hist.* 3:11, 32.

T

THADDEUS

See under **James son of Alphaeus**.

THEOPHILUS SON OF ANANUS

See under **Jonathan son of Ananus**.

THEUDAS

Theudas was a typical Jewish religious revolutionary who attracted a sizeable group of disciples during the procuratorship of Cuspius *Fadus (44–6 CE). His opponents, *Josephus recounts, called him a sorcerer or impostor, one of those false messiahs who are alluded to in the eschatological discourse of the Gospels. Theudas, in turn, presented himself as a wonder-working prophet. He led his gullible followers who, trusting him, were carrying all their belongings with them, to te River Jordan and promised them the repetition of the miraculous parting of the waters performed by Joshua at the start of the conquest of the Promised Land. It was meant to symbolize the liberation of the country from the Roman yoke. Fadus, the governor of Judaea, foresaw the implications and dispatched his horsemen to deal with the group. Many were slaughtered and others taken prisoner, among them Theudas, who was decapitated by the soldiers; his head was taken in triumph to Jerusalem.

The speech delivered by *Gamaliel the Elder, a leading member of the Sanhedrin, at the trial of the apostles contains an allusion to the slaying of Theudas and the dispersion of his 400 men (Acts 5:36). However Gamaliel, or rather the author of the Acts, misdates the event, which occurred in the mid-forties CE, by placing it before the uprising organized by *Judas the Galilean, which in fact took place at the time of *Quirinius' census in 6 CE.

Source: Josephus, *Ant.* 20:97–8.

THOMAS

The apostle Thomas (the name is the Greek transliteration of the Aramaic *te'ômâ* (Mk 3:18; Mt 10:3; Lk 6:15; Acts 1:13)) plays no part in the story of *Jesus of Nazareth in the Synoptic Gospels but is given a more prominent role in the Gospel of *John. Here his Aramaic name is regularly rendered in Greek as 'Didymus', the Twin (Jn 11:16; 20:24; 21:2). In John, the obscure Thomas of the Synoptics takes it upon himself to exhort his colleagues to accompany Jesus and die with him (Jn 11:16). Elsewhere he acts as the spokesman of the uncomprehending apostles (Jn 14:5). Indeed, he becomes the prototype of incredulity, refusing to believe in the resurrection of Jesus unless he could touch his living body with his own hands (Jn 20:24–8). Finally, he is presented as one of the seven disciples who witnessed the last apparition of Jesus by the Sea of Tiberias (Jn 21:2).

In the wake of John's Gospel Thomas became a leading figure in Gnostic thought. To him is ascribed the authorship of the Gospel of Thomas with its 150 sayings, which dates in its original Greek form to the second century, and survives in full in a third-to-fourth-century Egyptian Coptic translation. The work called the Acts of Thomas, probably written in Syriac in the third century, is also attached to his name. Needless to say, there is no valid evidence supporting the attribution of either of these writings to the apostle Thomas.

Christian legend, transmitted in the Acts of Thomas, reports that Thomas evangelized India, where he suffered a martyr's death at the hand of a local prince. Tradition asserts that in the fourth century his body was taken to Edessa (South-eastern Turkey) for burial. On the other hand, the Church historian Eusebius of Caesarea maintains that Thomas was the apostle not of India, but of the Parthians.

Sources: Gospel of Thomas: J. S. Kloppenborg et al., *Q Thomas Reader* (1990), 75–159. Acts of Thomas in M. R. James, *The Apocryphal New Testament*, 364–438. Eusebius, *Eccl. Hist.* 3:1.

TIBERIUS

Tiberius Claudius Nero was the stepson, adopted son and successor of *Augustus. As second emperor of Rome from 14 to 37 CE, Tiberius ruled over the Jews during the public ministry of *John the Baptist and of *Jesus of Nazareth. *Luke (3:1) dates the appearance of the Baptist to the fifteenth year of Tiberius (29 CE). Tiberius had no direct involvement with the New Testament story beyond the fact that he was responsible for the appointment of Pontius *Pilate as governor of Judaea in 26 CE. He also ordered Pilate to remove the votive shields carrying the emperor's name, which he had placed on the palace of *Herod (see the article on Pilate), and imprisoned the future Jewish king *Agrippa I for expressing the wish that Tiberius should soon die and be replaced by *Caligula (*Ant.* 18:179–204; *War* 2:180). Herod *Antipas, the tetrarch of Galilee, especially honoured the emperor by giving the name Tiberias to his new capital built between 17 and 20 CE.

The Emperor Tiberius

As far as Diaspora Jewry was concerned, Tiberius is remembered for expelling the Jewish community from Rome in 19 CE. The whole congregation had to suffer the punishment merited by a few swindlers, who had defrauded a rich Roman woman proselyte by embezzling her money, which they were meant to send to the Temple of Jerusalem (*Ant.* 18:84).

Sources: Josephus, *War* 2:168–80; *Ant.* 18.

TIMOTHY

Timothy was probably the closest disciple of *Paul. He was the son of a Jewish-Christian mother and a Greek father. As Timothy was not circumcised at birth, Paul, contrary to both his principles of not considering circumcision as of religious importance within the Church and opposing change in the run-up period to the Second Coming, ordered him to undergo the ritual operation because their common ministry was taking place in an area inhabited by many Jews.

Timothy accompanied Paul and *Silas during their mission to Macedonia (Beroea) and joined them in Corinth. He was with Paul when he wrote the letter to the Romans to which Paul adds greetings from Timothy. He took part in preaching to the Corinthians and was dispatched to Philippi. The letters to the Thessalonians are sent from Paul, *Silvanus and Timothy, and the letter to the Philippians from Paul and Timothy. Timothy's closeness to Paul appears in the epithets of 'fellow worker', 'brother' 'true child' and 'beloved child'. Timothy was still with the captive Paul, more likely in Rome than in Caesarea, when the letter to Philemon was written. Two pastoral letters are addressed to him. Church tradition attested by Eusebius regards Timothy as the first bishop of Ephesus.

Sources: Acts; Rom.; 1 and 2 Cor.; Phil.; Col.; 1 and 2 Thess.; 1 and 2 Tim., Philem. Eusebius, *Eccl. Hist.* 3:4.

TINNEIUS RUFUS

Quintus Tinneius Rufus was the Roman governor of Judaea at the outbreak of the second Jewish rebellion led by *Simeon bar Kosiba against Rome under *Hadrian in 132 CE. Rufus was no match for the revolutionaries and was decisively defeated. Hadrian had to bring in other generals, first Caius Quinctilius Certus Publicius Marcellus, and finally Sextus Julius Severus, summoned from Britain, to put down the revolt. The conflict was extremely bloody. Cassius Dio no doubt exaggerates when he speaks of 580,000 Jewish dead, but heavy

Roman losses are implicitly admitted when the standard formula 'I and the legions are well' was omitted by Hadrian from his letter to the Roman senate in which he announced his victory over the Jews.

The rabbis and Eusebius hold Rufus responsible for the religious persecution of the Jews during and after the rebellion, for the implementation of Hadrian's decree expelling them from Judaea, and for the ploughing up of the site of the Temple Mount (mTaan. 4:6; bTaan. 29a; Jerome on Zechariah 8:19). For reasons impossible to guess, a less hostile portrait of Tinneius Rufus is offered in the later layers of rabbinic literature. He is depicted there as a man familiar with the Jewish Bible, who regularly addressed tiresome and testing questions to the famous second-century CE Rabbi *Akiba such as, 'If God so loves circumcision, why is not every man born circumcised?'. Akiba is portrayed as never lacking an answer, a fact that naturally annoyed Rufus. According to a Talmudic legend, to attract the rabbi's attention and make him forget her husband, the wife of the governor set out to seduce Akiba. She did not succeed at first, but in the end she achieved her design by marrying him after duly converting to Judaism. Akiba thus gained a new proselyte and a very wealthy wife (bAZ 20a; b Ned. 50b)!

Sources: Dio 69:14. Eusebius, *Eccl. Hist.* 4:6.

TITUS

Titus Flavius Sabinus Vespasianus, son of *Vespasian (39/41–81 CE), was Roman emperor from 79 to 81 CE. Titus' fame, or in traditional Jewish eyes his ignominy, essentially derives from the successful continuation of his father's campaign against the Jews which ended with the capture of Jerusalem and the destruction of the Temple in 70 CE. If *Josephus is to be believed, Titus was not directly responsible for the burning down of the Sanctuary. On the contrary, while visiting the holy place in the midst of the battle, he gave orders to his soldiers to extinguish the fire, started accidentally, which was devouring the buildings, but not even his command could stop the frenzied destructiveness of the legionaries (*War* 6:260–66). During the triumph in

The triumphal arch of the Emperor Titus in Rome representing the seven-branched lamp-stand and other cult objects looted from the Temple of Jerusalem

Rome in 71 CE, celebrating the victory in the Jewish war, the spoils of the Temple of Jerusalem, the golden table and lamp-stand, the incense cups and the trumpets, were carried in procession before the triumphant emperor Vespasian and his two sons, Titus and *Domitian (*War* 7:148–52). The engraved images of these sacred objects can still be seen on the Arch of Titus in Rome. Dislike for the Palestinian rebels did not prevent Titus from acting fairly towards the Jews of Antioch in Syria. He firmly refused the request of the Gentile inhabitants of the city who petitioned for the abrogation of the civic rights of the Jews (*War* 7:100–11).

On a personal level, Titus maintained friendly relations with *Josephus during and after the war, as well as with the Jewish king *Agrippa II and with Agrippa's sister *Bernice. In fact, Bernice became the lover of Titus. Roman historians and gossip writers tell us that even after he had become emperor, Titus wanted to marry the Jewish princess, but in face of Roman opposition his nerve failed him. Suetonius reports that Titus had a 'notorious passion for Queen Bernice, to whom it was even said that he promised marriage'. Nevertheless he later sent her away from Rome 'against her will and his own' (cf. Tacitus and Cassius Dio).

For the Jewish tradition Titus was the prototype of the wicked. The rabbis accuse him of desecrating the Law and defiling the Holy of Holies of the Temple, where he availed himself of the services of two whores (bGit. 56b–57a). The Talmud's assessment of the victorious Roman is in striking contrast with that of Suetonius for whom the mature Titus was a faultless paragon of all the virtues.

Sources: Josephus. Suetonius, *Divus Titus* 7:1–2. Tacitus, *Histories* 2:1. Dio 66:3–4.

TITUS, PAUL'S COMPANION

Titus was one of *Paul's closest disciples, his 'true child', to whom one of the deutero-Pauline pastoral letters is addressed. He was a Gentile and his association with Paul goes back as far as the council of the apostles in Jerusalem in 49 CE. Paul deliberately brought Titus along as a kind of guinea pig in order to prove that admission of non-Jews into the Church did not require prior proselytization: 'Titus, who was with me, was not compelled to be circumcised, though he was a Greek' (Gal. 2:3).

Titus was used by Paul as an emissary in his dealings with Churches, especially that of Corinth (2 Cor. 8:6, 16, 23; 12:18). Paul missed him in Troas (2 Cor. 2:13); they met up in Macedonia (2 Cor. 7:6, 13–14) and Titus was sent later to Dalmatia (2 Tim. 4:10). He was a kind of itinerant ambassador of Paul. According to the letter addressed to him, Titus was entrusted with the Church of Crete and with its tiresome 'circumcision party' propagating 'Jewish myths' (Tit. 1:14) not to mention its equally difficult natives who were 'liars, evil beasts and lazy gluttons' (Tit. 1:12). The Church historian Eusebius calls Titus the first bishop of Crete.

Sources: Gal.; 2 Cor.; Tit. Eusebius, *Eccl. Hist.* 4:4.

TRAJAN

Marcus Ulpius Traianus (53–117 CE), the adopted son of Nerva, succeeded him as emperor of Rome in 98 CE and reigned until 117 CE. He was a much admired ruler, extending the imperial borders as far as Dacia (Romania) in the north-east and Armenia and Mesopotamia in the east, and improving the administration of the provinces. While he was engaged in the conquest of Mesopotamia in 115 CE, the Jews of Egypt and Cyrene revolted against Rome. Furious conflict developed in both countries – the Jewish leader of the rebellion in Cyrene was a certain Lucuas (Eusebius, *Eccl. Hist.* 4:2) or Andreas (Dio) – and many thousands of Jews lost their lives in the course of the hostilities, which occurred during the closing years of Trajan's reign.

According to the Church historian Eusebius, Trajan, in the footsteps of his predecessors *Vespasian and *Domitian, continued to hunt down Jews claiming Davidic descent whom he suspected to be potential leaders of revolution. The same author also reports the execution under Trajan of *Symeon son of Clopas, a cousin of Jesus, who was the second bishop of Jerusalem, the successor of *James the brother of the Lord.

The exchange of two letters between Pliny the Younger, governor (*legatus*) of Bithynia, and the emperor sheds interesting light on the legal status of Christians during Trajan's reign. Pliny inquired whether being a Christian was unlawful in and by itself, and as such punishable, or whether a specific criminal charge had to be proved in each case. Trajan replied by stating that simple membership of the Church was not sufficient cause for prosecution. Punishment was to be meted out only to persons found guilty, in the course of normal legal procedure, of breaking the law. Even though Christians were considered *prima facie* suspect of criminal behaviour, they were to be pardoned if they repented and renounced their religion.

Sources: Eusebius, *Eccl. Hist.* 3:32. Dio 68:32. Pliny the Younger, Letters x: 96 and 97.

The Emperor Trajan

V

VALERIUS GRATUS

Valerius Gratus was the successor of Annius Rufus as governor of Judaea from 15 to 26 CE. He was very active in changing Jewish high priests whose appointment was part of his duties. He removed *Ananus (or Annas) son of Sethi, an appointee of *Quirinius in 6 CE, who was to play a significant role in the trial of *Jesus, and replaced him with *Ismael son of Phabi for the period of 16/17 CE. He was then dismissed in favour of Simon son of Kamithus, who lasted no more than a year, and was replaced by Joseph *Caiaphas (27–37 CE), who was in charge of the case of Jesus. The high-priestly office was not a secure job in the days of the Roman governors: only Ananus (Annas) and Caiaphas enjoyed tenures of some length. In 26 CE Valerius Gratus returned to Rome and the vacant prefecture of Judaea was filled by Pontius *Pilate.

Source: Josephus, Ant. 18:33–5, 177.

VARUS

Publius Quinctilius Varus was Roman governor of Syria in the years 25–7 of the era of Actium, which began on 2 September 31 BCE. Therefore he held this office from 7/6 BCE until after the death of *Herod the Great in 4 BCE. His main role in Jewish history consisted in the savage suppression of the uprising which followed the death of Herod. During the prolonged quarrel among the sons of the deceased king over the succession to the vacant throne, several rebellions broke out. Varus promptly intervened and re-established the peace. However, the procurator Sabinus, sent by *Augustus to maintain law and order in Judaea, created further trouble and provoked an armed uprising in the capital. The disorder spread to Sepphoris in Galilee, where Judas son of *Ezechias (probably identical with *Judas the

Galilean or Judas of Gamala) took the lead in the revolt. There were revolutionary activities in Peraea and Judaea too. As a result, Varus felt obliged to step in again. He quickly brought calm to Galilee and when he arrived in Jerusalem with his two legions and Nabataean auxiliaries, the rebels lost heart and fled. Many were caught by the Romans. Varus crucified 2,000 of them and pardoned the rest before returning to Antioch. From then on the Roman cross was a sadly familiar sight in Jewish Palestine.

The Assumption of Moses (6:8) among the Pseudepigrapha, dated to the first century CE, probably alludes to Varus when it speaks of 'a powerful king of the west, who will conquer them [the Jews], and take them captive, and burn a part of their temple with fire, and crucify some of them around their city'. The same episode is remembered also in rabbinic literature (*Seder Olam*) as the 'War of Varus', provided that the corrupt reading 'War of *Asverus*', which preceded the 'War of Vespasian' by eighty years, is corrected to read the War of *Varus*.

Sources: Josephus, *War* 2:66–79; *Ant*. 17:286–98.

VESPASIAN

Titus Flavius Vespasianus (9–79 CE) was the first of the Flavian emperors and reigned from 69 to 79 CE. In 67 CE he was sent by Nero to Judaea to put down the revolt of the Jews. Having promptly conquered Galilee, he progressively occupied the rest of the country apart from the capital itself. While still engaged in war against the Jews, in 69 CE he was proclaimed emperor by the Roman armies in Egypt, Syria, Palestine and the entire eastern part of the empire. In December of the same year Vitellius, his rival for the imperial throne, was murdered and Vespasian was proclaimed the sole ruler by the whole Roman world. He returned to Rome, leaving his son *Titus to complete the Judaean campaign. Titus did so when he took Jerusalem in 70 CE. In the following year Vespasian and Titus celebrated a joint triumph in Rome during which the prize booties of the Jewish war, the golden Table of Shewbread and the Menorah or seven-branched lamp of the Temple of Jerusalem, were carried in procession. Both are visually commemorated on the triumphal Arch of Titus. The ceremony was terminated, according to Roman custom, by the execution of one of the main leaders of the revolt, the general of the Sicarii, *Simon son of Giora.

After the war, Vespasian converted the whole of Palestine into his private property, and transferred the poll tax paid by every Jewish man for the support of the Jerusalem Sanctuary to the coffer of the temple of Jupiter Capitolinus (*Josephus, War 7:216–18). He was also responsible for ordering the demolition of the Jewish Temple, built in c. 160 BCE by the high-priest pretender Onias IV in Leontopolis in Egypt to rival the Temple of Jerusalem (War 7:421). Historically less certain is the statement, reported only by the fourth-century Church historian Eusebius in the footsteps of Hegesippus, that Vespasian launched a persecution against the Jews in the context of a search for Jews of royal Davidic descent whom he proposed to execute as potential messianic revolutionaries. Apparently the same persecution continued also under two later emperors, *Domitian and *Trajan.

It is worth noting that according to Josephus, Vespasian during his stay in Palestine was the eye-witness of two peculiar Jewish religious phenomena. The first of these was the practice of exorcism, which was performed by means of the use of a foul-smelling root accompanied by the words of an incantation. Josephus refers to a Jew by the name of *Eleazar, possibly an Essene, who proved his prowess in the presence of Vespasian, his sons and a group of officers (Ant. 8:46–8). The other phenomenon was prophecy. Josephus himself claims to have foretold in the presence of Vespasian and Titus that both would rule over Rome: 'You will be Caesar, Vespasian,' he claims to have said to him, 'you will be emperor, you and your son here' (War 3:402). Josephus further recounts that while still a prisoner of war, his prophecy was fulfilled and Vespasian set him free. 'It is disgraceful that one who foretold my elevation to power and was a minister of the voice of God should still rank as a captive,' he is purported to have said (War 4:626). Rabbinic tradition ascribes the same kind of prediction to *Yohanan ben Zakkai, the religious leader of the Jews after the first war against the Romans who, after escaping from besieged Jerusalem, let Vespasian know that he would become 'king' in a typical Jewish

The Emperor Vespasian

way by interpreting a prophecy of Isaiah as announcing the future rise to the imperial throne of the Roman commander-in-chief. According to the talmudic story, Yohanan asked the legionaries: 'Where is the king?' They went to tell [Vespasian], 'A Jew seeks to greet you.' He replied, 'Let him come.' ... Yohanan said to him, '*Vive Domine Imperator!* [Long live my Lord the Emperor!].' Vespasian replied to him, 'Although I am not king, you give me a royal greeting. Should the king [Nero] hear this, he would kill me.' Yohanan answered, 'If you are not yet king, you shall be later. Indeed this Temple shall not be destroyed except by a king, for it is written, *And Lebanon* [=the Temple in Jewish tradition] *shall fall by a mighty one*' [=a king; Isaiah

10:34] (Lamentation Rabbah 1:5 [31]; bGit. 56a–b). The Roman historians Suetonius and Cassius Dio recollect that Judaean oracles foretold the elevation of Vespasian, and both mention explicitly the prophecy come true of Josephus.

Sources: Josephus, *War* 3–7; *Life.* Suetonius, *Divus Vespasianus* 5:6. Dio 66:2–4. Eusebius, *Eccl Hist.* 3:12.

VITELLIUS

Lucius Vitellius, consul in 34 CE and father of the future emperor Vitellius (69 CE), was appointed legate to Syria by *Tiberius in 35 CE, and recalled by *Caligula in 39 CE. An excellent administrator, he was repeatedly involved in Jewish matters. He was in particular responsible for relieving Pontius *Pilate of his governorship of Judaea in 36 CE and he dismissed also the high priest *Caiaphas from office, and replaced him by *Jonathan son of Ananus. Vitellius was ordered by Tiberius to capture the Nabataean king Aretas IV and punish him for the defeat he had inflicted on Herod *Antipas, tetrarch of Galilee. Vitellius, who disliked Antipas, half-heartedly obeyed the imperial command, but on hearing the news of the death of Tiberius in March 37 CE, while on his way with his army to the Nabataean capital, Petra, he stopped the enterprise and returned to Syria. His sympathy towards the Jews manifested itself in his dismissal of Pilate as a result of complaints received from the notables of Jerusalem. He further abolished the taxes on agricultural produce imposed on the city of Jerusalem by *Herod the Great, and he returned the vestments of the high priest from Roman to Jewish custody. Finally, he decided in early 37 CE not to march his army through the territory of Judaea in his campaign against the Nabataeans, to avoid upsetting the Jews by the standards displaying the images of the emperor. A statue of him erected in the Forum of Rome commemorated his unswerving loyalty towards Tiberius, *Caligula and *Claudius.

Sources: Josephus, *Ant.* 18:88–90; 115–26. Tacitus, *Annals* 6:32. Suetonius, *Vitellius* 3:1.

Y

YOHANAN BEN ZAKKAI

Yohanan ben Zakkai, usually entitled Rabban, 'our Rabbi', i.e. chief rabbi, was the religious leader who reorganized Judaism after the fall of Jerusalem and the collapse of the Jewish institutions in 70 CE. Few details relative to his life prior to the siege of Jerusalem have been preserved in rabbinic tradition apart from the statement that *Hillel and *Shammai were his teachers and that before coming to Jerusalem he resided in the Galilean city of Arav or Gabara where the uncouth provincials did not greatly appreciate his learning. This provoked, if the Talmud can be believed, the disillusioned exclamation, 'Galilee, Galilee, you hate the Torah!' (yShab. 15d). In Arav Yohanan is said to have been the teacher of the famous charismatic *Hanina ben Dosa.

A rabbinic legend, probably with some historical foundation, attests Yohanan's presence in Jerusalem during the siege and his escape from there. He lay motionless, pretending to be a corpse on a stretcher, and was carried out of the city into the Roman camp by two of his pupils. There he greeted *Vespasian in Latin, 'Vive Domine Imperator', and prophesied – as *Josephus, too, claims to have done (War 3:401) – that the commander-in-chief of the Roman army would soon become emperor (bGit. 56ab). The forecast came true in 69 CE. As a reward for the good augury Yohanan was allowed to set up his rabbinic academy in Yavneh (Jamnia). It was there that the teachers who survived the first Jewish war sought to reorganize under the guidance of Yohanan a Jewish religion without Temple and sacrificial worship. Some of the liturgical innovations necessitated by the destruction of the Sanctuary, such as the carrying of the lulab (palm branch) outside Jerusalem for seven days at the Feast of Tabernacles or the blowing of the ram's horn (shofar), are expressly attributed to Yohanan (mRSh 4:1, 3).

The substitution of the synagogue for the Temple ensured a swift transition in Jewish religious practice. The relatively painless change was due to the perspicacious wisdom of Yohanan ben Zakkai. Yet, his enormous merits notwithstanding, Josephus fails to record even the name of his outstanding contemporary.

Sources: Enc. Jud. 10:148–54. HJP II, 369–70.

Chronological Table

Dates	Roman History	Jewish History
BCE		
67		Death of Queen Alexandra Salome. Aristobulus II, high priest-king
65		Murder of Honi (Onias the Righteous)
64	Pompey conquers Syria	
63	Pompey conquers Judaea	Aristobulus deposed. Hyrcanus II, high priest-ethnarch The Idumaean Antipater, administrator
51–30	Cleopatra VII, queen of Egypt	
48	Julius Caesar defeats Pompey at Pharsalus	Hyrcanus and Antipater switch allegiance from Pompey to Caesar. Caesar confirms Hyrcanus II as high priest and ethnarch.
47		Antipater names Herod as governor of Galilee. Herod tried by Sanhedrin for executing the rebel Ezechias
44	Caesar assassinated	Menahem the Essene foretells Herod's kingship

Dates	Roman History	Jewish History
BCE		
41	Mark Antony rules the Roman East	
40	Parthians invade Judaea	Herod is appointed king by Mark Antony. Antigonus Mattathias named king and high priest by Parthians
40–37		Struggle between Herod and Antigonus
37		Herod and Sosius conquer Jerusalem. Herod marries the Hasmonaean princess Mariamme
37–4		Herod reigns
35		Herod appoints Aristobulus III as high priest. Aristobulus is drowned
31	Octavian defeats Mark Antony at Actium	
30	Mark Antony and Cleopatra commit suicide	Hyrcanus II executed by Herod
29		Mariamme executed by Herod
28		Alexandra, Mariamme's mother, executed by Herod
27–14 CE	Octavian becomes the emperor Caesar Augustus	
23	Augustus grants Herod Trachonitis, Batanaea and Auranitis	Herod constructs Caesarea
20/19		Rebuilding of Temple started by Herod
10		Caesarea completed

Dates	Roman History	Jewish History
BCE		
7	Augustus consulted on Herod's sons' disloyalty	Herod executes Alexander and Aristobulus, his sons by Mariamme
6		Herod's first will: Antipater to succeed
5		Second will: Antipas to succeed
c. 6/5		Birth of Jesus
4	Augustus consulted on Antipater	Antipater, Herod's eldest son, executed five days before Herod's own death
	Augustus reorganizes the government of Herod's former kingdom	
4–3	Varus, governor of Syria, crushes rebellion	Judas son of Ezechias and others rebel
4 BCE–6 CE		Archelaus ethnarch of Judaea. Hillel and Shammai flourish
4 BCE–33 CE		Philip tetrarch of Batanaea, Trachonitis, etc.
4 BCE–39 CE		Antipas tetrarch of Galilee
CE		
6	Quirinius organizes Judaean census. Coponius, prefect of Judaea	Archelaus deposed as predicted by Simon the Essene. Judas the Galilean rebels.
6–15		Ananus/Annas high priest
14	Death of Augustus	
14–37	Tiberius emperor	
18–36		Joseph Caiaphas high priest
26–36	Pontius Pilate prefect of Judaea	
29		John the Baptist and Jesus enter public life

Dates	Roman History	Jewish History
CE		
30		Death of the Baptist and of Jesus. Jesus movement starts. Gamaliel the Elder
36	Pilate dismissed	Caiaphas dismissed. Paul joins the Church
37–41	Gaius Caligula emperor	Paul visits Jerusalem
39		Antipas deposed and exiled
40–70?		Hanina ben Dosa
41–54	Claudius emperor	Agrippa I king James son of Zebedee beheaded. Council of the apostles in Jerusalem
44	Claudius appoints Cuspius Fadus as procurator of Judaea	Agrippa I dies. The rebel Theudas is killed
44–6	Tiberius Julius Alexander procurator of Judaea	Two sons of Judas the Galilean crucified
50–60?		Paul's letters
51/2	Gallio proconsul of Achaia	Paul in Corinth
52–60	Antonius Felix procurator of Judaea	
53		Agrippa II king of Batanaea, Trachonitis, etc.
54–68	Nero emperor	Agrippa II is given Galilee and Pereaea
58		The 'Egyptian' rebels. Paul arrested and kept in Caesarea. Meets Felix and his wife Drusilla
60–62	Porcius Festus procurator of Judaea	Paul meets Festus, Agrippa II and Bernice. Is sent to Rome for trial

Dates	Roman History	Jewish History
CE		
62–4	Albinus procurator of Judaea	High priest Ananus executes James the brother of the Lord. Jesus son of Ananias tried and dismissed
64	Fire of Rome	Persecution of Christians. Martyrdom of Peter and Paul
64–6	Gessius Florus procurator of Judaea	First war against Rome breaks out. Christians migrate to Pella (?)
67	Vespasian and Titus sent to Judaea to deal with the rebellion	Flavius Josephus, rebel commander of Galilee, captured
67–8		Zealots of John of Gischala in Jerusalem
68	Nero commits suicide	Simon bar Giora and Sicarii in Jerusalem
69–79	Vespasian emperor. Titus in Judaea	
70		Jerusalem taken and the Temple destroyed. Yohanan ben Zakkai and Gamaliel II at Yavneh
c. 70		Gospel of Mark
73/4	Flavius Silva governor of Judaea	Capture of Masada. End of the war. *Fiscus Iudaicus* imposed on all the Jews of the empire. Christians return from Pella (?)
79–81	Titus emperor	Josephus completes the *Jewish War*

Dates	Roman History	Jewish History
BCE		
81–96	Domitian emperor	Gospels of Matthew and Luke, Acts of the Apostles. Josephus completes *Jewish Antiquities*. Agrippa II dies c. 92/3
96–8	Nerva emperor	*Fiscus Iudaicus* mitigated
c. 100		Letter of James, 1 Peter, 1–3 John, Revelation
98–117	Trajan emperor. Younger Pliny consults him about the treatment of Christians	Bishop of Jerusalem, Symeon son of Clopas, cousin of Jesus, crucified. Ebionite or Nazoraean Jewish Christians survive
100–110		Fourth Gospel
117–38	Hadrian emperor	2 Peter
132–5	Second war led by Simeon bar Kosiba	
135–	Aelia built on the ruins of Jerusalem. Jews expelled from Jerusalem	Religious persecution of Jews by Hadrian

Glossary

Batanaea: a territory east of Galilee in Transjordan.

Chief priests: members of the leading priestly families out of whose members the high priest was usually chosen by the Herodian rulers or the Roman governors. See also **high priest** and **priests**.

Dead Sea (or Qumran) Scrolls: Hebrew, Aramaic and Greek manuscripts, mostly dating from the second century BCE to the middle of the first century CE, discovered in the area of Qumran by the Dead Sea between 1947 and 1956.

Eschatology: a Jewish doctrine flourishing between the second century BCE and the first century CE, relating to the expectation of the end of time in the near future.

Diaspora (dispersion): the collective designation of countries inhabited by Jews outside the land of Israel.

Essenes: an ascetic religious group of Jews, first mentioned in the second century BCE, some of whom embraced a life of male celibacy and common ownership or property. Mainstream scholarship identifies them with the community to which the Dead Sea Scrolls belonged.

Ethnarch: the head of a nation below the rank of a king.

Gaulanitis: a territory north-east of Galilee.

Halakhah: the rabbinic development of biblical law.

Hasmonaeans or Maccabees: a priestly family traditionally traced to an ancestor called Hasmon, who led the Jewish resistance against Hellenization under the Seleucid king Antiochus IV Epiphanes (174–64 BCE). The Hasmonaeans ruled the Jewish nation from 161 to 63 BCE.

Hellenists: promoters of Greek culture. In the New Testament the term refers to Greek-speaking Jews or to Jewish Christians of Diaspora origin.

High priest: the head of the Jewish priesthood in Jerusalem, president of the Sanhedrin and the principal religious teacher and judge among Jews. When Rome directly governed the country, he was also the political head of Judaean Jewry ultimately responsible for the maintenance of law and order. The office passed from father to son in the biblical period and again in the Hasmonaean era. From the time of Herod onwards the high priests were appointed by the Herodian kings or by Roman governors. See also **chief priests** and **priests**.

Idumaea: the territory situated south of Judaea, the biblical Edom.

Maccabees: see **Hasmonaeans**.

Messiah: literally someone anointed, a term most commonly understood as the designation of the Jewish king of the final age. The Dead Sea sectaries expected two Messiahs, one royal and one priestly, and possibly even a third prophetic Messiah.

Mishnah: the first code of rabbinic law compiled around 200 CE, but containing a great many older traditions.

Peraea: a territory on the east side of the Jordan (Transjordan).

Pharisees: a lay (non-priestly) religious party influential among Jews from the middle of the second century BCE. They were experts in traditional law and Bible interpretation. They are considered the ancestors of the rabbis of the Mishnah and the Talmud.

Praetor: a Roman magistrate subordinate to a consul.

Praetorium: the palace of the Roman governor of a province.

Prefect: the governor of a Roman province (in Judaea from 6 to 41 CE).

Priests: members of the priestly clan of the tribe of Levi who had the privilege to serve periodically and in rotation at the altar of the Temple of Jerusalem. When they were not on duty in the sanctuary, they acted as religious teachers in their towns and villages up and down the country.

Procurator: the governor of a Roman province (in Judaea from 44 to 66 CE).

Qumran Scrolls: see **Dead Sea Scrolls**.

Rabbis: see **Pharisees**.

Sadducees: a party of conservative upper-class Jews, first mentioned in the second century BCE. They were allied to the chief priests and opposed to the religious innovations propounded by the Pharisees, such as the belief in the Resurrection.

Sanhedrin: the Hebraized form of the Greek *synedrion*, designating a high court or council presided over during the Roman era by the high priest.

Seleucids: descendants of Seleucus, one of the generals of Alexander the Great, who ruled Syria from the end of the fourth century until the Roman conquest in 64 BCE.

Sicarii (daggermen): members of the revolutionary party founded in 6 CE by Judas the Galilean.

Synoptic Gospels: the designation of the Gospels of Matthew, Mark and Luke which reflect the same general point of view, follow the same story-line and use very similar wording.

Talmud: the enlarged code of rabbinic law based on the Mishnah and its interpretation, first compiled in Galilee *c.* 400 CE (Palestinian Talmud) and later *c.* 500 CE in Babylonia (Babylonian Talmud).

Tetrarch: the ruler of a (fourth) part of a territory.

Trachonitis: a territory in north-eastern Transjordan.

Bibliography

Bammel, E. and Moule, C. D. F. (eds), *Jesus and the Politics of His Day*, Cambridge University Press, Cambridge, 1984

Barclay, J. M. G., *Jews in the Mediterranean Diaspora from Alexander to Trajan*, T. and T. Clark, Edinburgh, 1996

Bauckham, Richard, *Jude and the Relatives of Jesus in the Early Church*, T. and T. Clark, Edinburgh, 1990

Bond, Helen, *Pontius Pilate in History and Interpretation*, Cambridge University Press, Cambridge, 1999

—— *Caiaphas: Friend of Rome and Judge of Jesus*, Westminster John Knox Press, Louisville, Kentucky, 2004

Borgen, P., *Philo of Alexandria*, Brill, Leiden, 1997

Crossan, John Dominic, *The Historical Jesus*, HarperSanFrancisco, 1991

—— *The Birth of Christianity*, T. and T. Clark, Edinburgh, 1998

Feldman, L. H., *Josephus and Modern Scholarship*, Walter de Gruyter, Berlin, 1984

Fredriksen, Paula, *Jesus of Nazareth, King of the Jews*, Macmillan, London, 1999

Freyne, Sean, *Galilee from Alexander the Great to Hadrian 323 BCE to 135 CE*, Michael Glazier and Notre Dame University Press, Wilmington/Notre Dame, 1980

Goodman, Martin D., *The Ruling Class of Judaea*, Cambridge University Press, Cambridge, 1987

—— *The Roman World 44 BC–AD 180*, Routledge, London, 1997

—— (ed.), *Jews in the Graeco-Roman World*, Oxford University Press, Oxford, 1998

—— (ed.), *The Oxford Handbook of Jewish Studies*, Oxford University Press, Oxford, 2002

Greenhut, Zvi and Reich, Ronny, 'The tomb of Caiaphas', *Biblical Archaeology Review*. 18/5, Sept.–Oct. 1992, 28–44

Griffin, Miriam, *Nero: The End of a Dynasty*, Duckworth, London, 1984

Hazel, John, *Who's Who in the Roman World*, Routledge, London, 2002

Hengel, Martin, *The Zealots*, T. and T. Clark, Edinburgh, 1989

Hoehner, H. W., *Herod Antipas*, Cambridge University Press, Cambridge, 1972

Hornblower, Simon and Spawforth, Anthony (eds), *The Oxford Classical Dictionary*, Oxford University Press, Oxford, 2003

James, M. R., *The Apocryphal New Testament*, Clarendon Press, Oxford, 1924

Jeremias, Joachim, *Jerusalem in the Time of Jesus*, SCM Press, London, 1969

Jones, A. H. M., *The Herods of Judaea*, Oxford University Press, Oxford, 1968

—— *Augustus*, Chatto and Windus, London, 1970

Jones, B. W., *The Emperor Titus*, Routledge, London, 1984

Lake, K. (tr.), *Eusebius, Ecclesiastical History*, Loeb Classical Library, London/New York, 1926

Lemaire, André, 'Burial Box of James, the Brother of Jesus', *Biblical Archaeology Review*, 28/6, Nov.–Dec. 2002, 24–33.

Meshorer, Y., *Ancient Jewish Coinage*, 2 vols, New York, 1982

Meyers, Eric (ed.), *The Oxford Encyclopedia of Archaeology in the Near East*, vols I–IV, Oxford University Press, New York, 1997

Millar, Fergus, *The Roman Near East*, Harvard University Press, Cambridge, MA/London, 1993

Murphy O'Connor, Jerome, *Paul: His Story*, Oxford University Press, Oxford, 2004

Neusner, Jacob, *The Rabbinic Traditions about the Pharisees before 70*, 2 vols, Brill, Leiden, 1971

Painter, John and Moody Smith, D., *Just James: The Brother of Jesus in History and Tradition*, Augsburg Fortress, Minneapolis, 1999

Rajak, Tessa, *Josephus: The Historian and his Society*, Duckworth, London, 1983, 2002

—— *The Jewish Dialogue with Greece and Rome*, Brill, Leiden, 2001

Richardson, Peter, *Herod: King of the Jews and Friend of the Romans*, Continuum, London, 1999

Roth, Cecil (ed.), *Encyclopedia Judaica*, 16 vols, Jerusalem, 1972

Safrai, S. and Stern, M., *The Jewish People in the First Century*, 2 vols, Van Gorcum, Assen, 1974–6

Sanders, E. P., *Jesus and Judaism*, SCM Press, London, 1985

—— *The Historical Figure of Jesus*, Allen Lane, London, 1993

—— *Paul and Palestinian Judaism*, SCM Press, London, 1977

Schäfer, Peter, *The History of the Jews in the Greco-Roman World*, Routledge, London, 2003

Shalit, Abraham, *König Herodes: Der Mann und sein Werk*, Walter de Gruyter, Berlin, 1969

Shanks, Hershel and Witherington, Ben, *The Brother of Jesus*, HarperSanFrancisco, 2003

Schiffman, H. L. and VanderKam, J. C. (eds), *Encyclopedia of the Dead Sea Scrolls*, 2 vols, Oxford University Press, New York, 2000

Schürer, Emil, Vermes, Geza, Millar, Fergus and Goodman, Martin, *The History of the Jewish People in the Age of Jesus Christ*, 3 vols, T. and T. Clark, Edinburgh, 1973–87

Schwartz, D. R., *Agrippa I: The Last King of Judaea*, J. C. B. Mohr, Tübingen, 1999

Schweitzer, Albert, *The Quest of the Historical Jesus*, SCM Press, London, 2000

Sherwin-White, A. N., *Roman Society and Roman Law in the New Testament*, Clarendon Press, Oxford, 1963

Smallwood, E. M., *The Jews under Roman Rule*, Brill, Leiden, 1976

Schneemelcher, W. and Wilson, R. McL., *New Testament Apocrypha*, 2 vols, Westminster John Knox Press, Philadelphia, 1991–2

Stern, Menahem, *Greek and Latin Authors on Jews and Judaism*, Israel Academy of Sciences and Humanities, Jerusalem, 1974–84

Suetonius, *The Twelve Caesars*, Penguin Classics, London, 2003

Syme, Ronald, *The Roman Revolution*, Oxford University Press, Oxford, 1939, 1989

Vermes, Geza, *Jesus the Jew*, Collins/SCM Press, 1973, 2001

—— The Changing Faces of Jesus, Allen Lane/Penguin, 2000/2001
—— The Authentic Gospel of Jesus, Allen Lane/Penguin, 2003/2004
—— and Goodman, Martin, The Essenes in the Classical Sources, Sheffield Academic Press, 1989
Williamson, G. A., Eusebius, The History of the Church, Penguin Classics, Harmondsworth, 1965
Winter, Paul, On the Trial of Jesus, Walter de Gruyter, Berlin, 1961, 1973
Yadin, Yigael, Masada: Herod's Fortress and the Zealots' Last Stand, Weidenfeld & Nicolson, London, 1966
—— Bar-Kokhba, Weidenfeld & Nicolson, London, 1971

Classical Sources

Cassius Dio, Roman History with an English Translation, by E. Cary, Loeb Classical Library, London and New York, 1916
Josephus, Flavius, Josephus with an English Translation, 9 vols, by H. St J. Thackeray and L. H. Feldman, Loeb Classical Library, 1926–65
Juvenal, Satires with an English Translation, by G. G. Ramsay, Loeb Classical Library, 1918
Philo of Alexandria, in Philo with an English Translation, by F. H. Colson and G. H. Whitaker, Loeb Classical Library, 10 vols, 1962
Suetonius, The Twelve Caesars with English Translation, by J. C. Rolfe et al., Loeb Classical Library, 1998
Tacitus, Cornelius, Annals with an English Translation, by J. Jackson, Loeb Classical Library, 1937
—— Histories with an English Translation, by C. H. Moore, Loeb Classical Library, 1925–32

Jewish Sources

The Complete Dead Sea Scrolls in English, Revised Edition, transl. and introduced by G. Vermes, Penguin Classics, London, 2004
The Mishnah, transl. by H. Danby, Oxford University Press, 1933

The Tosefta, vols I–VI, transl. by J. Neusner, KTAV, New York, 1977–80

The Babylonian Talmud, ed. I. Epstein, 18 vols, Soncino Press, London, 1935–52

Abbreviations

Ant.	Josephus, *Jewish Antiquities*
bAZ	Babylonian Talmud Abodah Zara
bBB	Babylonian Talmud Baba Batra
bBer.	Babylonian Talmud Berakhot
bGit.	Babylonian Talmud Gittin
bHag.	Babylonian Talmud Hagigah
bNed.	Babylonian Talmud Nedarim
bPes.	Babylonian Talmud Pesahim
bSanh.	Babylonian Talmud Sanhedrin
bShab.	Babylonian Talmud Shabbat
bTaan.	Babylonian Talmud Taanit
Eccl. Hist.	Eusebius of Caesarea, *Ecclesiastical History*
Enc. Jud.	*Encyclopaedia Judaica*, 16 vols
HJP	*History of the Jewish People in the Age of Jesus Christ*, by E. Schürer, G. Vermes, F. Millar and M. Goodman, 3 vols
JJS	*Journal of Jewish Studies*
Legatio	Philo, *Legatio ad Gaium*
Life	Josephus, *Life*
mAb.	Mishnah Abot
mBer.	Mishnah Berakhot

mGit.	Mishnah Gittin
mPar.	Mishnah Parah
mRSh	Mishnah Rosh ha-Shanah
mSanh	Mishnah Sanhedrin
mSheb.	Mishnah Shebiit
mSot.	Mishnah Sotah
mTaan.	Mishnah Taanit
mYeb.	Mishnah Yebamot
mYom.	Mishnah Yoma
tBer.	Tosephta Berakhot
tHul.	Tosephta Hullin
tNid.	Tosephta Niddah
War	Josephus, *Jewish War*
yBer.	Jerusalem Talmud Berakhot
yShab.	Jerusalem Talmud Shabbat
yYom.	Jerusalem Talmud Yoma
4Q169	*Discoveries in the Judaean Desert*, vol. V
4Q333	*Discoveries in the Judaean Desert*, vol. XXXVI
4Q468e	*Discoveries in the Judaean Desert*, vol. XXXVI

Index of Persons and Places

(Page numbers in bold type refer to main entries in the Who's Who)

INDEX

He just wanted a decent book to read ...

Not too much to ask, is it? It was in 1935 when Allen Lane, Managing Director of Bodley Head Publishers, stood on a platform at Exeter railway station looking for something good to read on his journey back to London. His choice was limited to popular magazines and poor-quality paperbacks – the same choice faced every day by the vast majority of readers, few of whom could afford hardbacks. Lane's disappointment and subsequent anger at the range of books generally available led him to found a company – and change the world.

'We believed in the existence in this country of a vast reading public for intelligent books at a low price, and staked everything on it'
Sir Allen Lane, 1902–1970, founder of Penguin Books

The quality paperback had arrived – and not just in bookshops. Lane was adamant that his Penguins should appear in chain stores and tobacconists, and should cost no more than a packet of cigarettes.

Reading habits (and cigarette prices) have changed since 1935, but Penguin still believes in publishing the best books for everybody to enjoy. We still believe that good design costs no more than bad design, and we still believe that quality books published passionately and responsibly make the world a better place.

So wherever you see the little bird – whether it's on a piece of prize-winning literary fiction or a celebrity autobiography, political tour de force or historical masterpiece, a serial-killer thriller, reference book, world classic or a piece of pure escapism – you can bet that it represents the very best that the genre has to offer.

Whatever you like to read – trust Penguin.

read more
www.penguin.co.uk